Alex Lord's British Columbia

Alex Lord, a pioneer inspector of rural BC schools, shares in these recollections his experiences in a province barely out of the stage coach era. Travelling through vast northern territory, utilizing unreliable transportation, and enduring climatic extremes, Lord became familiar with the aspirations of remote communities and their faith in the humanizing effects of tiny assisted schools. En route, he performed in resolute yet imaginative fashion the supervisory functions of a top government educator, developing an educational philosophy of his own based on an understanding of the provincial geography, a reverence for citizenship, and a work ethic tuned to challenge and accomplishment.

Although not completed, these memoirs invite the reader to experience the British Columbia that Alex Lord knew. Through his words, we endure the difficulties of travel in this mountainous province. We meet many of the unusual characters who inhabited this last frontier and learn of their hopes, fears, joys, sorrows, and eccentricities. More particularly, we are reminded of the historical significance of the one-room rural school and its role as an indispensable instrument of community cohesion.

John Calam has organized the memoirs according to the regions through which Lord travelled. He has included in his introduction a biography of Alex Lord, a brief description of the British Columbia he knew, a sketch of its public education system, and an assessment of the place Lord's writing now occupies among other works on education and society.

JOHN CALAM is a professor emeritus of the Department of Social and Educational Studies at the University of British Columbia.

EDITED BY JOHN CALAM

Alex Lord's British Columbia

Recollections of a Rural School Inspector, 1915-36

UBCPress
Vancouver

ISBN 0-7748-0381-9 (hardcover)
ISBN 0-7748-0385-1 (paperback)

Canadian Cataloguing in Publication Data
Lord, A. R. (Alexander Russell), 1885-1961.
Alex Lord's British Columbia

(The Pioneers of British Columbia, ISSN 0847-0537)

Includes bibliographical references and index.
ISBN 0-7748-0381-9 (bound). – ISBN 0-7748-0385-1 (pbk.)

1. Lord, A. R. (Alexander Russell), 1885-1961.   2. School superintendents –
British Columbia – Biography.   3. School supervision, Rural – British
Columbia – History.   4. Education, Rural – British Columbia – History.
I. Calam, John.   II. Title.

LA2325.L67A3 1991   371.2'011'092   C91-091347-1

This book has been financially assisted by the Ministry of Municipal Affairs,
Recreation and Culture through the British Columbia Heritage Trust
and BC Lottery revenues.

UBC Press
University of British Columbia
6344 Memorial Rd
Vancouver, BC V6T 1Z2
(604) 822-3259
Fax: (604) 822-6083

Printed and bound in Canada
by John Deyell Company

For Marie, Betty, and Susan

Contents

Illustrations

Maps

Acknowledgments

In 1985 Alex Lord's travel-worn briefcase containing long neglected papers was drawn to my attention, snatched from oblivion thanks to watchful intermediaries. With Lord's recollections now edited for public readership, the time has come to thank those instrumental in getting their preparation under way and sustaining its momentum.

First and foremost, I am deeply indebted to Alex and Muriel Lord's daughter, the late Helen Colls for treasuring her father's manuscripts. In the same connection, I greatly appreciate the strong contribution of her close friend Mary E. Inman. From the start she welcomed the enterprise, corresponded with me about possible sources of information and, at an early stage, invited to her home the late Dorothy McLellan, Marion McLellan Taylor, Janet McLeod, Enid Downton, and Jean Stonard, each of whom knew Lord and was willing to share memories to stimulate initial research. Similarly, I wish to thank Geoffrey Colls, Pat Hauck, and Anne Hoffman, proprietors of the Lord papers, who granted me permission to make use of their grandfather's observations in this book. I acknowledge with equal gratitude Colls's lending me photographs of Lord, personal papers, and hitherto-unpublished correspondence with or concerning such educational figures as S.J. Willis, Charles H. Judd, Frank Quance, Alexander Robinson, G.M. Weir, J.G. Althouse, and H.B. King.

For her initial consultative contribution, I recognize with gratitude the late Grace Louise Dolmage Bredin, a charter member of the University of British Columbia's Faculty of Education. The late Neville V. Scarfe, first UBC Dean of Education, likewise deserves credit for understanding at first glance the importance to British Columbia educational history of the Lord manuscripts and, despite serious illness, characteristically working in aid of their wider distribution. I am grateful as well to UBC Academic Vice-President Daniel R. Birch, then

Dean of Education, for finding the time during a university funding crisis to acquaint me with the Lord papers and invite me to participate in bringing them to light. That we can presently enjoy Lord's illuminating reflections on British Columbia schools and communities of an earlier day is due in no small part to the historical alertness of these three educators.

For a wealth of background material cheerfully offered me, I salute many regional institutions, including the Alberta Museums Association; Quesnel Paddlewheel Association; North Peace Historical Society; Fort St. John-North Peace Museum; South Peace Historical Society; BC Hereford Association; British Columbia Cattlemen's Association; Agriculture Canada (BC); Cariboo-Chilcotin Archives; Grande Prairie Pioneer Museum Society; Nechako Valley Historical Society; Vanderhoof Community Museum; BC Shorthorn Association; Archives of the Anglican Provincial Synod of British Columbia; Canadian Broadcasting Corporation Archives, Toronto; Royal Canadian Mounted Police Museum, Regina; Alcan Smelters and Chemicals Ltd., Kitimat; Fraser-Fort George Regional Museum, Prince George; Lakes District Museum Society, Burns Lake; Kamloops Museum and Archives; British Columbia School Trustees Association; British Columbia Teachers' Federation; School District 27 (Cariboo-Chilcotin); Bulkley Valley Museum, Smithers; Quesnel and District Museum; Kwinitsa Museum, Prince Rupert; Museum of Northern British Columbia, Prince Rupert; Port Clements Museum; Queen Charlotte Island Museum, Skidegate; Hazelton Historical Museum; Clinton Museum; Provincial Archives of Alberta; Royal British Columbia Museum, Victoria; Vancouver Museum; Hastings Mill Museum, Vancouver; Oblate Resource Centre and Archives, Vancouver; and Vancouver City Archives. In addition, I thank here and acknowledge in subsequent annotations those scores of individuals whose special knowledge rendered feasible my editorial task.

Finally, I am appreciative of resource use and counsel at the University of British Columbia, the University of Victoria, and the British Columbia Archives and Records Service; much obliged to Carolyn Smyly for her perceptive reading of an earlier draft; and profoundly indebted to Neil Sutherland, J. Donald Wilson, Thomas Fleming, and Patrick Dunae – four patient historians who helped me over innumerable obstacles. To Jean Wilson, ever generous in her encouragement and editorial advice, and Emma-Elizabeth Peelstreet whose copy editing so persuasively enhanced the manuscript, I convey my thanks and warm regards, as well as to Holly Keller-Brohman (associate editor), George Madisson (production), Arifin Graham (jacket design), and Angus Weller (cartography).

Alex Lord's British Columbia

Editor's Introduction

A prominent British Columbia educator, Dr. A.R. Lord is remembered as a raconteur with a passion for history and geography. In 1950 at age sixty-five, he retired as principal of Vancouver Provincial Normal School and began writing his memoirs. But as his daughter, the late Helen Colls, explained in 1982, prior commitments and waning health conspired against their completion.[1] Lord died in 1961 leaving some initial accounts edited for today's reader as *Alex Lord's British Columbia* and giving rise to a not-unknown editorial perplexity. On the one hand unfinished recollections deserve contextual introduction. On the other hand, such introduction may ruinously postpone a reader's direct engagement with the main text. Accordingly, readers are urged to pursue this book in whichever sequence best suits their interests.

Alexander Russell Lord – Alex Lord to friends – was born on 27 June 1885 in Merigonish, Nova Scotia. His grandfather, Dr. Alexander Maclean, was a respected minister in Canada's Maritimes and first moderator of the Presbyterian Church in Canada. Maclean married Sarah Matheson, daughter of a wealthy family, and their child Mary wed C.S. Lord, a Presbyterian minister whose last two pulpits were at Grafton and Fenelon Falls, Ontario. Alex was one of five sons who grew up among politically attentive relatives committed to religion, education, the professions, and public service.[2]

In his childhood Lord attended the Grafton and Fenelon Falls public schools and in 1904 qualified as a teacher at Northumberland County Model School. During two subsequent years he impressed his Fenelon Falls rural school board as a good teacher with a promising future. Craving further studies and perhaps swayed by a maternal uncle who had attended its medical school, he chose Queen's University, a proud institution historically rooted in Presbyterianism. There he tutored faculty children to meet expenses and graduated Bachelor of Arts in 1910. Then, teaching experience and qualifications in hand, he embarked upon a lifetime adventure in British Columbia education. Not that Lord and rural Ontario were incompatible, but the lure of the Canadian West proved irresistible. Professional challenges awaited the resolute young. Though modest enough, teaching salaries at times rewarded the competitive. Close relatives had also made the move. Uncle Isaac Maclean, cousin Courtenay Maclean, and brother James Lord worked in British Columbia as medical doctor, lawyer, and automobile association administrator respectively. Moreover, there dwelled dozens of Maritimers and others whom Grandfather Maclean had baptized or married and who 'held him in high regard.'[3] Most of all, thanks to his early promise, not to mention useful Queen's alumni connections, Kelowna offered Lord the principalship of its fast-growing, five-division Central Elementary School. Lord accepted, and in 1910 began a four-year term that earned him the firm support of the local board and the gratitude of an appreciative town. Concurrent with his marriage to Kelowna teacher Muriel McNair in 1914, Lord's growing reputation for authentic educational leadership drew the attention of Vancouver school authorities. They induced Lord to head Vancouver's twelve-division Grandview Elementary School, but only for a year. In the summer of 1915 he accepted a Prince Rupert-based provincial inspectorship. Despite strong incentives to settle down in Vancouver, his fascination with the inspectorate's sheer administrative reach punctuated his early career. Writing in retirement forty years afterwards, he noted with satisfaction that it 'was not difficult to feel ... that I knew at least by name everyone "north of fifty-three".'

Lord's first inspectorate was indeed vast, embracing elementary schools from Prince Rupert to the Alberta border, from Prince George to Soda Creek, and from Bella Coola to Stewart. It also included the Queen Charlotte Islands and British Columbia's Peace River Block. A steady influx of settlers characterized the entire region following completion in 1914 of the Grand Trunk Pacific Railway linking the Fraser headwaters, the Nechako Plateau, and the Bulkley and Skeena valleys with Prince Rupert on the Pacific. Even so, Lord observed that in 1915 'there were only forty-four schools' in this huge area, 'and only three of them had more than one room.' Most were 'assisted' schools whose teachers' salaries were paid by the provincial government, communities trying to meet other expenses. Struggling to get started, some of these schools suffered an 'utter dearth ... of simplest necessities ...'[4] Beginning teachers, moreover, could not receive the supervisory support they merited. Indeed the district, Lord declared, 'is almost wholly in the pioneer stage ... and necessarily has an isolated population; hence much of my time has been taken up with organization work. The tremendous distances covered – over 20,000 miles in all – coupled with infrequent and irregular means of transportation, rendered a satisfactory supervision of schools quite impossible.'[5]

Despite initial misgivings, Lord persevered. Those same attributes of professional brilliance and personal charm which had so impressed the Kelowna and Vancouver school boards at length prompted several colourful redeployments. In 1919 he returned as school inspector to Kelowna, a district of ample size, yet compact and agreeable compared with the endless reaches and stiffening winters of his maiden inspectorate. A sense of accomplishment also attended these contrasts in geography. Okanagan and West Kootenay schools proved relatively accessible. For example, in 1922 Lord reported that over the school year he had inspected every one of seventy-five schools once and afforded a substantial number a second visit.[6] With supervisory duties thus routinized, he could fret less over marginally sustained assisted schools or their inadequate inspection and address broader issues such as consolidation under which scheme, rural children could be transported to better-equipped schools in larger neighbourhoods. Nor were his trans-provincial experiences to end in Kelowna. In 1922 Superintendent S.J. Willis recalled him to District No. 8 then embracing schools in the city districts of North Vancouver and Port Moody, the rural municipalities of Burnaby, North Vancouver, and West Vancouver, plus the rural and assisted schools of Burrard Inlet, Howe Sound, the Pacific Great Eastern Railway from Squamish to Seaton Lake, and the coast and adjacent islands from Lund to Sayward. It was as if by then, scattered districts in need of help knew whom they should call – Alex Lord, youthful still at thirty-seven.

One good reason for these widespread requests for Lord's supervisory touch was the centrality of geography to both his personal and professional life. At Queen's University he had studied the subject, later teaching it to the higher elementary grades at Kelowna and Vancouver. To say he became well-acquainted with British Columbia is to put it mildly. He certainly knew where things were. But he also acquired a feel for why things were so, thinking as a geographer and, in his early reports, relating the fortunes of his schools to railway construction, land speculation and settlement, late growing seasons, early frosts, suffocating snows, spring morasses, isolation, fish canneries, mineral exploration, the lumber industry, agriculture, transportation, and other pertinent aspects of physical, economic, meteorological, historical, and human geography. What, moreover, proved so attractive to student, colleague, friend, and casual acquaintance alike was his brimming enthusiasm for the discipline. A sense of this passion appears in his splendid paragraph about how he reconnoitered his first inspectorate, his eye upon the geographical context of little rural schools rather than on the particulars of their daily rounds. 'As I gradually worked my way through the district,' he writes,

> I seemed to be coming constantly in touch with places and events of earlier days. My years of teaching in British Columbia schools, where 'The History and Geography' of the province was an important subject, had given me ... merely the dry bones of textbook knowledge. It was startling to find that the geographical centre of the province was a few miles south of Vanderhoof, that Fort George was due north of Vancouver, and that the British Columbia section of the Peace River Valley was east of the Rocky Mountains. Running Fort George and Blackwater canyons in a gasoline launch during June high water, when the crests of the current in the centre seemed several feet higher than the edges against the perpendicular rock sides, made Alexander Mackenzie's journey in a canoe appear almost a miracle, while a bicycle ride from Quesnel to Alexandria and Soda Creek replaced the romance of the fur brigade with what it undoubtedly was: drudgery and hard work.

One who valued such sensitivity to geographical data was Principal D.M. Robinson of Vancouver Provincial Normal School. To nobody's surprise he appointed Lord as geography instructor there.[7] From 1924 to 1929 – difficult times for an institution roundly criticized in the 1925 J.H. Putman and G.M. Weir *Survey of the School System* -Lord taught future teachers their geography, how to teach it, and what to expect of a novice teacher's life in some distant corner of the province.[8] As Irene Howard recalls of a later time, geographer Lord 'had a fund of stories about the Cariboo, which he loved, and ... gave a talk on how to cope ... say, at Lac la Hache.'[9] Lord's more formal geographical insights he wrote with George A. Cornish and V.L. Denton into *Canadian Geography for Juniors* (1934).[10] What normal school students seemed more vividly to remember, though, was his generous supply of geographical illustrations drawn with infectious humour from first-hand experience in a hinterland they themselves might inhabit for a time.

Lord's 1924 teacher-training appointment marked the beginning of a pendulum swing between Vancouver Provincial Normal School and the inspectorate. Up to 1929, he taught in the handsome normal school building at the southwest corner of 12th Avenue and Cambie Street. During the 1929-30 school year he exchanged jobs with Inspector T.R. Hall, a man he much admired.[11] This occupational switch allowed

Lord to re-establish daily contact with practical school administration, observe closely and continuously the work of normal school graduates, and enjoy Kelowna once again. The following year he was back at the Normal School, but it could not hold him. Though just forty-six years old in 1931, he had become quite senior in his métier. That year he rejoined the cadre of provincial inspectors. From 1931 to 1933 he took charge of Vancouver's elementary schools together with its superior schools – institutions described in 1929 as public schools 'established or maintained for the teaching of pupils enrolled in grades one to ten inclusive of the course of study . . .' [12] From 1933 to 1936 he supervised similar schools located in the city municipality of North Vancouver, the rural municipalities of Port Moody, Port Coquitlam, and Pitt Meadows, and rural schools along the PGE, in the Cariboo south of Williams Lake, and throughout the Chilcotin.

These last years of Lord's career as inspector were to prove especially strenuous. Besides attending to a scattered inspectorate there were other official tasks demanded of him outside his territory – advising government on industrial and educational politics; investigating serious parental complaints; acting as official trustee to a bankrupt school district; pressing for honorific recognition of outstanding teachers; assessing educational library holdings; and corresponding with foreign educational institutions. Even more taxing were the miseries of economic depression, certain of which prompted one of several historic attempts to redress fiscal inequalities in provincial public education – the 1935 H.B. King report *School Finance in British Columbia*. [13] With other inspectors in the field, Lord submitted to King descriptive accounts of, and recommendations concerning, educational conditions. [14] Time softened Lord's perspectives. In mildly romanticized retrospect circa 1956, he writes of assisted schools provided on the 'principle . . . that, wherever there were ten children six years to sixteen years of age, a school would be established.' 'Such a program,' he continues, 'was designed for, indeed *was essential for* [editor's emphasis] a district during its pioneer stage when money was scarce and labour abundant.' Though not perfect, Lord recollects, assisted schools produced good citizens 'respected in their communities for their character, their good sense, and their leadership.'

But Lord's private report to King was devoid of such nostalgia. A stunning appraisal of educational deprivation during the Great Depression, his 1935 assessment of conditions in rural extremities of his sprawling inspectorate tested the limits of the 'school wherever ten school-aged children congregate' principle governing the establishment of schools at the time. Indeed, in a passage relating to Depression days in the Cariboo/Chilcotin, he challenged the legitimacy not only of an absolute application of this principle, but also of the concept of freedom of settlement implied in its provisions. Specifically, he contended that no economic justification could be found 'for the existence of such communities as Lone Butte, Sheridon Lake, Willowford, Bridge Lake, Bradley Creek, Black Creek, High Bay, Fraser View and Tatlayoko.' In most of these settlements, he went on, 'it freezes eleven months in almost every year and cattle raising is the only form of farming that has a chance of success, yet in the last three years many settlers, without a dollar, have been *permitted and even encouraged* [editor's emphasis] to come from the cities to these areas. Then they demand roads, schools, and relief. So long as these regions are permitted to exist the cost of education must fall very largely on the government for the simple reason that the local people have no money.' Concluding that 'in a number of instances the securing of a school has been made too easy' and questioning whether 'the mere presence of ten children *entitles* the district to a school at government expense,' Lord was dismayed to learn that King wished to publish these sentiments verbatim and recognize him as their author.[15] In an explosive protest he aired his understanding that stating 'the truth and the whole truth' had been conditional on the promise that his communication was to enjoy strict confidentiality. 'The truth, however, contains dynamite,' wrote Lord, warning 'I am not quite able to see what especial good would be done by making some of my statements public but I can see that it might create a great deal of unpleasantness.'[16] Clearly, by the mid-1930s, he was hard pressed and signs of strain are perhaps implicit in Superintendent S.J. Willis' assurance in 1935 that Education Minister George M. Weir valued Lord's services and that 'at the end of this school year, we may be able to make some adjustment in the work which we hope will be more satisfactory to you . . .'[17]

In any event, Lord survived with customary aplomb the administrative severities of the early and mid-1930s. Then in 1936, Principal D.M. Robinson retired following sixteen years at the helm of the Vancouver Provincial Normal School. By then it was no secret who would take his place. Lord awaited official word, which came from Weir in a letter dated 31 July 1936 conveying the bare facts of the appointment as well as Weir's personal satisfaction. The appointment also mirrored Weir's own background as principal of Saskatoon Normal School, first professor of education at the University of British Columbia, first director of the UBC Department (later School) of Education, and co-author of *Survey of the School System*. In language echoing North American educational progressivism, he acknowledged a continuing (and disarmingly specific!) interest in teacher training under Lord's leadership. 'During your recent visit to my office,' he declared,

> we discussed the proposed organization of the Normal School during the year 1936-37. I have not had an opportunity to give this matter detailed consideration, but believe your organization is quite sound. My sugges-tion was that you might include a Problem Course on Canadian educa-tional matters. These problems would be considered from an evolutionary standpoint and would involve considerable collateral reading. Such a course would include History of Education from a functional standpoint.[18]

Lord brought to his new job two indispensable attributes – profound understanding of rural British Columbia, and a personable way of helping normal school students fathom its deeper meaning. In the first instance, the reader should remember that creating rural-minded teachers had been the quest of provincial educators for at least four decades prior to Lord's arrival at Kelowna, continuing through-out his lifework and on to modern times.[19] During his normal school principalship, contemporaries in the Education Department, Victoria, drew attention to such matters as the 1943 summer workshop on rural education, the need for teacher education in a rural setting, and the *Rural School Magazine*.[20] Through their Rural Elementary Teachers Association founded in 1938, rural teachers themselves called for a mode of teacher training sensitive to the realities of rural life. With colleagues at Victoria Provincial Normal School, Lord tried to keep these rural needs central to normal school affairs, his special response being to instigate several ungraded model classrooms where candi-dates could watch others' and attempt their own lessons. These train-ing units were under the direction of Zella A. Manning, an experienced instructor remembered as both 'a character' and 'a crack-erjack teacher.'[21] Perhaps risking intramural resentment, Lord went so far as to state that these 'rural' practice facilities contributed 'more to the success of teacher-training than does any other phase of the school's work . . .'[22] Yet he never considered Miss Manning's unit *the* solution to the many surprises beginning teachers encountered when they first measured normal school training against the realities of an initial country appointment. Accordingly, he never stopped pressing for some form of practice teaching in the rural schools themselves.[23]

In the second instance – telling novices about their province – few have forgotten his prowess. Some, like normal school associate Frank Hardwick, recall 'great yarns about the Cariboo and Chilcotin;' or, like summer school student L.B. Daniels, anecdotes with a purpose, such as how to avoid mistakes through knowledge of local customs.[24] These whimsical stories, their absurdities mostly turned upon himself, were woven into lessons in geography and school law, talks at larger gatherings, staff room exchanges, or private interviews. Lord, though, was no yarn-by-yarn compulsive storyteller. A humanitarian ethic unified these apparent digressions. Ex-student Edith Chamberlayne exposes the heart of the matter. 'If you wanted to be a teacher,' she remembers, 'you had to like children – not just bright children, not just pretty children, not just clean children,' but dull, deprived, and dirty ones too. In rural isolation, however, a host of factors could impede such affection. Collectively, Lord's anecdotes and the sympathy they represented helped novices 'morally, physically, emotionally' stand on their two feet, set a good example, and truly teach.[25]

Though committed to rural schools, Lord was by no means parochial. At times a quiet, reflective, even shy man, inbred sociability more often put him widely at ease. Not averse to travelling in style, he thought nothing of riding railway freight cars, work cars, or speeders and, where necessary 'got permission to flag freight trains . . . walked twenty-five miles a day,' or bicycled seventy-five.[26] This gift for intelligent affability caught the early and sustained attention of numerous organizations. He became a Freemason, a Kiwanian, and an executive member of the Canadian Club. He was an elder of Shaughnessy United Church, Vancouver, and a governor of Union Theological College, UBC. As normal school principal he sat on UBC Senate. Over the years he served as president of Vancouver Children's Aid Society, chairman of the Vancouver Community Chest budget committee and of its special committee on drug addiction, and chairman of the British Columbia School Radio Broadcast Committee. In 1947 he was elected and served two years as president of the Canadian Education Association, followed by a period as liaison officer between the recently founded UNESCO and public education in Canada. These and other voluntary endeavours, together with his professional contributions to public education, did not pass unnoticed. The University of British Columbia and Queen's University awarded him honourary doctorates in 1948 and 1950 respectively. In 1950 the British Columbia Teachers' Federation recognized his outstanding work by giving him the Fergusson Memorial Award. In 1953 the Canadian Education Association granted him honorary life membership for exceptional service to education in Canada. In 1964, over three years after he died, Vancouver School Board named a new Lillooet Street building the 'Dr. A.R. Lord Elementary School' in his memory.

Each year of his career presented Lord with its own special challenge,

but few turned out more adventuresome than those spent as rural
school inspector travelling the breathtaking upland reaches of the
Cariboo and Chilcotin or the wondrous valleys, plateaus, and prairies
'north of fifty-three.' In today's world of district and local *superintendents*[27] with headquarters in substantial inland, coast, or island towns;
reasonably reliable road, rail, air, and ferry connections; and routine
telephone communications with the fringes of their territories, with
the Ministry of Education in Victoria, and among each other, it is easy
to forget that Lord's British Columbia was unsophisticated by comparison. Nor was the province extensively populated. In 1911 the provincial total was 390,000, 57 per cent of which lived in greater Victoria,
Vancouver, or the lower Fraser Valley. By 1931 this provincial total had
risen to 694,000, but the proportion inhabiting the province's south-
western extremity had more than kept pace, climbing to 67 per cent.
Up country that same year, Prince George and Prince Rupert inhabit-
ants numbered 2,479 and 6,350 respectively. But most rural settlements
remained much smaller.[28]

As one gathers from Lord's narrative, these habitations engaged
initially in agriculture and trapping, later in lumbering, mining, fishing, or railway construction. In the case of agriculture, land sales
boosterism laid excessive claims to what the future promised, the
Winnipeg and London Grand Trunk Pacific public relations branches
alluding to newly laid British Columbia track as 'The Great Highway
to the Opportunities of the Golden West Via "The Garden of Canada."'[29] One might have supposed that these sanguine prophesies
coupled with the Zeitgeist of western Canadian settlement with its
image of the farmer 'as the symbol of national greatness and durabil-
ity;' the opening up of transportation routes; and the commitment to
sweat and solitude of individual pre-emptors, would together have
blessed agriculture and related occupations with prosperous futures.[30]
Such proved not the case, however, two economic setbacks coinciding
with Lord's travels as inspector.

The first – the First World War – fell upon the province despite earlier economic buoyancy under Premier Richard McBride's administration and the establishment of GTP terminus facilities at Prince Rupert, a
rush for timber licences, vigorous promotion of town lots and farm
lands, and initial development of the Pacific Great Eastern Railway.
However, the 'virtually unchecked optimism' such initiatives engen-
dered faded as the savage realities of European warfare took precedence. British, American, German, French, and Belgian capital
investments in British Columbia industry slumped. Land booms
accompanying railway construction collapsed through overcapitaliza-
tion. Metal prices fell. Lack of shipping led to unprofitable stockpiles

of lumber and canned salmon. The domestic fruit market shrank. Toward the end of hostilities, war contracts had, to some extent, stimulated certain canning, lumber, mining, and shipbuilding concerns, but these late and relatively short-range gains did little to forestall the decline of once-thriving communities. Nor did they satisfy returning war veterans welcomed home 'with flag-waving and speeches full of promise' only to face labour unrest and postwar unemployment.[31]

The second setback – the Great Depression – proved world-wide during the 1930s. As on the world scene, the onset of provincial hard times was sudden and unanticipated. Following the stock market crash of October 1929, Vancouver's building trade ground to a halt, seriously affecting the province's lumber industry. International protectionism, currency devaluation, and uncertain foreign markets wiped out world orders for British Columbia salmon, forcing corresponding layoffs in canneries, tin can and shipping crate factories, as well as longshore and other transfer occupations. Waterfront activities were likewise slashed because of a glut on the world grain market. Meanwhile, up-country British Columbia encountered shrinking demands for its coal, lead, fruit, beef, and other products, laying off workers in proportion.[32]

Though economic depressions during the second and fourth decade of the twentieth century did not entirely dictate legislative provisions for bringing formal schooling to rural British Columbia, it unquestionably limited the scale of education it was possible to deliver. Apart from several later amendments, the governing legislation in Lord's time was incorporated in the Revised Statutes of British Columbia, 1911, Chapter 26. Under Article 25 of this Public Schools Act, assisted schools – those often isolated, ungraded classrooms demanding so much of Lord's energy – employed teachers whose modest salaries were fixed by law and paid monthly from the provincial treasury. The rest was largely up to the community. The Act stated that 'the buildings in which the school is held, as well as the desks and furnishings, shall be supplied and incidental expenses in connection with its maintenance met, as decided at the annual meeting, either by voluntary contributions of parents and others interested or by local assessment.' Assisted schools were placed under a local board of three trustees who were British subjects and qualified voters. Their duties included teacher appointment and dismissal, reporting teacher resignations, school visits, providing books for needy children, and expelling pupils 'addicted to any vice.' They also had to acquire property or money to operate a school, purchase or build a school-house, equip and repair it, borrow funds for improvements, decide on a school site, and ensure children aged six to sixteen were charged no tuition.[33]

Nineteen thirty-six saw several additions to the 1911 Act which brought it in line with growing organizational strength among teachers, as well as with certain health and welfare provisions for rural children, some already in place for over a decade thanks to provincial health legislation and local voluntary efforts. For instance, boards could now suspend teachers only for stated cause and were obliged to follow set procedures in appeal cases. Teachers were guaranteed sick leave up to one day a month during term. Indigent children with defective vision were to be supplied with free glasses. Pupils would receive free medical and dental examinations including free dental treatment if unable to pay for it. And boards were required to convey pupils from remote homes to the nearest school and, where necessary, meet the fees for correspondence instruction, both rudimentary attempts to narrow the opportunity gap separating city and country schoolchildren. Here, then, were the assisted schools which, in Lord's opinion 'developed a sense of community pride and civic responsibility . . .' Upon local trustees depended their provision of basic instruction and minimal health care in a manner excluding no child on account of poverty. Such, at least, were the prevailing legalities.[34] Although they may not mirror the more severe deprivations of two economically depressed periods in British Columbia's past, they do testify to a waste-not, want-not morality at the local school level born of pinched circumstances and never wholly dispensed with.

When Lord tackled his maiden inspectorate in 1915, the teachers he visited were mostly women trained at the Vancouver or, a little later, the Victoria Provincial Normal School. In those days, teachers qualified by successfully completing two years of high school of the three needed for junior matriculation, plus the minimal four-month normal school course of lectures and practice prerequisite to a third-class teaching licence.[35] By 1920 the required normal school studies had been extended to nine months and, as of 1925, teacher candidates were first obliged to finish the three-year high school program. Toward the decade's end, Superintendent S.J. Willis reported with satisfaction that many normal school trainees were voluntarily offering first-, and even second-year university as well.[36] In short, during Lord's career as inspector, early provincial teacher preparation developed and stabilized, allowing a legal concept of teacher services the better to emerge and solidify.

Under the 1911 Act – up to the present in fact – the primary function of a British Columbia teacher was to teach 'diligently and faithfully' and 'maintain proper order and discipline . . .' A teacher who allowed property to be destroyed through 'gross neglect' had to pay for the damage. Because attendance was directly related to levels of government support, other clauses specified clerical functions such as calling the roll, maintaining an accurate register, and reporting on absences. Yet other provisos called for keeping a visitors' book, reporting children's progress to their parents or guardians, holding public examinations, apprising trustees of 'infectious or contagious disease or unsanitary conditions . . .' and, should all of this overwhelm the teacher, giving thirty days' notice of resignation, 'such notice to terminate with the close of school term.' This legal concept of the teacher as instructor/disciplinarian/healthworker/clerk remained mostly intact in the 1936 Act which added teacher trainer to the role, necessitating teachers to admit trainees to their classrooms, help them learn how to teach, and submit reports on their progress and suitability, these added responsibilities to be shouldered 'without additional remuneration or salary.'[37]

Within this embryonic system of public education where trustees hired, supplied, and managed, and teachers instructed, disciplined, and counted heads, it was up to school inspectors to ensure that the administrative and educational provisions of the prevailing Act were observed. To this end they were to visit and inspect each district school annually. Inspectors were nearly always men, invariably ex-teachers – usually ex-principals – thus presumed capable of sizing up the classroom scene, pointing the way to improvement (now and again by giving a demonstration lesson), bending at times a sympathetic ear, and reporting their findings. They also were expected to know the Public Schools Act backwards and forwards and to elucidate its finer points for the benefit of trustees, teachers, and parents. Essentially, British Columbia school inspectors were the superintendent of education's representatives in the field and messengers of educational uniformity. They served as decision makers and assumed local control if electors or their trustees faltered; advised on the establishment of assisted schools and their reclassification as components of 'regularly organized school districts'; and were expected to 'promote the advancement of education by holding public meetings as frequently as possible and encouraging the establishment of schools where none exist.' Nor was their labour ended when district affairs for the moment appeared well in hand. For, as Lord would discover, any lull in the yearly round placed them at the disposal of the Education Office in Victoria and, lull or not, the Act ensured they could be called upon at any time 'to visit and inspect' any school beyond the boundaries of their own inspectorates.[38] Up to 1919, expenses incurred during their official wanderings underwent the piercing scrutiny of Superintendent Alexander Robinson himself, though his successor, S.J. Willis, seemed less attracted to that level of accountability. Indeed, as the public school system developed in size and complexity, many broader aspects and all minor and manipulative functions of the inspectorate fell to the orchestration of a chief inspector of schools, a position first recommended in 1925 by Commissioners Putman and Weir, but realized only in 1939 with the appointment of H.B. King.[39]

To review then, public education in Lord's British Columbia was legitimized by the 1911 and 1936 Public School Acts. These statutes assigned *trustees* the job of initiating and maintaining a school. They required *teachers* to teach, keep order, check attendance, report illness, and assist teacher trainees. And they detailed *inspectors* to supervise teachers as well as to help parents and others get a school started and to keep it operating to everyone's satisfaction. A tidy arrangement, to be sure. However, it is one thing to create a statutory substructure, another to realize its intent in rural areas far removed from the legislative centre. Preliminary stumbling blocks loomed quickly and large.

For a start, depression-scarred trustees were prone to cutting costs, sometimes erecting school buildings which, viewed from later standards, Lord described as 'poorly heated, badly lighted, woefully equipped, unsanitary, and ugly.' Moreover, school-to-school inconsistencies were commonplace. Lord's 1933 school reports employ terms such as 'insubstantial,' 'unsatisfactory,' 'entirely inadequate,' 'faulty,' 'inferior,' 'poor,' and in one instance – Meldrum Creek – 'the poorest building in my inspectorate.' They also refer to schools that are 'satisfactory,' 'comfortable,' 'well-finished,' 'very good,' 'substantial,' 'neat,' 'excellent,' and, at Dog Creek, 'an unusually attractive building.'[40] Under adverse circumstances, moreover, even knowledgeable, well-intentioned rural trustees (and there were many) faced obstinate local resistance. Some parents refused to pay their share of the assessment or to help fix a broken schoolhouse window. Other parents withdrew their children to work at home, threatening their marginally enrolled local school with closure. Equally frustrating to conscientious, able trustees were disputes over their just share of school taxes among loggers, miners, or railway construction workers who worked and moved on, and ranchers, homesteaders, or fruit growers who tended to stay put. Curious reverse effects sometimes ensued, the more transient interests tending to urge a higher level of support which their nomadic lifestyles enabled them in the long run to evade. As for ill-intentioned trustees, in 1935 H.B. King, a determined exponent of strong central control, left a classic account of 'local administration at its worst,' the saga about a rural school bully 'whose wholly-supportive mother and uncle constituted a majority of the Local School Board' and whose unbridled misbehaviour terrorized his classmates, intimidated the teacher, and prompted the third board member to resign 'in disgust.'[41] Meanwhile, as some communities increased, thrived for a time, and eventually dwindled, the essential fragility of assisted school attendance was to become readily apparent. In 1945 Maxwell A. Cameron showed that 301 of 828 rural schools were closed through chronic under-enrolment.[42]

For another thing, when Lord assumed his maiden inspectorate in 1915, the novice teachers he visited were very young, very inexperienced and, sometimes for good reason, very frightened. It was not at all uncommon to find assisted schools staffed by teenaged novices, a few of whom, given their early entry to normal school and short preparation there, might still be only sixteen years of age – near-contemporaries of their older students! A young teacher so situated often experienced a world of back-country teaching in sharp contrast to the gentler realm of the normal school. The working year could prove an anxious one. In absolute if not comparative terms, salaries were low – about fifteen dollars a week in 1917, twenty-two in 1923, and twenty in 1931.[43] Many schools were remote. Teaching conditions were often primitive. At best, novices taught in log buildings with snugly chinked walls and properly secured and maintained shake or sod roofs, or in small, but sturdy frame structures. At their collective worst, these buildings and their denizens endured the distractions of wood rot, ground subsidence, structural sag, ill-compacted earth or wobbly split-pole floors, spiders, cobwebs, mice, rats, termites, carpenter ants, flies, wasps, mosquitoes, nesting birds, bats, tadpole-infested water crocks, marauding bears, visiting moose, makeshift furniture, indifferent illumination, frozen inkwells, smoking wood stoves, and that threat to urbane refinement, the precarious, oh-so-visible outhouse.[44] By city standards, books were scarce, ungraded timetables were tough to design, tougher to implement; and, in the tenureless order of things, the question 'Shall I be rehired?' nagged the unconfident schoolteacher day and night throughout the vicissitudes of the school year.

As with the schoolhouse, a teacher's personal circumstances could also give rise to deeply felt uncertainties. Often the newest member of a community divided on such disparate questions as recipes and religion, a teacher required exceptional tact, particularly regarding room and board. Some were lucky. Authors Joan Adams and Becky Thomas tell of rural teachers happily settled in Cariboo ranch houses, Peace River homesteads, or Monashee farm dwellings. Others, however, faced cold comfort and domestic sullenness, the blight of rural depression when rivalry over a fee for room and board could engender jealousies beyond the ability of an eighteen-year-old normal school neophyte to cope. Worse, historian J. Donald Wilson relates the shocking case of Loretta Chisholm, 'a twenty-one year old teacher at Port Essington' found murdered in May 1926, and the appalling demise of Nixon Creek teacher Mabel Estelle Jones whose pathetic suicide note declared that what 'a few people' said about her 'almost broke my heart.'[45] Granted, these last events represented the extremes; other accounts lend balance to the history of rural schooling as recalled by one-time practitioners through presenting the pleasant as well as the more tragic side of rural school teaching.[46] Nevertheless, the limitations of a rural community's human and economic resources and the initial doubts surrounding a country teacher's working and private life, when in conflict, undeniably induced chronic teacher turnover in rural areas. Just how chronic the problem was Lord confirmed in 1922 when he wrote of his Kelowna inspectorate that 'the usual changing of teachers took place. In September there were new teachers in seventy-four of the eighty-eight rural classrooms and in January, an additional thirteen.'[47]

Then, too, inspectors themselves were hard pressed to fulfil their obligations under the Public Schools Act. Adams and Thomas speak of their absences from home and family, solitary journeys, uncomfortable temporary lodgings, and 'scuttlebutt that boiled up in the community' about the teachers who needed to be evaluated objectively.[48] Stories abound of inspectors outmanoeuvred by local sentinels heralding their arrival, resourceful teachers armed with well-rehearsed emergency lesson plans, disarming children of uncertain hospitality, even gruff dogs trained to discourage well-dressed men carrying government-crested briefcases. As writer Thomas Fleming explains, trustees increasingly approached the inspectors with their problems, considering them 'educational experts and men of practical affairs' with ready solutions up their sleeves. In their many duties, such as quantitative assessments of 'pupil absenteeism and retention rates, pupil and teacher performance, enrolment increases, and school operating costs,' inspectors were periodically thwarted by prolonged travel via unreliable transportation facilities.[49] The Grand Trunk Pacific Railway was a case in point. Lord recalls 'a train arriving in Prince Rupert from the east "on time" was rare enough to cause comment, and lateness was likely to be stated in days rather than hours...'

Nor when inspectors met their many responsibilities were their efforts necessarily acknowledged. The teacher reports they composed on the run were said by commissioners Putman and Weir to consist of bland, colourless prose describing an educational scene that was per-

petually 'satisfactory.' Some teachers whom inspectors visited saw
them as faddists preoccupied with a single subject, concept, or device
to the exclusion of all else. Others considered them out of touch or
sympathy with up-to-date practice. 'Trustees and other ratepayers'
complained that it was impossible to acquire 'reliable insights into
actual classroom conditions from reading ... [inspectors'] reports;'
that their classroom visitations were too infrequent to do any good
and that those most in need of supervision – rural teachers – received
least.[50] Of course, as with Lord, other inspectors doubtless enjoyed
on-the-job compensations. Many teachers 'remembered ... inspector[s] with gratitude' and occasionally with affection in that they were
at times the sole educational professional in whom they could confide
during an entire school year.[51] The feeling was not unreciprocal. Lord's
own recollections contain vibrant sketches of teachers whose company and service to children he clearly appreciated – people such as
Bill Sykes, L.V. Rogers, Elizabeth McNaughton, Paul Murray, and
Clarence Fulton come to mind, as do such unnamed teachers as the
young man at Dunster, the 'personable young woman' at Chilco, and
the Mennonite youth near Vanderhoof possessing 'latent qualities of
excellence.' For these and other reasons, Lord and his peers seem to
have enjoyed their jobs, hardships notwithstanding. They com-
manded respect in many communities; savored travel and a change of
scene; worked far removed from close departmental supervision;
made decisions as they saw fit and confronted their consequences;
and developed a knack of recounting their adventures in colourful
detail. In Lord's case, this professional satisfaction appears best
expressed in his love of wide horizons and diverse company as
reflected in the fact that the bulk of his memoirs speak not of schools
but of the richly varied societies that sustain them. Just the same,
being a school inspector in Lord's day was no sinecure, as Putman and
Weir themselves observed in 1925, agreeing that, contrary to its
innocent-looking statutory description, the inspector's task stretched
its incumbent beyond reasonable limits.

In this context, *Alex Lord's British Columbia* invites attention to its
inherent value system. Implicit among its observations is Lord's over-
riding conviction that British Columbia educators ought to know British Columbians. To this end Lord selected a cast of memorable
characters – Cataline, irrepressible Hazelton packer; Dr. H.C. Wrinch,
pioneer Hazelton physician; Ootsa settler Harry Morgan and Grassy
Plains pioneer John Bostrom; Vanderhoof expediter Joe Redmond;
Herbie Taylor, slayer of bears and 'Big Dan' Maclean, scourge of bank
robbers; Henry Koster, incisive Chilcotin rancher; Barney Brynildsen,

imaginative Bella Coola merchant; Father Coccola, comforter of the dying; and dozens of others. Together they share certain unmistakable attributes. They are self-assured, adventuresome folk, taking risks but not reckless, patient, courageous, willing to learn. They are strongly independent, at times intelligently non-conformist. Ambition, ability, thrift, and energy permeate their lives. Their toughest problems yield to a blend of perseverence, resourcefulness, and common sense. Thrown together in an economically depressed hinterland, they have occasion to differ, and differ they do with a vengeance. Day to day they endure because they must, sometimes with wit, normally with tolerance. Over the long haul they bind their lives together with compassion and a sense of justice. Throughout, a remarkable hospitality touches their existence. Sometimes Lord describes it as bed and board at the going price. More often he conceives of it as openness to any shared experience be it time, thought, joy, or sorrow. At its most romantic, hospitality is Lord wrapped in the mellow comfort of some Chilcotin hearth trading yarns till stars pale with the dawn. At its most poignant, it is Father Coccola treading the frozen trail to Cheslatta to bury the Indian dead.

Less abstract, maybe, than these very human qualities which Lord admired so much are certain incidental beliefs concerning law, politics, and society. Himself an agent of school legislation, he adopted a surprisingly resilient stance when confronted with several legal situations. At bottom, the true object of his respect was the law-abiding citizen like Henry Koster who, despite his indignation over an invidious provincial tax, paid it anyway as the moral obligation of one who helped elect the government which imposed it. Yet Lord appeared neither morally superior nor legally rigid when he or others might justifiably have thrown the book at offenders. Several sketches are of police officers dealing with trapline poaching, prohibition infringements, pornography, and the like. He seemed to approve of the ingenious and often personal solutions to such alleged misdemeanors that some officers came up with. As for his own legal ethic, developed over years of purchasing railway tickets, counting schoolchildren, and mediating local quarrels, his code might be expressed as 'play fair, circumvent conflicting regulations, and close the official eye in a good cause.' Though politically a confessed 'Grit,' Lord confined his analysis of government policy to a single, mildly acerbic comment on the federal Liberals' misplaced optimism over the Grand Trunk Pacific Railway's ability to pay its own way. In a more general manner, however, he left no doubt over his conviction that knowledge of politics lies at the heart of informed citizenship. Lord introduced this theme in an account of a Port Hope, Ontario, political meeting at which he heard

Sir Wilfrid Laurier speak. He pursued the theme in a yarn about H.B. Thomson's inept performance during his Prince Rupert campaign speech; augmented it in a glimpse at Fort George ballot-count irregularities; elaborated upon it by alluding to Pouce Coupé settlers bent on conveying their political concerns to newly elected Premier H.C. Brewster; and concluded with a touching portrait of Superintendent Alexander Robinson whose dogged refusal to distinguish cabinet from civil service prerogatives terminated in summary dismissal and alarming decline, followed by suprising and happy regeneration.

Lord's intention was not to submit the places and people he knew so well to searching sociological examination. Nevertheless, *Alex Lord's British Columbia* does not lack for social comment. According to Lord, certain farmers, business people, school trustees, MLA's, medical doctors, judges and others – community leaders all – as graduates of their rural schools went forth to set new standards of civic pride. Social change was not their objective. They sought no New Jerusalem. Instead Lord gave us farmers and police officers, doctors and lawyers, railway workers and trappers, riverboat captains and clergy, politicians and ranchers, children and housewives, all accepting their social milieu. No aspect of Lord's account renders this perspective more evident than his overall picture of a multi-ethnic British Columbia. Persuasively drawn in the foreground appear the well-schooled or self-educated British, some, like Norman Lee and David Lloyd, with impressive English university or 'public' school associations. In middle distance are nationals merging expediently with the general scene, such as Barney Brynildsen, drawn as a sober, industrious man of 'high reputation;' or Henry Koster's father, the German miner who taught his son to read – not Goethe, but Thackeray. Toward the background emerge certain stereotypes – an outspoken Jewish fur buyer; intractable Mennonites clinging to their German language; French Canadian, black, and Chinese minority figures each uttering music hall versions of standard English. In the background, meantime, tarry nameless Indians either carving, weaving, or thwarting the law. Granted, notable irregularities crop up in this otherwise socially ordered landscape, such as Koster, a middle-distance man painted in the foreground. Nor is it unlikely that fairly sharp social divisions apparent in *Alex Lord's British Columbia* perhaps might have blurred had Lord written to conclusion. As the manuscript stands though, Lord's enthusiasm for British institutions cannot pass unnoticed.[52]

As well as his views on human nature, law, politics, and society, Lord expressed decided opinions on education.

First, Lord contended that the *purpose* of education is citizenship which, in his opinion, the rural school shows such promise of engendering. Curricula, he insisted, come and go, but like a textbook or a building, a curriculum is 'merely an instrument' to help teachers shape pupils into good citizens. In this sense, then, education is the touchstone of social integrity. Such being the case, it is of paramount social importance to be able to recognize the well-educated person. Here Lord gave direct advice. Koster, he said, is such a person. The wellspring of Koster's enlightenment was his grasp of language, which was 'precise and exact' like a 'university graduate with a major in English.' Richly experienced, he conversed knowingly along the spectrum of subjects from cattle diseases and beef prices, communism and religion, to trees, placer mining, and the magnificence of the Cariboo. He was clear, uncomplicated, able to strip a topic of all but essentials and drive home rational conclusions with solid arguments. He also possessed such attributes as hospitality, manners, good taste, and ambition, hallmarks in Lord's view of the well-educated person and valued citizen.

Second, Lord held that such a citizen ideally starts to grow when guided by a *good teacher*. After a few months, for instance, Bill Sykes' schoolchildren wrote copperplate, a requisite skill in a letter-writing society. Presumably, pupils taught by the resolute young man at Dunster acquired similar proficiency. However, in Lord's mind there was more to good teaching than fundamental instruction. For him, the good teacher had somehow to fit the community, serve it, learn from it – not merely as a matter of strategy but because of enjoyment. The classroom, too, should reflect the enthusiasm a good teacher brought to the job, creating a bright, co-operative atmosphere, both for its own sake and because children in ungraded schools need to work on their own. Setting this 'tone' (a category, incidentally, on the inspector's standard teacher report form) called for special character traits. Sykes had generosity; the young man at Dunster, courage. Elizabeth McNaughton combined knowledge and professional modesty with an amiable disposition. L.V. Rogers embodied the best in determination to succeed. Clarence Fulton displayed a streak of creative non-conformity, though it landed him in trouble. Paul Murray radiated benevolence and wisdom. All six excelled in classroom rapport not because of what they knew – and they knew a lot – but of who they were. Lord was explicit on this point. 'Teachers are much more important than what they teach,' he declared.[53]

Although the above qualities of the good teacher emerge only through inference from Lord's occasional mention of such matters, they square remarkably well with his more deliberate statements on the subject such as 'A Canadian Looks at Teacher Training' (1937) and 'Changes in Vancouver Normal School' (1938), both published during his early years as principal of the Vancouver teacher-training institution. The emphasis here was classroom methodology. In the 1937 publication, Lord observed that 'the true teacher is a leader and guide. His classroom reveals a situation which is pupil-centric, where he is conspicuously in the background quietly guiding and directing, where pupils are industriously working for themselves; his curriculum is only a means; he deals with large units of work, not with fragments; he "teaches" nothing that pupils can find for themselves.' In the 1938 piece, Lord deplored a normal school program demanding an 'excessive student load of thirty or thirty-four periods per week.' Such a burden, he declared, 'made adequate evening preparation by the student impossible and therefore forced instructors to adopt a lecture method' which 'penalized initiative and placed a premium on good memory.' He further explained that the reduction of this load by nine periods a week resulted in more preparation time for trainees, discussion of assigned reading as a basis for class instruction, unification and consolidation of general principles, and room for the notion that 'teaching is more of an art than of a science . . . '[54]

To his assumptions about educational purpose and the nature of the good teacher Lord added other provocative educational comments largely contained in his section entitled 'Curricula in 1910.' Bear in mind that during his British Columbia career (1910–50) three related educational developments affected the province: (1) the many-faceted progressive education movement, a western phenomenon whose American form significantly influenced British Columbia schools; (2) a change in the aims and ambience of British Columbia high schools; and (3) a growing preference for curricular centralization. His early inspectorates in predominantly rural areas, his sympathies much in support of the character-building power of well-run rural schools, Lord was at odds with the first two tendencies, ambivalent on the third.

Though he did not name it as such, the progressive education movement which Lord played down as creating in British Columbia only a 'mildly revolutionary atmosphere' was, he said, derivative, an imitation of American theory and practice fraught with the 'objectionable educational jargon' Americans used to explain new psychological concepts.[55] He gave examples, minimizing them as inconsequential 'variations' or 'revisions' first tried out in reforms of the 1930s under Curriculum Director H.B. King. They included discursive statements of educational aims; subject time allotments with corresponding 'credit' values; division of subject matter into teaching 'units;' new evaluation procedures involving 'objective' tests; and systematic, cumulative school records for each student. Subsequent changes after

King's retirement in 1945, Lord observed, 'bore little resemblance' to previous ones, his contention being no doubt that many progressive ideas abroad in his time as inspector proved to be fads.

Lord's reservations over a new role for British Columbia high schools constituted a reaction to curriculum changes initiated in 1945 by King's successor Harold L. Campbell. Earlier on, Lord noted, just getting to high school was a personal triumph. He conceded that dispensing with the high school entrance examination made no discernable difference to a student's subsequent performance, but regretted its desuetude on the grounds that, 'human nature being what it is,' a provincial exam serves as a singular motivator. More to the point, the demise of the entrance exam signified a new 'social attitude' which Lord recognized, but accepted with reluctance. This attitude rested upon two principles new to British Columbians: (1) the *right* of *every* child to attend high school, rendering this institution a people's college in the American sense; and (2) a high school's responsibility to hold each student as long as possible, academic standards notwithstanding. The curricular manifestations of such principles Lord clearly considered hurtful. Under their persuasion, hard-nosed subjects such as chemistry supposedly yielded to 'life situation subjects' such as general science, scant preparation Lord thought for students struggling with first-year university chemistry. Equally deleterious, he believed, was filling in a bright high school student's uncommitted timetable slots with art, typewriting, or music, subjects which, in the progressive context, he mentioned with little enthusiasm despite earlier joy over Bill Sykes' prowess as a teacher of elementary school music. Yet another feature of this all-embracing high school of great wonder to Lord was its eligibility for 'accreditation,' an arrangement whereby, once endorsed as a fit institution, a high school could graduate deserving students on the basis not of province-wide, but of school-set examinations. This scheme, he said, got out of hand and graduated a 'considerable' number who would have failed had they sat 'an external examination of a rigorous form.' In other words, the university was obliged to accept and cope with as best it could certain high school graduates who, in Lord's opinion, had no business being there. In short, as late as 1956 when he set down his thoughts on the subject, Lord perceived the British Columbia high school not as a place chiefly engaged in propagating a widely accommodating, well-informed citizenry but rather, as an institution intended for preserving academic standards and screening its students for university entrance. To such a marked extent, he distanced himself from 'progressive' reforms of the 1940s and 1950s, by distinguishing between an elementary school that teaches citizenship, articulateness, civility, even happiness, and a high school far more concerned with subjects and standards than his remarks on educational purpose and the nature of the good teacher at first blush might imply.

On curriculum centralization, Lord's support of Departmental examinations raises a substantial problem of inconsistency which, if his uncharacteristically laboured prose at this point is any indication, he was not unaware of. Implicit to his remarks on accreditation was the suggestion that high school teachers cannot be trusted to set sufficiently rigorous internal tests. Contrariwise, he saw a provincially centralized curriculum as a threat to 'that most valuable of all teacher traits, initiative.' Admittedly, he recognized certain advantages in centralization. It allows for closer monitoring of classroom work, facilitates record-keeping, and ensures uniformity, hence fairness, in issuing graduation diplomas and, in a pinch, provides a 'comforting' crutch for novice as well as 'most mediocre teachers' whatever their tenure. The temptation for gross misuse (such as dictating detailed course outlines as class notes), however, is compelling among timorous, unimaginative, or incompetent teachers. A far better scheme, he maintained, would have been a program stating 'general essentials' for teachers to use 'in accordance with their own intelligent conception of what is best for the pupils in the local district,' a very British approach, by the way. Under such a system of shared central and local curriculum jurisdiction, Lord argued, central authorities could list recommended texts and teachers could select those most appropriate to their circumstances. Anything less, he concluded, smacks of the assembly line, an industrial technique unworthy of true education, though (and here Lord wavered), maybe unavoidable in the large modern high school, that 'regrettable' new place compelled to offer courses tailored 'to fit the abilities and even the *inclinations* [editor's emphasis] of the average..."

Such, in short order, are the human, legal, political, social, and educational values inherent in *Alex Lord's British Columbia* and they are the counterpoint of his narrative. It remains to locate Lord in British Columbia educational history.

Since the mid-1930s several kinds of historical analyses of provincial education have appeared. For their fuller appreciation, readers should consult such books as J. Donald Wilson and David C. Jones (eds.), *Schooling and Society in Twentieth Century British Columbia* (1980). Briefly, though, earlier studies brimmed over with optimism; a little later, sceptics challenged such optimism; and coincidentally, articles, monographs, and popular narratives added to a growing general literature. F. Henry Johnson's biography, Alan H. Child's thesis, and Thomas Fleming's analyses, each suggesting practical methodologies and ready sources, furnish stimulating historical studies in aspects of school inspection, as do other works, scholarly and popular alike.[56] Much, however, remains to be done. Several unique features of *Alex Lord's British Columbia* help close the gap.

First, here is new material. Unlike annual reports, regulations, curriculum outlines, and other official documents, Lord's comments on curriculum reform wind the topic to a higher pitch because they lay bare the retrospective doubts of an ex-civil servant once duty bound to implement, now free to criticize provincial educational policy. This same humanizing effect applies equally to Lord's portrait of the redoubtable Alexander Robinson. Official histories say Robinson was 'removed,' and newspaper headlines proclaim 'he told the premier off.'[57] Lord adds flesh to these bare bones, giving us an intimate sketch of 'the most dynamic personality who ever stood in a British Columbia classroom.' In other respects, too, Lord supplies fresh data and original thinking. To date, few have matched his finesse in employing transportation as the leitmotiv of a work on British Columbia education. Lord is constantly on the move, and the reader moves with him day and night, around the seasons, along road, rail, and water routes; on foot, horseback, and bicycle; in flivvers, day coaches, sleeping cars, canoes, launches, sternwheelers, and coastal steamers; in the company of settlers, police officers, trappers, traders, hunters, railway conductors, steamboat captains, priests, and judges; to meet teachers, trustees, schoolchildren, ranchers, politicians, bankers, packers, farmers, members of the business community, physicians, lawyers, government agents, telegraphers, and bootleggers. The outcome is an original and touching account of the hopes, fears, and fortunes of early British Columbians and of a way of life public schooling was intended to render secure.

Second, Lord's reminiscences possess a stimulating heuristic quality. They tantalize, whet the appetite, introduce themes worthy of historical elaboration. They are rich in timeless educational issues such as rural schooling, supervision, mass education, central versus local control, curriculum reform, teacher initiative, educational purpose, and so forth. As for personalities, in rescuing Alexander Robinson from temporary obscurity, Lord points the way for writers interested in readable biography, with a flair for characterization, and willingness to master the voluminous data.[58] Beyond Robinson, a roster of subjects ripe for biographic rediscovery would not be hard to compile. One might profitably start with Margaret K. Strong, first woman inspector of British Columbia schools.[59]

Besides being new, or more correctly, previously unpublished, *Alex Lord's British Columbia* intersects interestingly with several other histories.

Consider, for example, Fleming's elegant 'Our Boys in the Field.'[60] Lord fits to a T Fleming's pre-Depression British Columbia school inspector. Born and educated outside the province, Lord was a gentleman and a scholar expecting high standards; he had come out to British Columbia as a teacher in the early 1900s and certainly 'took great pride in the province's educational development' even though he turned a blind eye to a few local deviations. On Fleming's choice of 1925 as the boundary between old school 'individuals of high character' and a new breed of 'educational experts and men of practical affairs,' however, Fleming and Lord complement each other. Note that Lord's tenure as inspector extended from 1915 to 1936 with interruptions as normal school instructor from 1924 to 1929 and 1930 to 1931. Nor was he alone. Seventeen other inspectors appointed before 1925 held their positions well beyond that point, the most striking, chronologically speaking, being A. Sullivan (1909-43), J.B. DeLong (1913-46), and G.H. Gower (1913-44).[61] Indeed, in 1936, a year of extensive educational reform under Education Minister George M. Weir, fourteen of twenty-nine British Columbia inspectors (48 per cent) had been initially appointed prior to 1925.[62] In light of Lord's retrospective misgivings over large high schools, accreditation, general science, promotion by age, the 'fetish' of high school retention, and other progressive hallmarks, one wonders how many of his contemporaries in the inspectorate shared his views, what effect a lingering conservatism might have had on the kind of executive solidarity requisite of educational reform, and ultimately whether this caution in the face of changing educational perspectives might have impeded the realization of a more sweeping progressive education than the one Weir and several of his successors were ever able to introduce. Such questions are worth pursuing.

Or, take for instance Timothy A. Dunn's 'The Rise of Mass Public Schooling in British Columbia, 1900-1929,' a persuasive analysis which identifies citizenship as the purpose of pre-Depression British Columbia education, describes an educational bureaucracy calculated to achieve that purpose, and concludes that, as elsewhere, early provincial public schooling was 'part of a larger "search for order" directed at preserving [social] stability,' three observations which conform quite closely to Lord's stories.[63] Where Dunn and Lord diverge, though, is in their account of the provincial inspectorate and its Victoria headquarters back-up. For Dunn, this cadre of educational civil servants is a rigid instrument of efficiency and control, an enduring pyramid of subordination with the superintendent of education commanding its apex. For Lord, it is a far looser association of outstanding educators who normally conduct their affairs in an amicable way, take professional initiatives, sympathize with teachers, and trade yarns with the locals. In his searching treatise, 'Agriculture, the Land, and Education: British Columbia, 1914–1922', David C. Jones takes up much the same point, showing British Columbia Director of Elementary Agricultural Education J.W. Gibson and his provincial supervisors working on behalf of a rural population which they wanted not 'to subjugate or control . . . but to elevate and enlighten.' Such findings are consistent with those of James Collins Miller, whose *Rural Schools in Canada: Their Organization, Administration and Supervision* (1913) showed that 'in much of Canada the growth of the administrative staff barely kept pace with the growth in the system as a whole;' that the effect of school inspectors on rural schools was the *gradual transformation* of central policy to classroom practice; and that, in historian Neil Sutherland's words, local inspectors 'prodded . . . rural school boards into hiring better teachers, providing better sanitary facilities, putting schools into reasonable repair, keeping them open for a moderate length of time, and building teacherages.' Inspectors so occupied seem not to fit the image of that inflexible, opinionated arm of government under whose dominion, as Michael Katz once put it, 'schools were . . . divorced from the communities they served and laymen had progressively less power. . .'[64]

Because of its protagonists, emphases, and analytical bite, Jean S. Mann's 'G.M. Weir and H.B. King: Progressive Education or Education for the Progressive State?' serves as another foil for *Alex Lord's British Columbia*.[65] Fascinating is the notable difference in degree of self-consciousness separating their authors' treatment of the concept 'progressive education.' Mann, a post-progressive scholar, roots her argument in the Putman/Weir *Survey* which she considers a 'melange' of progressive educational theories circa 1925. She depicts Weir as 'best known for his advocacy of the "new education"' and King as an enthusiast for 'those facets of progressive education to which the label "scientific" could be attached.' She thinks about instances of British Columbia progressive education – junior high schools, vocational guidance, wide course choice, for example – neither as humanitarian gestures nor as devices to enhance learning, but rather as conscious attempts to condition children to a stable provincial order progressive chiefly in its commitment to 'social and industrial expansion.'[66] By contrast, beyond passing reference to a 'mildly revolutionary atmosphere' and a whimsical apology for using 'a bit of objectionable educational jargon – the word "motiva-

tion",' Lord, who had lived throughout this period and worked with
confessed British Columbia progressives, seemed oblivious even to
the issue as Mann, with hindsight, conceives of it. He never
employed the term 'progressive education.' He made no mention of
the Putman/Weir *Survey*. He presented Weir, who appointed him
principal of the Vancouver Provincial Normal School, merely as 'Liberal Education Minister.' He wrote rather huffily of King as 'a prominent and controversial figure ... with pronounced opinions on
practically all matters having to do with schools ... ,' who 'knew
what he wanted and ... intended to get it.' In short, progressive
education as a mode of social and economic manipulation seemed
the last idea in Lord's mind. Yet, precisely in the manner of the
educational progressives Mann describes with such dash, Lord took
no exception to the established social, occupational, or industrial
workings of early British Columbia. Quite the contrary. He envi-
saged and clearly approved of a 'great power development pro-
gramme' which some day will give rise to 'a second Kitimat at
Tatlayoko,' in Mann's terms a very 'progressive' vision indeed! To
this extent, then, the conservative relates after all to the progressive,
leaving one to inquire whether in reality educational philosophy and
educational practice necessarily (or at all) determine social and economic policy, or whether 'progress' as a function of social stability
and industrial expansion can perhaps prove the common dream of
educational progressive and conservative alike.

On these same questions – the nature of British Columbia progressive education, what it supposedly replaced, and the intent and
extent of its realization – three other historical analyses converge upon
Lord's writing. George Tomkins' comprehensive *A Common Countenance: Stability and Change in the Canadian Curriculum* (1986) confirms
that in British Columbia, as elsewhere, 'the rhetoric and reality of
change were far apart,' and the implementation of progressive ideas
'selective.'[67] Such, indeed, is the difference between progressive cru-
sader H.B. King, whose public utterances fuelled the debate as he
'attacked his new [curriculum] responsibilities with zest,' and Lord's
unpretentious stories of field visits never cast in 'progressive' dis-
course. So, when Lord told of the joy, the fun, the satisfaction incidental to Bill Sykes's music lessons, or intimated what a great experience it
must have been to take part in one of Clarence Fulton's physical
education classes, he did so, not as a theoretician expounding some
abstract notion of child psychology or rural sociology dredged from
the literature of progressive education, but as a cultured professional
with a mature respect for human dignity and a kindly sense of
humour. As for what critics have alleged progressive education super-

seded or sympathizers argued it accomplished, Sutherland offers two brilliant insights. In his 'The Triumph of "Formalism": Elementary Schooling in Vancouver from the 1920s to the 1960s,' he inquired of Vancouverites who went to elementary school in those days how their teachers taught and what they themselves learned. In a crushing rejection of Hilda Neatby's *So Little for the Mind* (1953), he concluded that, throughout the twentieth century, Canadian education 'did not and never had done much to train the mind it served.' And in his methodologically similar 'Everyone seemed happy in those days: the culture of childhood in Vancouver between the 1920s and the 1960s,' Sutherland proposes an alternative explanation for childhood cheerfulness, unrelated to their teachers or their lessons, progressive or otherwise. These children he asserted, enjoyed the 'culture of childhood,' which is to say 'the knowledge, customs, expectations, beliefs, norms, values, and social roles that governed relationships between them,' which were of *their own* making, and which, despite pressures within their classrooms, allowed them on the playground or in other meeting places between school and home to find 'some moments in which they delight in themselves and their lives.'[68]

Among works most closely related to the historical particulars of *Alex Lord's British Columbia*, by far the best scholarly companions are '"May the Lord Have Mercy on You": The Rural School Problem in British Columbia in the 1920s' by J. Donald Wilson and Paul Stortz, and Wilson's 'The Visions of Ordinary Participants: Teachers' Views of Rural Schooling in British Columbia in the 1920s.' Based on a rich array of reports, recollections, and questionnaire returns for 1923 and 1928, the first documents the rural teacher's point of view – a perspective as grim as Lord's is hopeful. It not only reveals the frustrating details of parental jealousies, amorous importunities, personal danger, and heartrending loneliness tormenting less fortunate rural teachers, but also speculates on why such cries for help often went unheeded by an education department convinced rural schooling improved year by year. The second piece, a tight account of 'the interplay between intentions and consequences' in provincial educational policy, probes ethnicity in British Columbia society, a question inherent in Lord's narrative, but lacking conscious inspection. According to Wilson, teachers' observations on this matter 'conformed to the racial hierarchy ... of that day. Apart from British and American immigrants or settlers from eastern Canada,' he continues, 'the preferred immigrants were those from the nations of northern and western Europe. Slavic immigrants from central and eastern Europe ... were acceptable, but not preferred. Among the non-preferred were those from southern Europe.... Those from Asia were considered non-assimilable . . . ,' a rank ordering not unlike that inferable from Lord's incidental comments.[69]

Finally, one last genre of literature – full biography – calls for attention because of its value for comparative purposes. A fine example is R.J.W. Selleck's *Frank Tate: A Biography* (1982), an Australian classic of great wit and erudition relating 'the journeys of a school inspector . . . significant in themselves . . . ' and holding as well the power to 'illuminate the shadowy values and hopes of past generations.' Tate's Australian experience as inspector, 1895-9, predates Lord's initial northern British Columbia posting, 1915-9, by twenty years, moving it that much closer to Victorian England's tastes and standards. Otherwise, the parallels are striking. Both Tate and Lord became inspectors via the rural teacher-rural principal path. Both taught at training institutions, eventually becoming principals. Each described the discomforts of extreme climates, although at opposite ends of a Fahrenheit scale, Tate telling of an 'almost unbearable' classroom at Koonung Koonung where the mercury soared to 104 degrees [40°C], Lord terming 'uncomfortable and dangerous' teaching at Fort Fraser where the temperature plummeted to sixty degrees below zero [-51°C]. At first overcome by a certain social directness and mental insularity born of regions barely recovered from gold rush fever, each man came to appreciate life in rugged isolation, Tate growing 'very much wiser about the rough pioneering life of our mallee settlers . . . ,' Lord discovering throughout 'the entire Chilcotin . . . the genial welcome . . . , the direct, innate courtesy . . . , the blunt expression of opinion which always seemed to get down to essentials . . . ,' qualities he came to prize. Such a citizenry, they independently concluded in early career, deserves well-trained, committed teachers and neither, as Tate insisted, the 'immature and inexperienced . . . who groped their way forward . . . nor the older . . . who had dropped into a dispirited routine,' or those who Lord, on occasion, observed keeping order through dread of reprisal. Many other similarities mark their adventures in the field, a timely reminder that life along the world's frontiers is seldom unique.[70]

However, the careers of these kindred spirits also featured some remarkable differences. During his inspectorship, throughout long service as Victoria State deputy minister of education, and beyond into retirement, Tate remained the more professionally assertive, sharply critical of 'the old and well-worn ruts of ancient conservatism,' stubbornly opposed to paying teachers according to their students' examination results, firmly supportive of high schools where 'the all-round development of all is desired.' Quite unlike Lord, who regretted de-emphasis on British Columbia government exams, feared comprehensive high schools would debase standards, and was less than inspired by a 'mildly revolutionary atmosphere which followed The First World War . . . more in imitation of the United States than original,' Tate took keen interest in the 'new education,' *especially* its American form. In 1925 he established connections in New York City at Teachers College, Columbia. By 1930, thanks to his 'drive, his speed of mind, and his ability to persuade colleagues to ignore [Australian] interstate rivalries,' he acquired important Carnegie funding to set up the Australian Council for Educational Research, an organization whose chief executive K.S. Cunningham – himself a Teachers College, Columbia graduate – saw education as a science better informed by American than by British example. The irony is not hard to recognize. Tate, the older Australian raised to observe Victorian English values and employed within an ultra-centralized public school system seized hold of progressive education, not Lord, the younger Canadian and United States neighbour who, despite the 1925 Putman/Weir advocacy, was little inclined to espouse its 'progressive' cause. As with ironies in general, this one is easier to identify than to explain. It serves, though, as a caveat against the easy assumption that educational influence varies directly with the geographical proximity of its source of innovation.[71]

Since Lord first measured its reaches over seventy years ago, British Columbia has changed dramatically both in the ever-widening scope of city existence and in the increasing complexity of communication networks enhancing rural life. Yet, in spite of such changes, *Alex Lord's British Columbia* asserts its currency in two arresting ways.

First, it inquires once more into the manner of the province we inhabit. It answers that we inherit certain sobering realities of geography – far-flung political boundaries, unyielding topography, unforgiving winters, disabling back roads, inhospitable seaways, scattered and uneven settlement. It stresses that, despite transportation and communication developments, local perspectives remain fixed and political views fiercely sceptical. It emphasizes that, in their quest for the good life, British Columbians have survived the undulations of boom-and-bust economics, pinning their faith more often than not upon some single, localized component of the economic whole – a homestead, a farm, a ranch, an orchard, a road, a railway, a cannery, a sawmill, a mine, a speculative venture, or a government subsidy. And it reminds us, allegiances in evidence to be sure, that we are a province of diverse national, cultural, religious, and racial origin; a province, moreover, in which educational efforts to preserve, comprehend, and tangibly recognize such diversity periodically founder on the trident reef of prejudice, bigotry, and political expediency.

Second, *Alex Lord's British Columbia* instinctively points to where British Columbians by tradition believe they will acquire power and inspiration to confront and overcome the economic and social ills that menace their daily lives and threaten their general well-being – the school. No other institution enshrines for Lord and his contemporaries such high hopes for a better future, hopes undiminished by economic and social problems neither of the school's making nor always in its capacity to remedy. On behalf of this school, citizens like Joe Redmond exercise their considerable political wits. Within this school, children lay the foundation of their own, hence, the province's future. The lucky ones do so with the guidance of an Elizabeth McNaughton or a Paul Murray. Helped by such outstanding teachers they will acquire not only knowledge and skill but also, those qualities of morality, good conduct, cheerfulness, and patriotism intended to advance community, provincial, and national cohesiveness.[72] From this school, too, will go forth those good citizens respected in Lord's words 'for their character, their good sense and their leadership,' destined to leave their economic, social, and spiritual environment a little better than they found it. A tall order, perhaps, albeit consistent with a latter-day provincial administration contending that the 'quality, effectiveness and relevance of the Province's schools ... have enormous impact on our success' and directing its Education Commissioner, Barry M. Sullivan, QC, to recommend a school system designed to help British Columbia compete in a world facing 'unprecedented ... economic and technological change.'[73]

With charm and humour, *Alex Lord's British Columbia* explores those intimate relationships between British Columbia society and the schools it created. We are indebted to its author for reminding us of these vital connections in such colourful fashion.

John Calam
Fulford Harbour, BC

Alex Lord's British Columbia

BRITISH COLUMBIA

KLONDIKE

YUKON

NWT

PACIFIC

Atlin

Telegraph Creek

Mackenzie R.

Liard River

QUEEN CHARLOTTE

Stewart

①

Peace River Block

Fort Simpson
Prince Rupert
Inverness
Terrace

Skeena R.

Hazelton

Smithers

G.T.P.

②

ISLANDS

Fort McLeod

Burns Lake
Fort Fraser
Ocean Falls
Bella Coola

③

④ Fort St. James
Vanderhoof
Prince George
Fort George

Peace River

⑥
⑦

⑤

⑧

ALBERTA

OCEAN

⑨

LEGEND

1 Omineca District
2 Skidegate Inlet
3 New Caledonia
4 Stuart River
5 Nechako River
6 Cascade Inlet
7 Burke Channel
8 Fort George Canyon
9 Blackwater Canyon
10 Rocky Mountains
11 Cariboo
12 Chilcotin
13 Thompson rivers

Quesnel

Williams Creek
Barkerville

⑩

*VANCOUVER
ISLAND*

Union Bay

⑫

⑪

Fraser River

Fort Alexander
100 Mile House

Columbia R.

Soda Creek
Ashcroft

⑬

P.G.E.

Kamloops

Newcastle
Nanaimo
New Westminster

Vancouver

Victoria

U.S.A.

Brewster (Wash.)

0 kilometres 300

0 miles 150

Fort Vancouver (Wash.)

ARW/91

Map 1

CHAPTER ONE

North of Fifty-Three

During the autumn of the year 1904 Canada was in the midst of a general election with the Liberals using the construction of a second transcontinental railroad, the Grand Trunk Pacific, as their main argument for retention of power. I was then attending model school, the lowest rung on the Ontario teacher-training ladder of those days and went one evening to a political meeting in Port Hope. The speakers were the Liberal Chieftain, Sir Wilfrid Laurier, his Minister of Finance and first lieutenant the Honourable W.S. Fielding, and the local candidate A.B. Aylesworth. In bursts of oratory such as are seldom heard these days they pictured the heights to which this country – and particularly northern Canada – would rise with the completion of the railroad. The most significant statement that evening and, as events turned out, the most inaccurate prophesy, appeared on a banner stretched above the platform. It read 'The Grand Trunk Pacific will never cost the people of Canada one dollar.'

While the GTP was under construction and to some extent because of it, another railroad, this time entirely in British Columbia, was undertaken. Its purpose was to connect the coast with the vast areas of productive land in the central and northeastern parts of the province. Named the Pacific Great Eastern, this railroad was to have its southern terminus at Vancouver, to meet the GTP in the vicinity of Fort George, and then to continue into the Peace River region. It was an ambitious and far-sighted undertaking which soon ran into difficulties which were to plague it for fifty years but which have no place in this record. Suffice it to say that by the summer of 1914, when the first railroad was completed, the second, with track laid on most of the southern third and the grade completed on another third, had suspended operations and little optimism was in evidence concerning its future.

It was in those days that I began inspecting schools in the area served by both railroads. The inspectorate was a new one and covered a considerable territory. In addition to 700 miles on the GTP from Prince Rupert to the Alberta border and 150 miles south from Fort George along the hoped-for PGE, it included the British Columbia coast and adjacent islands from Bella Coola to the Yukon and, in the northeast of the province, the Peace River Block. While there were times in the ensuing years when the total miles involved seemed extreme, yet the population was not in proportion. In 1915 there were only forty-four schools, only three with more than one room. It was not difficult to feel four years later that I knew at least by name everyone 'north of fifty-three.'

This was a country that saw the beginning of British Columbia or, at any rate, of its recorded history. Long before Victoria or New Westminster had been brought into existence, Fort St. James was the capital of New Caledonia, the administrative headquarters of a fur-bearing empire. Earlier still, in 1793, an officer of the North West Company, Alexander Mackenzie, had journeyed 'from Canada by land' by a route which led him through what is now the Peace River Block, Fort George, the upper Cariboo, and overland to Bella Coola. Other explorers followed, and trading posts were opened at such strategic points as Fort McLeod (1805) and Fort George and Fort St. James (1806). It is appropriate here to mention that these were North West Company establishments; the Hudson's Bay Company entered the scene only after the union of the two companies in 1821.

The province's first 'arterial highway' commenced at Fort St. James and ended when it came to the Columbia River near the present town of Brewster in the State of Washington. Its purpose was to provide a more convenient route for bringing in supplies and taking out furs than the long, arduous trip by way of the Peace, Athabasca, and Saskatchewan rivers to Lake Winnipeg which the explorers had followed.

By the new route supplies were secured from Fort Vancouver near the present city of Vancouver, Washington on the Columbia, and brought up that river by boat to the mouth of the Okanagan. There they were transferred to the horses of the fur brigade for the long trek which followed the Okanagan to the head of the lake, thence west and north, across the Thompson River and on to Fort Alexandria on the Fraser. The rest of the journey was by water on the Fraser, the Nechako, and finally the Stuart rivers. The entire distance, more than 700 miles, required most of two months to complete and sometimes even more. Reverend Modeste Demers, the first missionary in New Caledonia, left the Columbia River early in July 1842 and arrived at Fort St. James on September 16th. This was the chief and almost the only artery of travel from 1812, when the North West Company bought John Jacob Astor's Columbia River interests, until after 1847, when the establishment of Victoria as Hudson's Bay Company headquarters made more direct connection necessary.

Nor was the coast section of the inspectorate lacking in historic interest. Alexander Mackenzie had been in Bella Coola in July 1793. He had missed meeting Captain George Vancouver by less than a month, for in June Vancouver sailed into Burke Channel and found and named Cascade Inlet near which the pulp centre of Ocean Falls stands today. The next half century saw much of the coast and many of the islands surveyed by ships of the British Navy, while the Hudson's Bay Company extended its interests until it came into contact with Russian establishments in Alaska. Fort Simpson, for instance, was built in its present location [now Port Simpson] in 1834, but had existed earlier at the mouth of the Nass River.

The Queen Charlotte Islands were visited by Captain George Dixon, after whom Dixon Entrance is named, in 1787 and ships called frequently thereafter to trade for sea otter skins until that beautiful animal was all but exterminated. Gold was found on the shore of Skidegate Inlet in 1850 and the argument is still unsettled whether this was the first or the second discovery of that troublesome metal in British Columbia. Of great importance were the arrival in 1847 at Fort Simpson of Reverend William Duncan whose missionary effort was to result in an industrial Indian community and, in 1875, of the first salmon cannery at Inverness near the mouth of the Skeena River.[1]

As I gradually worked my way through the district I seemed to be coming constantly in touch with places and events of earlier days. My years of teaching in British Columbia schools, where 'The History and Geography' of the province was an important subject, had given me, I soon discovered, merely the dry bones of textbook knowledge. It was startling to find that the geographical centre of the province was a few miles south of Vanderhoof, that Fort George was due north of Vancouver, and that the British Columbia section of the Peace River Valley was east of the Rocky Mountains. Running Fort George and Blackwater canyons in a gasoline launch during June high water, when the crest of the current in the centre seemed several feet higher than the edges against the perpendicular rock sides, made Alexander Mackenzie's journey in a canoe appear almost a miracle, while a bicycle ride from Quesnel to Alexandria and Soda Creek replaced the romance of the fur brigade with what it undoubtedly was: drudgery and hard work.

Of course, in 1915 there nothing was left of the fur brigade days except the stories and an occasional relic such as the old freighting canoe under a shelter on the river bank in Quesnel.[2] More was in evidence of the Cariboo gold rush; many roadhouses and their furnishings were still in use and in much of their original condition; 100 Mile House dispensed hospitality through doors which retained their long, handmade strap hinges; the buildings which had been Barkerville's Court House and Opera House still stood, but unused and almost buried by the tailings from the workings higher up Williams Creek. Time had been kinder to buildings than to their makers, but even of these a very few remained. The 'Duke of York' [entrepreneur William Houseman] with his beard and his white puttees was a familiar figure as he accepted a free ride on the stage as his inalienable right, and Cataline, too old for packing, still drank rum in Hazelton's Omineca Hotel after pouring some on his shoulder-length iron-grey hair.[3]

Everything else was new or becoming new for this was a period of transition. The second decade of this century produced greater changes than any other period in Canadian history partly because of the added impetus given to science and industry by the First World War. The most far-reaching was the replacement, for many purposes, of an economy based on draft animals and human strength by one dependent on electricity and the internal combustion engine. Cities and populous areas felt the impact first and experienced relatively little distress in the change-over, but in the remote hinterland progress was slower and much more painful.

Consider the Cariboo Road for example. For much of its 220 miles from Ashcroft to Quesnel it passed through good agricultural land from which have been developed such noted ranches as the 70 Mile, the 100 Mile, the 142 Mile, the Onward, the Australian, and the Kersley. All had large acreage and raised crops to suit their market – the Cariboo, the mines, and the freighting trains. Every ranch had a roadhouse, and most of its produce was sold in the form of food on the spot, with no charges for freight or handling to be deducted.

Receipts were substantial. The tariff was reasonable enough – fifty cents for a bed, a meal, a horse feed or, when bars were legal, a drink – but there were many customers. Six-, eight-, and twelve-horse teams were constantly travelling up the road hauling supplies to the mines. The mail stage drove from Ashcroft to Quesnel in three days but was able to make seventy miles a day only by changing horses every ten or twelve miles.[4] With all the drivers, passengers, and horses to be fed small wonder that some ranches banked the cheque for the autumn sale of beef as the roadhouse had paid operating expenses.

The automobile and the motor truck changed all.[5] Stagecoaches were replaced by seven-passenger cars, and trucks with canvas-covered bodies which operated at first from spring until fall and later, with better roads, throughout the year. Times of departure from and arrival at Ashcroft and Quesnel were governed by the mail contract which required three days for the trip by horse-drawn coaches, but only a day for a motor vehicle. In time, the contract was altered to allow for the trip to be completed in one day and when freighting teams disappeared, the roadhouses fed no horses and only the occasional traveller.

With the local market in decline ranchers looked for others to take its place, but with little success against the obstacles of long distances and high transportation costs. Different farm products seemed to offer a solution and experiments were tried with these. It was a slow and tedious process and a good many years were to pass before the Cariboo economy was once more firmly established. When that time did come, farming was largely cattle-raising, only one of a half-dozen industries being carried on. Hundreds of newcomers had settled on pre-emptions or had purchased small pieces of land, some large ranches noted in earlier days for hospitality and food had changed ownership, and roadhouses had been largely replaced by motels and auto courts.[6]

With the passing of the roadhouse went much of the freedom and ease which played so large a part in the charm of the Cariboo. It was pleasant to know when you were hungry that you could walk in, hang up your hat, and sit down at the family table or, if it were nightfall and you wished a place to sleep, to take the first unoccupied bed. You paid fifty cents. It was the custom of the country and it applied to everyone, local residents as well as transients. The Quesnel bank manager who was invited by a customer to drive out for duck shooting over the Labour Day weekend asked jokingly, 'How much do I owe?' He was taken aback to be told 'three nights, eight meals for yourself; six feeds for the team: $11.50.'

For the stranger it could be embarrassing. On my first trip down the road we stopped at a prosperous ranchhouse. The owner, learning from the stage driver that I was the school inspector, told me that there had been some talk of starting a school there. We discussed the details and as there seemed to be some difficulties, he asked if I would stop overnight with him on my return five days later and meet the local parents. This was done and arrangements were completed as a result. The next morning, refreshed by a good night's sleep and a bountiful breakfast, I thanked my host, said goodbye, and left.

Six months later I met him on the street in Quesnel. He gave a curt nod in reply to my greeting and walked on. It worried me but as I came to know the country better, I thought I knew why. On my next visit I stopped at his house for dinner. When paying for it I said, 'and I owe you for two meals and a bed a year ago.' He gave me a warm hand-shake as he took two dollars.

Development along the line of the Grand Truck Pacific was a very different matter for this was largely a new country. True there were settlements but they were small, few, and widely separated. Hudson's Bay Company posts at Fort George, Fort St. James, and Fort Fraser, while over a century old, were still confined to a few buildings and a small area of cultivated land. A few prospectors, trappers, or people with wanderlust had found a favoured location in the area, built a log house, and called it home. Seekers for Omineca gold went into that district through the Skeena and Bulkley valleys, and one route to the Klondike in 1897 passed near the present Vanderhoof. Still later, the builders of the Yukon Telegraph line followed much the same route as the railroad from Fort Fraser to Hazelton. Among all of these adventurers, some men and an occasional woman found the country attractive and remained. They were few indeed; for purposes of industry and railroad revenue it was an unpopulated country.

Two major obstacles impeded settlement. First, large blocks of land had already been sold and were not available for newcomers. Companies in eastern Canada, anticipating that the completion of the railroad would be followed by a substantial increase in land values, bought the best they could procure in the largest blocks possible. They were in no hurry to sell, hoping first for a profit and later that they might at least get their money back. To the provincial government who were the original owner, it was gratifying, until the matter became an election issue in 1916, to receive substantial payments and to place these properties on the tax roll as well, but to the impecunious land seeker it was disheartening to examine a pre-emption map and discover how few quarter sections were available.

Secondly, the nature of the country itself was a drawback. Many thousands came to the Canadian Prairies with little money, secure in the knowledge that they could produce a crop and make a living in a year. But in this section of British Columbia, trees were everywhere. In a way, this was an advantage for little money was needed to build a log house, and there was no scarcity of fuel, but it required years of hard work to cut down trees, take out stumps, and prepare land for cultivation. In the meantime there was no cash return, the family had at least to secure the necessities, and the head of the house was obliged to obtain wage-paying work wherever possible, thereby further delaying land clearing.

Hence it is not surprising that population increase was slow. Six years after the last spike had been driven, less than half of the 125 stations on the British Columbia portion of the railroad had any permanent population except section crews and there were less than a dozen of those with over a hundred people. Prince George (replacing the much older Fort George), Vanderhoof, Burns Lake, Smithers, Hazelton, and Terrace, with populations ranging from 300 to 1,000, served districts which were vast in area but pitifully small in people. The railroad carried few passengers and less freight. Almost the only profitable train was the 'Halibut' which, like the CPR 'Silk Specials' of the same era, was a wonderful revenue producer. It carried fresh halibut, caught by United States boats and landed in Prince Rupert, in refrigerated cars to New York and Chicago. Revenue from all sources, however, was inadequate to meet operating expenses and interest on the tremendous cost of construction. A few years later, the Grand Trunk Pacific and its companion in misfortune, the Canadian Northern, were taken over by the Canadian government and amalgamated into the Canadian National Railway.

The manner in which schools were provided during these difficult years entitles the BC government of the day, and in particular Alexander Robinson the then-head of the Department of Education, to more credit than they have received.[7] The basic principle was that, wherever there were ten children six years to sixteen years of age, a school would be established. It was known as an assisted school, a considerable misnomer since the government paid the salary of the teacher in full and the local residents had to meet only maintenance costs. These were small, for fuel and janitor services were usually donated and fifteen or twenty dollars a year would pay for the few items to be bought.

The school house was erected by 'the contribution of parents and others interested.' In practice, it was often built of logs, and all labour, both in securing the logs and in constructing the building, was donated by the residents. Windows, a door, lumber for the floor, and a blackboard were purchased and wherever it seemed necessary, paid for by a grant which the government made under the provision 'others interested.' Seats and desks, maps, a globe, and textbooks were also supplied without any cost to the local people. The completed building was primitive enough, but it was a school and seldom failed to have a teacher.

Such a program was designed for, indeed, was essential for a district during its pioneer stage when money was scarce and labour abundant. Some districts never got beyond that stage and remained assisted, but most increased in population and prosperity until they were able to meet a larger share of school costs and become rural school districts. A building of good design and construction was then provided by the government which thereafter made an annual grant amounting to less than half the teacher's salary, the additional amount required being secured by a tax on local property.

They were not perfect, these little one-room schools. According to 1950 standards they were poorly heated, badly lighted, woefully equipped, unsanitary, and ugly. All elementary school grades were taught, often one or two years of high school were available, and occasionally a pupil took matriculation.[8] Too many of the teachers were misfits whose reputations barred them from positions in the more prosperous southern communities; the rest were beginners fresh from four months of normal school training, and they changed schools every year.

Yet those same schools produced good citizens. Today, forty years later [circa 1956], their graduates are influential, respected in their communities for their character, their good sense, and their leadership. They are farmers, business leaders, school trustees, and occasionally members of the legislature. Two or three are doctors, and one is a highly regarded justice of the Supreme Court. For this the one-room school is entitled to some credit for it trained its graduates to work for themselves, and also developed a sense of community pride and of civic responsibility fast disappearing in this era of increasing centralized control.[9]

This was the central British Columbia of 1915 in broad outline. It was a country rich in colour, of lakes and valleys, of rivers and mountains, of flowers and trees, but also in colourful history, legend, and characters. The land itself remains, vivid and clear, for all who wish to see; its history has all but disappeared. True, there are relics in archives, in museums, and in historical records, but much is still untold and remains only in the memories of a few. Succeeding chapters endeavor to bring these bits and fragments together. They are written the only way they can be written – from memory – and memory is often unreliable; but while the accuracy of some detail may be questioned, the spirit of the times and places may not.

CHAPTER TWO

Northern Interior Episodes

'ONE GOOD DRINK EVERY MORNING'

The Judge and I were travelling on the train to Hazelton when he recognized an old acquaintance, Mr. Charles Barnes, who announced, 'I am on my way to Hazelton to get my commitment papers to the Old Men's Home in Kamloops to die.'[1] The following afternoon being Sunday, we left the hotel and walked over to the British Columbia provincial police station to pass the time of day with Chief Constable Sperry Cline.[2] Half an hour later Barnes arrived and soon after he was joined by his old friend Jimmy May.[3] For the rest of the afternoon the three of us listened to a conversation which was not only interesting because of the stories, but also because, while May's language was of the expressive and forceful type common to frontier people, Barnes' was precise and rarely included a word unsuited to a drawing room.

A few months earlier Barnes had sold the only piece of property he owned, a pre-emption on the Skeena River, and with the proceeds had returned to England to die. The money passed out of his hands far more rapidly than he had expected; when there was just enough left to pay the fare, he bought a ticket to Hazelton.

May, an old-time prospector, now too old to go out into the hills, was spending his declining years in Hazelton. Each morning he went over to the Hudson's Bay Company store to get his drink of rum and with the day thus satisfactorily started, returned to his cabin to do chores and to sit in the sun. He suffered from a simple though painful ailment which a minor operation and two or three days in hospital would remedy but always found some excuse when treatment was proposed. At last the superintendent of the Hazelton Hospital, Dr. H.C. Wrinch, who, in addition to being an ordained cleric of the Methodist church and an

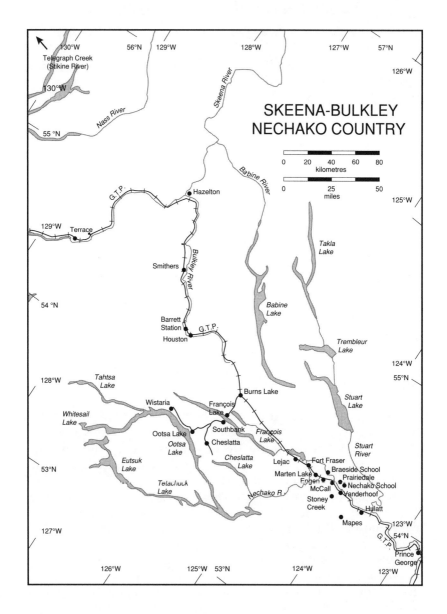

Map 2

expert psychologist where old prospectors were concerned, found a solution.[4] It was merely to suggest that 'for a man like you who has been drinking rum for fifty years, the hospital will have to supply one good drink every morning.' When he was able to be around again, May told his cronies: 'That young feller Wrinch is a smart doctor. He's the only one could find out what was wrong with me.'

The conversation that afternoon soon turned to Hazelton's early days and to a one-time government agent whom Barnes held in high regard. 'Once,' said he, 'I decided to spend the Christmas season among the fleshpots of Victoria. On a certain afternoon I was so unfortunate as to meet a socialist member of parliament who questioned me about the government agent. I replied that he wa a perfect English gentleman, to which his answer was, "Does that entitle him to misbehave with Indian women?" I said, "Sir, when I first arrived in Canada I enquired in Montreal as to the charges on excess baggage. I was informed they were fifteen cents a pound. I accordingly checked my reputation in Montreal and have left it there ever since having no further need of it. I have no doubt the government agent did the same."'

Barnes had been in Atlin during that district's more prosperous days and expressed regret at what he felt was a lack of consideration show there by the relatively wealthy, especially women, to those who were less fortunate. He brought his point home in connection with a New Year's Eve festivity. The affair, a concert followed by a dance, was held in a hall, and the only seats were long benches. Barnes arrived early and was followed a few moments later by a woman whose reputation was not beyond criticism. She took a seat halfway up the room on an empty bench which, as the audience arrived, was left empty until Barnes went up and sat beside her. At the end of the concert he invited her to remain for the dance and, when she declined, escorted her home.

The next afternoon Atlin dispensed New Year's hospitality. Two prominent ladies called on Mr. Barnes in his cabin and as he entertained them with cake and a glass of wine, one said, 'Mr. Barnes, you did make an exhibition of yourself last night.' 'What do you mean, madam?' 'Why, sitting with that woman and taking her home.' There was nothing irreverent in Barnes' reply, nothing but the code by which he lived. 'Madam,' he said, 'if Jesus of Nazareth had been in Atlin last night he would have done as I did; in His absence I took His place.'

THE FINAL WORD IN HOSPITALITY

A welcome letter arrived from Ootsa Lake, giving the names of ten children who were at last in the district and expressing the hope that a school could be started soon. In the 2,000 square miles of country between Burns Lake and Ootsa Lake there were forty youngsters for whom no school was available because they were too widely scattered. Occasionally two families would settle within a mile or two of each other but more often would be eight or ten miles apart. Correspondence courses had not yet come into use and my suggestion that a boarding school might be a solution brought a Departmental rebuke and the query, 'Did you never hear of Cache Creek?' I had not but it seemed wise to do so. Enquiries revealed that years before a government-supported residential school had been maintained at Cache Creek and that it had been closed because of conditions embarrassing to those in authority.[5] The official position was easy to understand and made the Ootsa Lake news all the more gratifying.

Don M. Gerow, proprietor of the Burns Lake Hotel, was at the railroad station when the train arrived about midnight. With him was his new Ford car, new to him and to Burns Lake – for he was learning to drive the first automobile in that district – otherwise far from new but nonetheless luxury compared with the prospect of driving forty miles in a wagon drawn by a slow team. We soon made a bargain to leave at eight o'clock next morning.

Three other passengers who could not well be refused arrived earlier than that seeking transportation: the sergeant of provincial police in charge of that district, the local constable, and an Indian prisoner. The sergeant explained that he held a warrant for the arrest of two Indians charged with having beaten up an Ootsa Lake settler whom they suspected of having stolen a silver fox from their trapline. One Indian had been arrested during the night in the local rancherie, but the other was believed to be near Ootsa Lake.[6] Sharp at eight o'clock we set out with the prisoner in the rear seat between the two officers.

At its best, the road was not designed for automobile traffic and that day it was far from its best for the spring break-up was not over and there had been several days of rain. Our driver's experience was limited but for several miles he had no trouble. Then, while we rounded an especially muddy corner, the rear wheels skidded part way down the bank and the car was saved from overturning by crashing into a stump. Examination showed the only damage to be a fender which was so wedged against the tire that it had to be removed. The driver and I took off our coats and went to work.

In this country mosquitoes are a real plague and that day they seemed to be bigger, more numerous, and more vicious than usual. The police fought them for a few moments and then, taking their prisoner, got out of the car and announced that they would walk up the road. Half an hour later repairs were completed and we were ready to proceed when the sergeant returned and without any comment sat down once more in the rear seat. The car was started and in about a mile overtook the constable who also resumed his seat in silence. We waited for instructions which seemed to be necessary but none were forthcoming, so at last the driver said, 'Where's the Indian?' The terse answer was 'He beat it.'

We crossed beautiful François Lake by ferry on a glorious May day.[7] On the other side the road grew steadily worse and it was seven o'clock when we reached Bostrom's, the only established ranch in that district.[8] There we learned that it would be impossible to go farther by car and a team and driver were available, but we must start immediately if we hoped to return to Burns Lake the following night. 'Immediately' did not mean precisely that for no one ever left Bostrom's without partaking of a generous meal and it was after eight o'clock when we were ready to leave.

A gentle rain was falling, the night was pitch-black, and we were riding in an open wagon. The road was full of holes so it was fortunate the team of heavy horses never left a walk. About midnight we reached the Ootsa Lake stopping place which, though in darkness, soon gave a cheerful greeting to be followed by 'Sorry, we're full up.' 'May we sleep on the floor?' 'The floor's full too; you'd better go back to Harry Morgan's.'[9]

Harry Morgan's was around two sides of a square but one of us knew a short cut and into it we started in the darkness and the rain. It led into a bog. By the time we had managed to turn the team and wagon around, get back to the main road, and drive on to Morgan's, it was three o'clock in the morning and we were wet, cold, and dirty. Our shouts brought a light in the window and in fifteen minutes we huddled in comfort before a blazing fire drinking hot coffee. After forty years I still think Harry Morgan to be the final word in hospitality for he gave me his bed for the rest of the night.

Arrangements for the establishment of the school were completed the following morning without any difficulty since the prospective pupils were there and all the parents were willing to make some sacrifice in order to have a site for the building which would be fair for everyone.[10] The police were not so successful. When their enquiries satisfied them that both Indians had left Ootsa Lake several days before and that little help would be furnished by the local people who were inclined to feel that robbing a trapline was a serious offence, they decided to resume the search at Burns Lake.

We had dinner at noon. As we sat at the table Morgan asked, 'Do you know Ontario?' When I said I did, he hesitated a moment and

then enquired 'Did you know M.J. O'Brian in Renfrew?'[11] M.J. O'Brian
may be said to be the man who made Renfrew famous for with his
Cobalt-made millions, he secured for that town one of the first and
surely one of the most celebrated Canadian hockey teams. I told
Morgan that I had never met O'Brian but in common with everyone in
Ontario I knew who he was. When their relationship was shyly mentioned, I asked, 'Have you ever been back?' 'Yes,' said Morgan. 'M.J.
sent me a ticket and gave me a job. I kept the job just long enough to
earn the price of a ticket back to Ootsa Lake.' I couldn't resist asking
why. The answer was 'This is the finest country on earth. You build
your own house and cut your own fuel; you get your own meat with a
fishing rod and a rifle and your trapline brings what little money you
need. There's no one to boss you and you can do as you like. Where
else can you get all that?' The sergeant and I, both government servants, looked at each other and silently said 'Amen!'

We drove back to Bostrom's under a cloudless sky and with a warm,
drying wind. After another of those satisfying meals, we transferred
to the car and began the last stage of the journey in the none-too-
sanguine hope that we might catch the train at Burns Lake. The roads
dryer, the car running better, our driver more expert, we arrived with a
half hour to spare. As I boarded the train, someone whispered in my
ear, 'Those Indians are over in the rancherie and I hope they never
catch them.'

LATENT QUALITIES OF EXCELLENCE

The arrival of a group of Mennonite settlers was not welcomed by the
older residents of the Nechako Valley. They were 'foreigners,' a term
freely used to describe any who were not Anglo-Saxon, and that alone
was enough to create a prejudice but, in addition, most spoke a
language very close to German and we were at war with Germany.
Worst of all they had brought with them everything they needed for a
year or more and were spending nothing locally, a practice little short
of treason in a district which depended on the purchases of new pre-
emptors for much of its cash income.

The party had arrived in the summer and had gone at once to blocks
of land located for them earlier. The labour which lay ahead would
have daunted most for there was nothing there but land and trees
and, before the snow fell, dwellings of some sort and shelter for
animals had to be provided. Sites had to be cleared, and trees felled
and sawn into logs as a preliminary but essential step to the actual
work of construction, so it was little wonder that the provision of
schools was delayed. Arrangements were made for their establish-

ment as soon as buildings could be available, which, it was agreed, could scarcely be before the following summer.

Early in April a disturbing letter came from the superintendent of education. From his point of view at a desk in Victoria, it was a reasonable letter granting permission to the Mennonites to open two schools immediately with two of their own people as teachers. But to me it meant a wonderful opportunity for the Nechako people to engage in added criticism if, as I feared, these two teachers were of less-than-average ability, particularly in their use of English. An immediate visit to the community appeared essential if unfortunate rumours were to be forestalled.[12]

One school, about twenty miles from Vanderhoof, was connected with that town by a road which, never good, was so difficult in April that a horse could not make the round trip in one day, while the second was on the other side of the Nechako River, still frozen but dangerous to cross.[13] There was an alternative which seemed better than spending four days on this problem, and in my ignorance I took it by getting off the train at the railroad flag station nearest the first school about four o'clock in the morning.

The sun soon rose and, shortly after, smoke appeared from the only house within sight where, in response to my knock, I received a friendly welcome and an invitation to breakfast as well as some complimentary remarks about 'our teacher.' When I had spent a couple of hours in the school I found how well-deserved these were. The young man in charge, a graduate of a Manitoba normal school, displayed latent qualities of excellence, and I left at noon for the second school wishing that all our schools were as fortunate.

The ice on the Nechako was firm enough until almost the opposite shore. Fortunately, the water was shallow and my only inconvenience was getting wet to the knees, a misery quickly forgotten when I reached the second school where the situation was very different. The teacher, who looked to be about eighteen years old, was personable and, so far as I could tell, liked by her pupils, but could understand scarcely anything that I said and, when she spoke, only an occasional word was intelligible to me. Her high school certificate recorded high marks in English but her ability was obviously confined to reading and writing the language. It was even difficult to make her understand that she could not remain in charge.

That information had to be conveyed to the chairman of the school board by whom it was so unfavourably received that at five o'clock, I found myself on the road with nowhere to go but Vanderhoof and no way to get there but to walk. The evening was pleasant, though, the temperature just about freezing point, and as darkness came on, the stars shone with a brilliance that seems equalled nowhere else. All this, however, could barely compensate for the road which scarcely deserved the name, being merely two tracks, without a grade, and ankle-deep in slush and mud except where it dipped into a hollow, where if one were lucky, it reached only to the knees.

About ten o'clock I saw a light and after some mental adjustment decided it must be John [Joe] Redmond.[14] A year before a school had been started in this district through his initiative and I had received an invitation to spend the night at his house whenever it was convenient. Now seemed an excellent time to accept. The house was set in what seemed to be the centre of a twenty-acre field; unable to find a gate, I climbed the fence to find myself in a ploughed area. Stumbling across the furrows and occasionally going down on hands and knees, I reached the house and knocked. The door opened and Redmond, lamp held high in his hand, stared for a moment and then shouted, 'Mother, come here. It's the Master!'[15]

Mother came with her kindly sympathy, fitted me out with dry clothes and carpet slippers, provided in unbelievable time a meal which I still remember, and then said to her husband, 'Take him to bed and don't start talking.' Redmond led the way and as we entered the bedroom asked, 'What do you think of home rule?' I answered, 'I don't know anything about it and I don't care anything. I'm going to bed.' I did and as I went to sleep Redmond was still in the centre of the room talking about home rule for Ireland.

Next morning all my clothes had been cleaned and pressed and my shoes polished. After breakfast I thought I would spend the morning at the local school half a mile away, but the hundred yards of muddy field to be crossed almost prevented me.[16] Then as I was standing in the doorway looking at it, Redmond appeared, squatted down on his heels, and said, 'Climb on my back.' I did and he carried me through the mud to the road. At noon we drove to Vanderhoof. After dinner at the hotel as I was trying to express the thanks I felt, I asked the question which experience had taught me was always wise, 'How much do I owe you?' For a moment I thought he would hit me. Then his fists unclenched. He smiled and said, 'You don't know any better but don't say that again.'

CATALINE

Among all the stories true and legendary that have come out of the Cariboo and northern Interior, perhaps no name is better known than that of Cataline the packer.[17] He is to that country what Paul Bunyan is to Minnesota though Bunyan's monument at Bemidji has no duplicate along the Cariboo Road while unlike Bunyan, Cataline actually lived and his exploits need no embellishment. He travelled on the Cariboo Road for many years, transporting on the backs of his horses and mules everything that miners required, but this was work which did not require any special ability and which the freighting teams and wagons could do better. It was on the trails, too narrow and often too precipitous for wagon traffic, that he gained his reputation. Nothing was too bulky, too awkward, or too heavy for him to undertake, and his record included packing a complete sawmill almost a hundred miles.

Cataline's character contributed to his reputation even more than his prowess as a packer. He was commonly supposed to be Castilian by birth and his ordinary language gave some support to that belief though not enough to provide any certainty, for French, English, and Chinook were intermingled with Spanish. He wore the best white 'boiled' shirts procurable in Hudson's Bay Company stores and literally wore them out for he never took one off until it fell off. His favorite drink was rum always taken with a ceremony which consisted of first pouring some on the top of his head and then rubbing it in thoroughly with the tips of his fingers. Haircuts were rare, washing only by accident, and drinks frequent. The cumulative result over several months was certainly impressive.

In his later years he had the contract for packing supplies to the cabins on the Hazelton-Telegraph Creek section of the Yukon Telegraph line. His headquarters were in Hazelton where he spent his last days after his retirement and where I first met him. On a Saturday morning in the winter of 1916 I was comfortably seated in front of the wood-burning stove in the old Omineca Hotel and grateful that I did not have to face the thirty degrees below zero [-34°C] weather outside. The sitting room was separated from the barroom by an archway through which loud voices could be heard though their owners were out of my line of vision. A figure appeared, tall, square-shouldered, erect, the face almost hidden in beard, and with long grey hair falling below his coat collar. He strode over and standing above me began to wave his arms and to shout in loud angry tones. The words were beyond me but clearly I was being damned in several languages. Suddenly he burst out in a roar of laughter, clapped me on the shoulder, and returned to the bar. It was Cataline, telling me a story.

A year later the Omineca Hotel burned to the ground. Cataline got out safely and then remembered that his treasured boots had been left in his room. He went back for them just as the burning roof collapsed. It was an end which seemed to fit an adventurous life.[18]

MOST CHRIST-LIKE MAN

November 11, 1918 marked the end of the war which we called 'Great' in our cheerful ignorance. It brought peace and relief to many places but little to Prince Rupert and central British Columbia where the flu was raging in epidemic proportions.

How this disease got its hold on these areas is still a mystery, for the techniques of modern medical science were not then available if, indeed, they were even in existence. Certainly, there was a cause and a source but the first outbreaks were so unusual and so far removed from an apparent origin of infection that any explanation could be little more than a guess. Vancouver papers had reported a serious condition for almost a month, but Prince Rupert was breathing a sigh of relief at its own escape when a halibut fishing boat came into port with the entire crew sick; they had been stricken almost a thousand miles out to sea. On almost the same day in the Interior, Dr. Ross Stone of Vanderhoof left for Fort McLeod with a pack-horse outfit in response to a call for help because 'Indians were dying like flies.'[19]

These were the first reported cases, but in less than a fortnight, flu was everywhere. In Prince Rupert with a population of 4,000 there were 1,500 cases and over 300 deaths. Some, perhaps many, died from sheer fright for, in a small town where everyone knew everyone else, the mental effect of attending the funerals of 100 friends in a week could be overwhelming. But Prince Rupert had doctors, nurses, and a hospital. For the 700 miles of railroad line and the country north and south of it, there were hospitals only at Hazelton and Prince George, one doctor at Hazelton, one at Vanderhoof, and two in Prince George. Thus, those sick at Burns Lake had to depend for medical help on Hazelton, 130 miles to the west, or on Vanderhoof, 80 miles to the east. There were no through roads to either place so the journey had to be made by rail on but two trains each week. The hospitals were crowded far beyond the point of safety and doctors worked for days on end without removing their clothes, reduced to snatching bits of sleep as they drove their sleighs along country roads. Yet in the more remote places patients recovered or died without any other help than what the family or a neighbour could provide.

Just when it seemed things could be no worse, the Canadian Pacific ss *Princess Sophia* went down a few hours sail from Prince Rupert where both she and her crew were well-known. That story has been told many times; it is enough to say that there were no survivors.[20] One steward had been taken off ship suffering from flu on the *Sophia*'s northbound trip only to succumb a few days later in the Prince Rupert hospital.

'A Raconteur with a passion for history and geography.' Alex Lord in late career

'The lure of the Canadian west proved compelling.' Alex Lord as a young man

'You could walk in, hang up your hat, and sit down at the family table.'
141 Mile Roadhouse, Cariboo Road

'Our shouts brought a light in the window and in fifteen minutes we huddled in comfort before a blazing fire ...' Harry Morgan's cabin at Ootsa Lake

'Travelling on ... the Grand Trunk Pacific ... was something of an adventure ...'
An early passenger train at Mile 45 from Prince Rupert

'The captain ... could not attempt the canyon in darkness.'
ss *BX* in Cottonwood Canyon, 1910

'*There were three schools at each end of Graham Island.*'
First Masset School c. 1909. Miss Jessie Peck, teacher, with *(front row)* Laulee (Spud) Millard, Donald Fraser, Bill Millard, Freddy Ives, Douglas Fraser, Aileen Fraser, Lucy Millard, and *(back row)* Budd Millard, Tom Fraser, Harold Orr, and Betty Fraser. Copyright K.E. Dalzell, *The Queen Charlotte Islands 1774-1966*

'*Inspection of Island schools necessitated making a choice.*'
Sandspit children playing on the school grounds

'He persuaded the Post Office Department to establish a mail service against
its will.' Captain David Lloyd at
Tatlayoko Lake

'They were lucky people to live in that house.'
Tatla Lake c. 1934-5. *(Back row)* Mrs. Margaret
Graham, Tom Duncan, Bill Graham; *(front row)*
Mr. Robert Graham, friend 'Gerry,' Alex Graham,
Betty Graham

'On Friday, [I boarded] a slow train to Okanagan Landing.'
Rail terminus with SS *Okanagan* in dock at right

'We spent the better part of a week in Prince George with visits to several outlying schools ...'
Olive M. Clarke, first teacher at Beaverly School, with students, 1918

'Herbie Taylor lived some ten miles downstream from Fort St. John ...' D.H. Taylor and son Charles in front of the old house at Taylor

'*When one rail was several inches higher that the other ... cars were likely to be derailed.*'
Wreck on the Edmonton, Dunvegan and BC Railway c. 1914

'*A flat-bottomed boat came in sight around a bend ...*'
Peace River cruise of the premier's party. With their guides, left to right, are Minister of Lands T.D. Patullo, UBC Dean of Agriculture L.S. Klinck, Provincial Premier H.C. Brewster, and seated, Surveyor-General J.E. Umbach

'The most dynamic personality who ever stood in a British Columbia classroom.' Alexander ('Sandy') Robertson, Superintendent of Education, 1899-1919

'They were not perfect, these little one-room schools ... Yet those same schools produced good citizens.' Farrell Creek School, Peace River Block, 1920s [see Map 6]

One day in November, Father Nicolas Coccola stood on the railroad station platform at Burns Lake with his pack on his back.[21] I asked him where he was going and he said, 'To Cheslatta; my people are sick and there is no one to help them.' It was a cold, raw day as I watched him start on that fifty-mile walk to help his Indian brothers with his early medical training and with those spiritual values which to him, and perhaps to them, were of more importance.[22] Father Coccola reached Cheslatta, nursed his Indians, prepared their food and, to those who did not recover, administered last rites. Then he buried them. I think of him whenever I read [those words of Scripture]: 'I was sick and ye visited me' for, to me, Father Coccola was the most Christ-like man I have known.

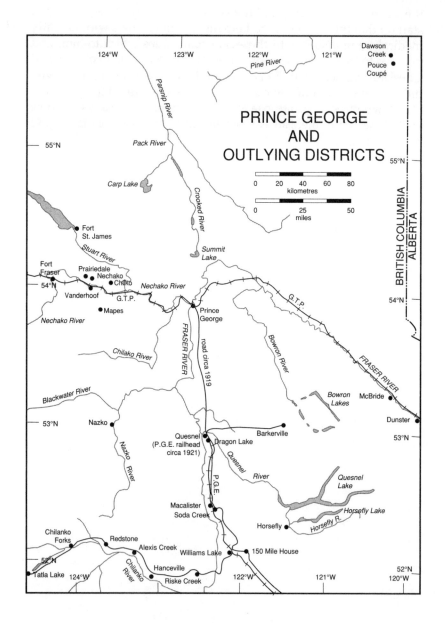

Map 3

CHAPTER THREE

Politics and Personalities

'SHE CAN'T UNHITCH THEIR HORSES'

The hotel clerk led me down the hall to my bedroom. As he stood in the opened door he said, 'I suppose you're going out to Chilco?' 'Why should I go to Chilco?' I asked in surprise. 'Why,' he replied, 'there's quite a row there and aren't you the new school inspector?'

He was right as I found out when I drove to Chilco the next day.[1] The previous February – it was now October – Chilco's first school had been opened using a pre-emptor's abandoned cabin as a building, and an interim school board of the usual three members had been elected. Under the School Act of the time it had to be interim until the second Saturday in July, the official date for annual school meetings, when all school business was transacted. In the meantime, a school site was selected and a permanent schoolhouse begun.

Annual school meeting notices, among other things, must state the place of meeting. Samuel Cocker, the Chilco secretary, scarcely knew how this should be carried out for there were two possible places: the temporary building, and the new one which had walls but no roof. He compromised by stating that they would meet in the new school if the day were fine, and in the old one if it rained. When the day came it was neither one thing nor the other with the result that two annual meetings were held, one in each building, and each meeting elected three trustees.[2]

A few days later, one school board met and appointed as teacher a personable young woman who was well-recommended, a graduate of normal school, and the sister of a local resident.[3] About the same time, the other board appointed a middle-aged man who had neither training nor experience but who had promised the chairman a substantial sum in return for being located on a quarter section of vacant land, it being tacitly understood that the payment would be made from his salary as teacher.[4]

To resolve this stalemate each board appealed to the superintendent of education who, coming to the sensible conclusion that one meeting had been as legal as the other, cancelled the proceedings of both and ordered the holding of a new one 'to elect three trustees for the Chilco Assisted School District.' The decision was the only one possible, but its results were unexpected.

When the new meeting was called to order the attendance was surprisingly large, every bachelor for many miles coming to elect the board which would appoint a lady teacher. Their right to vote was questioned and angry discussion followed. 'These were outsiders and this school was no concern of theirs.' 'Who is an outsider when there are no boundaries?' Fortunately the secretary was prepared with a ruling from the superintendent of education, namely, 'Anyone who is qualified on the provincial voters' list may vote if he lives closer to that school than to any other school.' East, west, or north, there was no other school for a hundred miles. The bachelors voted, their favoured trustees were elected, the young woman became teacher, and the opposing faction refused to send their children to school.

I found six children in attendance and the School Act required an average of eight if a school were to be kept open. The parents of another five refused to consider sending them; when I asked for a reason they replied, 'That girl isn't fit to teach.' To a suggestion that my opinion on that point might be of more value than theirs, the rejoinder was, 'She can't unhitch their horses.' After hours of argument, during which I found that their knowledge of school law was at least as good as mine and that resorting to the Compulsory Attendance Act was in vain, I gave up.

Fortunately there was an alternative. Six miles away lived a family with four children who would gladly go to school if some means could be found to get them there. All youngsters in this country rode horseback, the teacher's brother had a surplus of riding ponies which he loaned for the rest of the term, and the school continued.

The teacher, unhappy over a situation which she could not improve, resigned at the end of June. The school board appointed as her successor the man who had been the nominee of the opposing board a year earlier. When I asked why, the chairman's answer was, 'We thought we would give those beggars what they wanted to stop the row.' The real reason developed later; as the man had not become the teacher, the promised fee had not been paid, and he and the leader of the other faction were no longer on speaking terms.

The saintly Bishop of Caledonia told this story.[5] He received an anonymous letter which made serious charges against the Chilco curate.[6] They were so serious that he investigated and found no grounds for them. Then he called a meeting of the congregation and urged that before repeating any story they make sure of two things, that the story be true and that some good purpose be served by telling it.

His listeners were attentive and, he felt, impressed. As he concluded one man jumped to his feet and said, 'Bishop, you are absolutely right,' and pointing across the room cried, 'There's the snake in the grass!'

'JUST MAKE A NOISE LIKE A FISH'

The Provincial election of 1916 was of more than ordinary interest. Viewed from today [circa 1956], it marked the beginning of over thirty years in office for the Liberal party and of a general disintegration of the Conservatives, but even in 1916 there were unusual features.

During the 1915 session of the Legislature, Conservative Premier Sir Richard McBride announced its dissolution and an election on an unstated date, with further aid to the Pacific Great Eastern Railway as the major policy of his party. Strong opposition was voiced by influential Conservatives and after several months of bitter internal dissension, Sir Richard was safely installed as agent general in London's British Columbia House, never to return during his lifetime to his native land.[7] The new head of the party was Attorney General W.J. Bowser.[8] As a result of all this and of further delay occasioned by cabinet reorganization in which some familiar figures disappeared, the election was not held until September 1916.

Northern BC took its elections seriously and political meetings were strenuous affairs, with heckling developed to something of an art, especially in Prince Rupert which owed its very existence to Liberal naval policy and Liberal railroad policy, both of which had met with strong Conservative opposition. In a province-wide tour Bowser and a recently appointed cabinet minister, Henry Broughton Thomson, spoke at Prince Rupert.[9] Bowser, an old campaigner, held his own and a little better with his many interrupters but Thomson, with little platform experience, was soon in deep water. He began with his worry over a suitable topic for an address in Prince Rupert and quoted the advice of a friend: 'In Prince Rupert, just make a noise like a fish.' Next day, *The Empire*, edited by rugged individualist Sam Newton, reported the address verbatim to that point, adding, 'He did it.'[10]

Much of the election controversy centred around land settlement policy. Some months earlier two Vancouver clergy, Reverend John McKay and Reverend A.E. Cooke, had published a pamphlet entitled 'The Crisis in B.C.' in which the government had been blamed for the slow development of the North through having sold substantial land to speculators, particularly in large blocks.[11] The authors claimed that this made it difficult for prospective settlers with little money to find satisfactory land for pre-emption, hindered the construction of roads, and frequently made it impossible to locate enough families for a school in any one district. The pamphlet had wide circulation, its charges were quoted extensively from political platforms, and undoubtedly it had considerable influence in constituencies which were affected.

An unusual election problem occurred in the Fort George constituency where the main candidates seeking election were Conservative Minister of Lands, the Honourable William R. Ross, and Socialist John McInnes.[12] Both were newcomers to the riding, Ross coming from Fernie where he had been elected for four legislative terms, but deemed it inadvisable to attempt a fifth; and McInnes, from the Boundary country. The unusual situation concerned an Election Act provision for the use of what was known as a 'tendered' ballot by electors whose right to vote was challenged by a scrutineer acting on behalf of a candidate. In former elections a challenged person could, if so wished, make an affidavit before the deputy returning officer about being entitled to vote, then cast the ballot. This time, however, the tendered ballot was printed on specially coloured paper, had to be sealed in an envelope, placed in the ballot box, and could only be counted by a judge in the event of a recount being required.

Fort George was a riding of great size extending to the northern and eastern boundaries of the province so it is not surprising that in some of the more remote polling districts, Returning Officer Sheriff E.S. Peters found difficulty in securing competent election officials. When the ballot boxes were returned to him he was disturbed to find that a number contained only tendered ballots which had been polled as ordinary ones. Worse, if these were not counted Ross had a small majority, but counted, McInnes had a larger one. The sheriff obeyed the Election Act and did not include them in his final report but notified both candidates of the situation.

McInnes applied to the county court judge for a recount. Many matters, legal as well as others, were handled in a free and easy manner in those days and there was considerable delay in this case. When the day of the hearing came, Ross's solicitor asked that the application be dismissed on the grounds that the Election Act placed a time limit on the application for a recount and the hearing. The judge studied the Act for a few moments and then ruled the application dismissed.

John McInnes's political record had been unusual. First elected to the legislature in 1907 to represent Grand Forks, he lost in 1916, but in

1945 defeated the Liberal Education Minister H.G. Perry to become the member for Prince George.

Politics had small place in educational matters back then but during an election day they did occasionally intrude, especially when a cabinet minister was running in a new riding. Ross received several requests which ranged from a new school building to a high school entrance certificate for a student who had failed. Most demands he turned over to the inspector with the injunction: 'If you can't do it, don't let them know until after the election.' One was handled differently, however.

A week before the election I went to a district a few miles across the Nechako River north of Vanderhoof where a school had been requested.[13] Everything was in order: The children were there. A site had been selected. Arrangements had been completed for the building. When I promised to secure a grant of $300 their leader, Joe Redmond, asked, 'Will we get it before the election?' I pointed out the obvious: the election was six days away, my recommendation had to go to Victoria, and there were two trains a week. I assured them that election or no election, they would get $300, but Redmond glumly shook his head. Perhaps his Irish upbringing explained his lack of faith, for he went to a political meeting the following evening where Ross was the speaker. Afterwards all adjourned to the bar and at a convenient moment he asked Ross for a grant for their school. 'Sure,' said the Minister, 'will $1,000 be enough?' Redmond was wise enough to see that a notation was made in the ministerial notebook.

A letter to me from the superintendent of education three weeks later stated, 'I have been advised by the Honourable, the Minister of Lands, that he has promised a grant of $1,000 to a school in the vicinity of Vanderhoof. He has no further information. As it will, of course, be necessary for me to implement the Minister's promise kindly ascertain to whom this money is to be paid and for what purpose.'

In due course Redmond received a cheque for $1,000 and the district, which would have been satisfied and happy with $300, quarrelled for the next year over its expenditure.[14]

At length the election was over and a new régime begun. The outgoing legislature had included forty-two Conservatives and two Socialists, Parker Williams from Newcastle and John Place from Nanaimo, while the new one was composed of thirty-nine Liberals, eight Conservatives, and Parker Williams.[15] The new Liberal premier was Harlan Cary Brewster, counting among his supporters from northern BC two, T.D. Pattullo and A.M. Manson who in later years were to become well-known.[16]

Bowser was never again to hold cabinet rank.

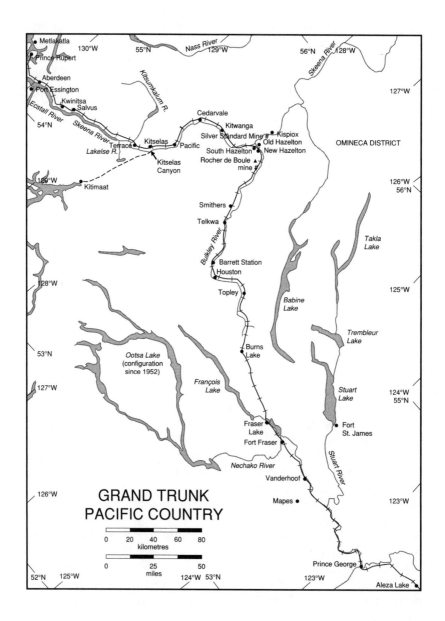

Map 4

CHAPTER FOUR

'Dig Yourselves Out'

Travelling on that part of the Grand Trunk Pacific Railway which ran through British Columbia was something of an adventure for several years after 1917. Construction had been completed three years earlier with the driving of the last spike near Fort Fraser, but almost immediately financial difficulties beyond the scope of this narrative began to plague operations. There was little deterioration in passenger accommodation and none at all in the friendly efficiency of train crews, but, in several other respects, conditions seemed steadily to worsen. The roadbed was poorly maintained, while slides, floods, and heavy falls of snow caused delays which, to the passengers at least, appeared unnecessarily long. A train arriving in Prince Rupert from the east 'on time' was rare enough to cause comment, and lateness was likely to be stated in days rather than hours; 'two days late,' 'three days late,' and 'cancelled' were not uncommon. When you would reach your destination, at least in times of heavy snow and high water, was unpredictable and you could only hope for the best.

One train left Prince Rupert on a Saturday morning in early May with the usual sprinkling of commercial travellers, a couple of mining engineers bound for Hazelton where the Rocher de Boule and Silver Standard Mines were providing some interest, and two or three fur buyers hoping to pick up the last of the winter's catch.[1] Most on board, however, were prairie farmers and their families returning home for the spring work after spending the winter in Victoria or Vancouver.

My own destination was Smithers, or so I hoped, for this involved some co-operation on the part of the conductor to circumvent conflicting regulations of the railroad and of the provincial auditor general. The railway would not allow stopovers on return tickets, while the auditor general refused to honour expenditures for the purchase of two single tickets for what, in his opinion, should have been a return trip. With only two trains per week in each direction a good deal of doubling back and forth was necessary which, ordinarily, would have made it difficult to avoid breaking one regulation or the other if Bill Moxley, the conductor, had not found a solution.[2] On this trip, for example, I planned to go straight through from Prince Rupert to Smithers and to stop off on my way back at Hazelton and Terrace. Accordingly, before leaving, I bought a return ticket from Prince Rupert to Terrrace and, when Moxley collected the 'going' half of this, I explained my plans to him and at the same time purchased a Pullman car seat to Smithers. When we left Terrace he punched out a conductor's receipt for a return ticket to Hazelton and collected the fare and, had I ever left Hazelton, another would have been issued to Smithers.

In the early evening we reached Kitwanga, 150 miles from Prince Rupert. Usually the train stopped here for only three or four minutes, but this time it was almost an hour before Moxley told us that the road ahead was blocked and that we would spend the night where we were. At the same time he asked me, 'Do you want a berth?' I replied that I had one. 'Oh no!' he said, 'You have a seat.' When I asked, 'What is the difference?' the answer was '$1.50.' I paid it and secured another receipt.

The next day was Sunday and after breakfast someone suggested that we go to church, as there was no chance of the train leaving before evening. All the passengers agreed. Shortly after ten o'clock we were on the station platform ready to begin the half-mile walk when one of the passengers, a Jewish fur buyer, mounted a box and demanded attention. When he got it, 'Folks,' he said, 'you're getting a lot for your money on this trip for you're eating at the expense of the GTP. There are going to be a lot more free meals, so remember that, when the collection plate comes round, nothing goes in but paper money.'

Kitwanga, one of the many Indian villages along the Skeena River, was better known than most because it possessed many unusually well-preserved totem poles. These, having attracted the interest of specialists in Indian lore from both the Department of Indian Affairs and the Smithsonian Institution, were occasionally described in illustrated magazine articles and had been used generously by the railroad in its advertising material.[3] Passenger trains stopped briefly to allow tourists to examine the poles and perhaps also to enable the Indians to sell their wares, chiefly baskets and miniature totems.

The entire Skeena River from the Pacific to the junction with the Bulkley River at Hazelton had been strongly influenced by the Church of England, an influence which began in 1862 when Reverend William Duncan opened his remarkable undertaking at Metlakatla. The

Kitwanga church was of that faith and, while most of the congregation were Indians, a few as well as the clergy were white. The building was small, equipped with benches, unadorned, and plainly furnished, save for the necessary requirements of the Anglican service.⁴ On this Sunday the church was crowded, with our group from the train making up one-third of the congregation. The sermon and the reading of the lesson were given in English, but in the singing of hymns, which were all familiar ones, the Indian words rang out clear and true. As one watched the Indians' faces, something akin to rapture was so evident as to leave no doubt of its sincerity.

When the collection was taken up the admonition of our fur buyer bore abundant fruit. Two Indians, one on each side, passed the plates and, as they marched up the aisle to present them at the altar, their faces were as expressionless as Indian faces are mistakenly supposed to be, despite the fact that each plate was piled high with bills and not many were ones. There seemed to be a twinkle in the cleric's eye as he prepared to receive the offering and his handshake at the door when the service ended was warm.⁵

Late in the afternoon Conductor Moxley came to tell us that the line ahead was still blocked and we would spend a second night in Kitwanga. Then he asked me, 'Do you want a berth?' 'I have one,' I answered. 'No,' he replied, 'that was for last night.' I found the receipt he had given me the previous evening, and we read all the small print, finally agreeing that, since none of it disproved that my receipt was punched 'Berth, Pr. Rupert to Smithers,' I could occupy it till I got there.

The next morning the train once again started and made the thirty-mile run without incident to New Hazelton. Half an hour after our arrival I was congratulating myself that, as it was only forty-five miles to Smithers, we should probably arrive there at a reasonable hour in the evening. Then the conductor arrived. 'Folks,' he said, 'there are forty slides in the next forty miles and we're staying here indefinitely.' Then he turned to me and added, 'You haven't any right to be on this train.' I knew this, but I also knew what would happen if I left the train and went to the hotel half a mile away. Moxley's term 'indefinitely' was a literal one, for no one knew when that train would start and in all probability no one would know more than a half hour in advance. At the hotel I would sit up most of the night, perhaps most of several nights, waiting. When I had finished explaining all this, Moxley grinned and said, 'You go back to South Hazelton and, if the agent will sell you a ticket to Smithers, I'll pick it up.'

South Hazelton was one of three 'Hazeltons.' The oldest, the best known and, at that time, the most important, was locally known as

Old Hazelton. Major William Downie had visited its site at the junction of the Skeena and the Bulkley rivers in 1859 while investigating the possibility of gold in the Omineca; later, the Hudson's Bay Company established a post.[6] It gradually became an important fur-trading centre and outfitting post with government offices, several stores, the Ingenika and Omineca hotels, and the only hospital between Prince Rupert and Prince George.

When the railroad was built, it followed the south bank of the Bulkley while Old Hazelton was on the north. Thus the station serving the district was named 'New Hazelton' and soon gained some population and great ambition. In the main it was a raw, unfinished pioneer town, though 'Blackjack' Macdonald's hotel was in decided contrast. Macdonald, who once operated a hotel in Port Essington with a bar 125 feet long ('the longest bar in the British Empire'), expressed his confidence in New Hazelton by erecting a large, modern building provided with most amenities including hot-water heating.[7] Unfortunately, in my time, lack of patronage compelled economies and the heating plant was in use only during the more extreme weather.

New Hazelton also possessed a bank which had been held up on two occasions, the second experience providing one of the north's more unusual stories. The Presbyterian missionary for the district at the time was 'Big Dan' Maclean who, in addition to being an ordained minister was also a competent veterinarian and an excellent shot. Eight bandits entered the bank in daylight and secured all the available cash. As they came out, Big Dan, crouched behind a stump with a rifle, opened fire. He was soon joined by others and by members of the provincial police with the result that seven were either killed or died later in hospital. That the lone bandit who escaped had the money did not lessen Maclean's fame.[8]

South Hazelton was little more than a name on the railroad timetable. In common with many other station sites it had been the scene of a real estate 'townsite' promotion. This one had the unusual feature of lots being offered as premiums with subscriptions to an eastern Canadian magazine, the catch being that the recipient was required to meet the cost of a survey. South Hazelton had a station. Customarily stations were six to ten miles apart, and very few had resident agents, yet South Hazelton was only three miles from New Hazelton.[9]

The agent was an old acquaintance and readily sold me a return ticket to Smithers. Moxley collected it and I returned to my comfortable accommodation.[10] Tuesday and Wednesday were spent in the two local schools thus completing at least part of what I had set out to do.[11] Thereafter time began to drag even though the weather was at its best, the fishing was good, and several passengers were excellent bridge players. At last, on Saturday morning, our fifth day in Hazelton and our seventh from Prince Rupert, a relief train arrived and with it a message from the rail management. Passengers who so desired might return to Prince Rupert, travel on the ss *Prince George* to Vancouver, and from there to their prairie homes by Canadian Pacific; they were advised not to do so, however, as management felt sure that there would only be another two or three days' delay.

Our fur buyer and I were the only ones to accept the offer. As I was about to board the train, Moxley said to me, 'You owe the railroad for a week's board and lodging.' 'Just for that,' I answered, 'I'm going to get a refund' and, on my return to Prince Rupert, I did. After all, I had paid for a ticket and a berth from Hazelton to Smithers which I had been unable to use. Later I learned that the prairie passengers were thirty days in travelling from Prince Rupert to Edmonton.

Nine months later, in February, I spent twelve days in another 'tie-up,' but this time I had myself to blame for being on that train at all as I missed the preceding one at Fort Fraser. It had been unusually cold even for the Nechako Valley, with the thermometer registering forty-five degrees below zero [-43°C] when I arrived at midnight on Saturday and dropping to sixty degrees below [-51°C] during the next three days. Below-zero temperatures were common enough, even forty degrees below [-40°C], but sixty degrees below [-51°C] was both uncomfortable and dangerous. Fortunately there was no wind.

The Fort Fraser Hotel had been erected during that community's brief townsite boom and had been cheaply constructed, with little between the bedrooms and the outside save the siding nailed to the two-by-fours. It was heated by two stoves. One warming the combined office and sitting room was a typical northern stove, a gasoline drum resting on a cradle of bricks, with a door cut in one end and a hole for the stovepipe in the other. It took several sticks of cordwood, retained the heat, and provided comfort for anyone within twenty feet. The other was the usual hotel-type kitchen range. It served well for cooking but gave out so little heat that I became convinced that a story I had never believed was in fact true. As the dining room was much too cold we ate our meals in the kitchen. After breakfast one morning the cook placed a pail of dishwater on the back of the range; when we returned at noon for lunch it had a half-inch of ice on the top. It had frozen on the stove.

When I had registered, Dave, the black proprietor, took me upstairs to my room. 'Boss,' he said, 'I sho' hopes you'll be warm. I'se put six blankets on that bed.' He had, but they weren't enough. Even though I left most of my clothes on, I could not get warm and sleep would not come. At last I got up, went downstairs, and dozed in a chair till morning.

I stayed in that chair most of Saturday and Sunday night. On Monday I went to the school and found all the youngsters there for this was before the days of the legendary regulation that schools must close if it is twenty degrees below [-29°C].[12] That night I again sat beside the stove counting the hours until Tuesday midnight when the train was due to arrive, but the next morning it was reported to be four hours late. During the day Dave installed a sheet-iron heater in a bedroom and after dinner said, 'Boss, you go to bed. The boy, he's got an alarm clock an' he'll call you.' The room was delightfully warm, I was asleep almost immediately, and heard nothing until I was awakened by the train stopping at the station two blocks away. There was nothing I could do except turn over and go back to sleep.

On Saturday night, four days later, the next train arrived on schedule. We continued on time until we reached Pacific, the first divisional point east of Prince Rupert, where we learned of heavy snow conditions ahead that would detain us at Pacific for twenty-four hours. At the end of that time we again started, running 'on block' with the snowplough ahead of us, meaning that our train stopped at each station until the crew of the snowplough at the next station called to say that the line was clear. It was a necessary safety device to prevent the train from running into the snowplough.

There is a peculiar weather condition below Terrace in the lower Skeena Valley. As is well known, Prince Rupert has the rather heavy annual precipitation of about 120 inches, most of it falling as rain. The same climatic factors which exist at Prince Rupert continue for some eighty miles up the Skeena but, farther inland, the temperature in winter drops sufficiently to convert the rain to snow. Since one inch of rain makes ten inches of snow, heavy daily falls are common, and by late February five feet of snow on the ground is usual. A short distance below Terrace this condition is abruptly stopped by a cross current of air which comes down the Kitsumkalum Valley on the north and the Lakelse Valley on the south to cross the Skeena at right angles. There may be deep snow five miles away when the ground is bare at Terrace.

Our journey proceeded successfully through half-a-dozen stations until we reached Salvus, sixty miles from Prince Rupert. There we waited for word from the snowplough crew and continued to wait until they arrived, having tramped over the drifts on snow shoes. The news they brought was gloomy; the mouth of the Kwinitsa Tunnel was blocked to the top, the plough could make no progress, and snow was still falling.[13] A telephone message to Superintendent Allan Kilpatrick in Prince Rupert had brought the reply, 'Dig yourselves out; all our equipment is east of you.'[14] Since burly 'A.K.' was not only held in high regard by the railroad workers, but also knew that his wife was on our train, that seemed final.

For eight days there was no change. Then the temperature rose, and rain came, first gently, but soon in typical Prince Rupert fashion. On the morning of the twelfth day the plough forced its way through the tunnel and found a clear track ahead. The train followed, arriving in Prince Rupert thirteen days late. The next morning four passengers boarded an eastbound train to return to their prairie homes – a GTP trainman and his wife on their annual holiday and a bride and groom on their honeymoon.

We had been comfortable enough on the train. The crew were friendly and companionable and, through long experience, had learned to be unconcerned about a few days delay. There was an abundance of heat and plenty of well-prepared food. Light was the only problem, for it gave out. At that latitude [Kwinitsa, 54°15'N; Hazelton, 55°15'N] in February, artificial light is necessary for reading until ten o'clock in the morning and after three in the afternoon, leaving a long time to sit in the dark. Even smoking loses much of its satisfaction when the smoke cannot be seen.

Such delays might have been annoying, even seriously inconvenient, to one who was on the train but to one who was waiting for its arrival at a flag station they were considerably worse. Most stations were of that type and while they possessed well-built station-houses, they had neither agent nor anyone else with information on when a scheduled train might arrive.[15] It was likely to be late, but the risk of depending on that was too great when missing it meant waiting either three or four days for the next one. To make matters more difficult, hotels or even stopping places did not exist near most stations and the occasional visitor had no alternative but to impose on one of the three or four settlers who, as often as not, lived perhaps two miles distant.

Aleza Lake was a flag station about thirty-five miles east of Prince George. On Tuesdays the eastbound train arrived at nine-thirty in the morning and the westbound at seven in the evening, thus allowing most of the day for visitors to transact their business. Such a convenient timing of trains existed only in the division east of Prince George and was taken advantage of whenever possible.

Before leaving Prince George on a Tuesday morning in late March I learned from the dispatcher that the westbound train would be six hours late leaving Edmonton. 'However,' he added, 'don't count on that, for it may make up some of it.' I had a busy day in Aleza Lake, finished my work in late afternoon, had supper with a hospitable settler, and set out on the mile-and-a-half walk to the station shortly after nine o'clock in the faint hope that the dispatcher might have been right. He was not, for the train did not arrive until noon on Thursday. Somewhere along the way it had lost an additional thirty-six hours.

The waiting room was furnished with nothing else but benches along the side wall. There was no stove, and each night it was cold enough to freeze a half-inch of ice on the top of the water barrel on the platform. My fellow would-be passenger and I spent the first night attempting to sleep, listening for the whistle of the train and pondering the probable fate of the railroad until day dawned and the sun rose. An hour later, down the track came an old trapper, 'Packbelly Bill,' on his way to Prince George with his last catch of furs. He had all we lacked, for he fed us with his coffee and bacon, kept us warm with the fire he built, and entertained us with hard-to-credit stories of his adventures until shortly after noon on Thursday, the train at last arrived.

CHAPTER FIVE

By River to Quesnel

In 1916 anyone who wished to travel from Prince George to Quesnel between May and November had two routes from which to choose: the road and the river. The road was available throughout the year in theory, but long stretches of deep mud in autumn and spring as well as occasional heavy falls of snow in winter seriously shortened the period of effective use. It had been built to satisfy the needs of the very few people who required land transportation to Fort George which, only a few years earlier, was merely a Hudson's Bay Company trading post. While it probably served those needs, at least to the extent of providing a path to follow, it did so by a roundabout route. The Cariboo Road from Ashcroft to Quesnel was then, as it had been for over fifty years, the great and almost the only means of access to this entire area, but several branch roads led from it. One, which followed the old telegraph line (originally built in the late 1860s as part of an abortive plan to unite New York and London by wire) northwest to Stony Creek and beyond, crossed the Blackwater River some forty-five miles from Quesnel. From that point another branch led fifty-five miles to Fort George.

The river route was much older. Alexander Mackenzie followed it in 1793 to a point somewhere between the present Quesnel and Alexandria before turning back to ascend the Blackwater. Fifteen years later Simon Fraser, from whom the river takes its name, found it to be navigable as far as Soda Creek and so established a pattern for the fur brigades to follow as long as they existed. The next century saw greatly increased water transportation not only between Soda Creek and Fort George but also far up both the Nechako and the Fraser. The early dugouts first used by the Indians and copied by miners and settlers were the most common craft, but freighting canoes, locally built boats of various shapes and sizes, and even rafts were in service.

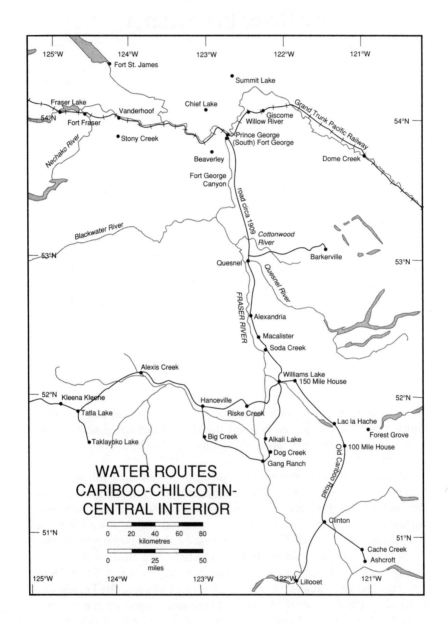

WATER ROUTES
CARIBOO-CHILCOTIN-
CENTRAL INTERIOR

Map 5

Later sternwheeler steamers powered by wood-burning engines and complete with such refinements as staterooms and dining saloons went into operation and continued until the depression preceding the First World War, together with competition from automobiles and trucks, forced their replacement by smaller, more economical gasoline launches.

The *Circle W*, the *Rounder*, or the *Viper* left Fort George, recently [circa 1910] named South Fort George through some strange disregard for both accuracy and fairness, reasonably early in the morning and completed the ninety-mile run to Quesnel in about nine hours. The fare was ten dollars for transportation and nothing else. The launch's main purpose and chief source of revenue was freight which was considerable since it was cheaper for Quesnel merchants to order supplies from Edmonton, then pay rail charges to Prince George and launch rates down river, than to buy in Vancouver and meet the combined costs of rail transport to Ashcroft and 220 miles of Cariboo Road freighting. Passengers were a minor consideration and their comfort was their own affair. If they were wise, they brought their own food and if they were fortunate, they could find seats on packing cases or gasoline cans. None of this was of any great importance on the downriver trip but a different matter on the thirty-hour journey upstream.

The Fraser is a turbulent river. Even where it is wide, as at Prince George or New Westminster – and to the casual eye the width seems about the same at both places – its current is so considerable that anyone attempting to cross in a dugout or a rowboat is likely to reach the other side half a mile lower down. When that great volume of water must pass between the rock walls of a narrow, 100-foot wide canyon, its speed and its power are tremendous even at low water; with a rise of forty feet or more during the spring freshet, it becomes an uncontrollable torrent. One June, when unusually high water had covered the railroad tracks below North Bend, I watched a small red section house floating along until it reached a canyon. Halfway through, it began to swing round and round in a steadily narrowing circle until at last it disappeared under the surface. Ten minutes later it reappeared in bits and fragments; the force of the water had torn it to pieces.

There are two canyons in that section of the river between Fort George and Quesnel. Both have been navigated many, probably hundreds of times, and were safe enough in a boat directed by anyone as competent and riverwise as the captain of the *Circle W* yet, to the inexperienced, each time would bring a thrill of exhilaration or of fear according to the condition of the passenger's nerves or conscience.[1]

Fort George Canyon fifteen miles below the town was the more awkward to run because of enormous rocks near its entrance. The usual practice was to keep well to the left until about 100 feet from the mouth and then, at right angles to the river with the spray dashing over the boat, to cross to the other side. It was a manoeuvre more easily carried out against the current than with it and, on the down trip, was sometimes made with the engine in reverse.

However, Cottonwood Canyon, eighteen miles above Quesnel, was a box canyon, a mass of water shooting straight ahead between two high rock walls with nothing between to impede its progress. To me, the river seemed to form an arc from side to side, and, in high water, the difference in height appeared to be several feet. With the current the run was completed in a few seconds; against, progress was painfully slow, the boat sometimes gaining difficult inch after inch, sometimes only holding its own then, finding less violent force, shooting ahead at what, by contrast, seemed the rapid rate of a mile or two an hour.

Four o'clock on a November morning is an early hour to start on a journey. I boarded the *Circle W*, tied to the Quesnel river bank, in bad humour, for my three-day-old cold was worse, ice was running in the river, the *Circle W* had no heat, seats, or food; and I had little hope that the dozen aspirin in my pocket would give much relief during the thirty hours of misery ahead. It was dark when we left and, when dawn came, the sun was hidden by banks of heavy clouds which intermittently dropped as rain or snow. Bundled up in sweater and overcoat, seated on the floor with my back against a box, and occasionally dropping off to sleep, I managed to get through the day until we tied up beside the bank, when it was dark again.

It was then the engineer offered me his 'bunk' for two dollars.[2] As a sleeping place it was not attractive being merely a hole in the wall immediately behind the engine furnished with a pillow and some gray blankets, but I gladly accepted, crawled in, and swallowed another aspirin. Twenty-four hours later I woke up in the Prince George Hospital. The 'bunk' had no ventilation; when the engine had started at four o'clock the next morning I had not wakened and had continued to breathe fumes for the next nine hours. Though an effective way of completing the trip in comparative comfort, it scarcely compensated for the highly unpleasant after-effects.

Three-and-a-half years later I made the round trip for the last time, but under quite different circumstances. As a result of improved business conditions and a government subsidy, one of the sternwheel steamers, the *BX*, had been overhauled and put on the run when navigation opened the previous spring, making it possible for my wife to come with me.[3] We spent the better part of a week in Prince George with visits to several outlying schools, and to John Henderson's at Beaverley for a dinner of brook trout.[4] It was the latter part of May, the weather was delightful, and our accommodations at the Alexandria Hotel (later to become government offices) were comfortable.

The *BX* left South Fort George, three miles away, early in the morning so we decided to board the previous evening and have a comfortable night's sleep. In doing so, we began to meet the kindness and hospitality which were as common to the Cariboo as its cattle and its lumber. I went to the hotel desk to settle our account and was handed a bill for one person. When I pointed out that there were two of us the proprietor, rough-and-ready J.H. Johnson, informed me in emphatic Prince George language that my wife could pay for nothing there.

The steamer fare was ten dollars each way, with no reduction for a return ticket. I gave the purser a fifty-dollar bill and asked for two return tickets to Quesnel.[5] When I received thirty dollars in change I said, 'My wife is with me.' 'I know that,' was the reply, 'but she is the guest of the company.' We left our baggage in the stateroom and went out to sit on the deck in the gloaming. Soon the stewardess appeared – an old friend, for in the winter she lived near one of my assisted schools – and after a few minutes' chat, she asked the number of our stateroom. Her comment when I told her was, 'He should have known better.' Later we found that we had been moved to the bridal suite.[6] So it went on the river and along the Cariboo Road until we arrived back in Prince George.

We were due to leave Quesnel for the return trip to Prince George in mid-afternoon on Friday. Three days earlier, however, we had read a news bulletin which caused us concern even though it was indefinite. Radio broadcasting was in its infancy and unknown in central British Columbia, while daily newspapers which came up the Cariboo Road by mail stage arrived several days after publication. The government telegraph system, however, supplied a welcome service by issuing news bulletins at all its offices; these were necessarily brief and lacking in detail but did furnish important news.

Thus we learned that the general strike under One-Big-Union auspices had commenced in Winnipeg and was receiving wide publicity because of its national significance and of its unusual leadership.[7] For several days news bulletins carried strike reports, then a brief sentence suggested that the railway unions might go out in sympathy. Two days later such action was 'probable.' To us in Quesnel this was disturbing. Two passenger trains per week operated between Edmonton and Prince Rupert, and one passed through Prince George on Saturday evening. If we failed to catch it and a strike occurred, we would be delayed indefinitely and catching it depended on our steamer making the upriver run in less than the usual thirty hours.

The captain was sympathetic, but pointed out that the duration of our run depended on when we reached Cottonwood Canyon.[8] If he could get through during daylight, he would continue for several hours thus assuring a short run for the next day, but he could not attempt the Canyon in darkness. We had to be content with that, and to hope for no delays, but, just two hours after leaving Quesnel, one came. We were seated on the upper deck; on the deck below, the captain's collie dog lay on a coil of rope, head resting on his paws, eyes closed, apparently asleep. Suddenly, without a sound and for no evident reason, he sprang to his feet, ran to the side, jumped into the river, and swam strongly toward the shore. He reached it, shook himself for a moment, and began to climb the steep 100-foot hill a short way back from the bank. Then for the first time we saw the reason: a deer was half-visible among the jack pine and cottonwood at the top. It disappeared almost at once with the dog in full pursuit.

In the meantime the captain had worked the steamer in against the bank, and the crew had put out the gangplank. Half an hour went by. Following two short blasts of the whistle, the dog reappeared, trotted down the hill and up the gangplank, lay down on the coil of rope, and went to sleep again. The delay, far more interesting than annoying, made no difference, for we passed through the Canyon without difficulty and travelled considerably farther before tying up for the night. The next day, with a clear sky and a light breeze, was restful and pleasant; even the second canyon seemed much less menacing when watched from a deck twenty feet above it. We reached South Fort George early in the afternoon, the train was several hours late, and the rail strike did not materialize. As usual, my worries had been of no avail.

CHAPTER SIX

Peace River Memories

SIXTY BUSHELS TO THE ACRE

The Peace River District has a considerable history as history in western Canada goes, and a longer one than most of British Columbia. Alexander Mackenzie spent the winter there, at the junction with the Smoky, before making his journey in 1793 'from Canada by land.' During the next thirty years, his became the route followed by the fur traders taking supplies to New Caledonia and bringing out furs. Thereafter, until almost the turn of the century, settlement was slow and consisted chiefly of trappers, traders, prospectors, missionaries, and mounted police, some of whom have left behind them almost legendary tales of heroism and achievement or of basic goodness. Witness the monument to 'Twelve-Foot' Davis which stands on a bluff in Alberta overlooking the confluence of the Smoky and Peace Rivers; its inscription reads: 'Pioneer, Pathfinder, Trapper, Trader. He was every man's friend and never locked his cabin door.'[1]

One trader tired of a bachelor life, was anxious to secure a wife on his annual outfitting trip to the Hudson's Bay Company post at Fort Edmonton. Women, however, were scarce there and he had given up hope when, on the evening before he was to start the return trip, an overland party arrived from Fort Garry. At nine o'clock he approached a woman whose appearance pleased him and said, 'You don't know me, but if you will marry me I'll promise you the best house in the north country and half of everything I have will be yours. We'll have to leave tomorrow morning.' In the morning she said, 'Yes,' and forty years later added, 'Neither of us has ever had a regret.'

This was one of the more difficult, often tragic routes by which miners or those hopeful of becoming miners sought to reach the goldfields of the Klondike. Some went up the Peace, crossed over to

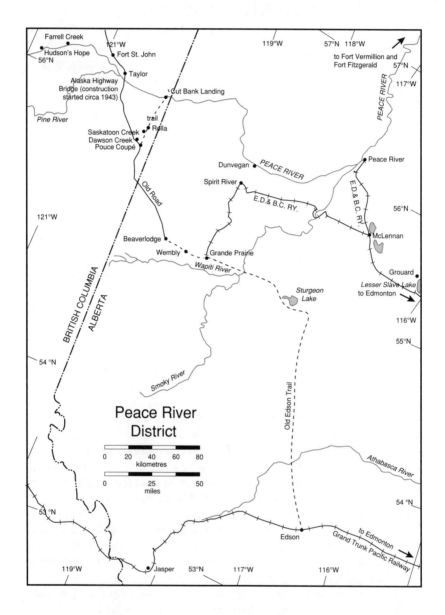

Map 6

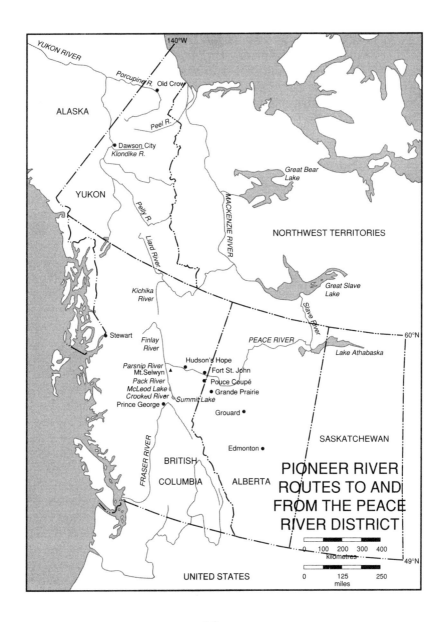

YUKON RIVER

140°W

Porcupine R.

Old Crow

ALASKA

Peel R.

Dawson City
Klondike R.

Great Bear
Lake

Pelly R.

YUKON

MACKENZIE RIVER

NORTHWEST TERRITORIES

Liard River

Kichika
River

Great Slave
Lake

Slave River

Stewart

60°N

Finlay
River

PEACE RIVER

Lake Athabaska

Hudson's Hope

Parsnip River
Mt. Selwyn
Pack River
McLeod Lake
Crooked River
Prince George

Fort St. John
Pouce Coupé
Grande Prairie
Summit Lake

Grouard

SASKATCHEWAN

Edmonton

FRASER RIVER

BRITISH

COLUMBIA

ALBERTA

PIONEER RIVER
ROUTES TO AND
FROM THE PEACE
RIVER DISTRICT

0   100   200   300   400
kilometres

UNITED STATES

49°N

0   125   250
miles

Map 7

the Liard, and followed that river to another divide which led them to the Pelly and the Yukon. One party which spent two years on the way went down river almost to the mouth of the Mackenzie, then ascended the Peel and went down the Porcupine. Some never got through, and those who reached the Klondike came away in a year or two with far more memories than gold.

The worth of the Peace River District, however, lay in its climate and in its wonderful soil, both of which were well suited for farming, especially for growing wheat. Its fame spread far afield and, shortly after 1900, landseekers began to arrive, at first singly or in pairs, but later in numbers as word went back of no crop failures and of 60 bushels of wheat or 120 bushels of oats to the acre. They came by various routes but always in wagons or sleighs hauled by teams, for the first railroad was not to arrive until 1914. Some followed the old road from Edmonton past Lesser Slave Lake and then north, northeast, or northwest. Others took the difficult Edson Trail straight north from that town [see Map 6] and usually lived to regret it. The shortest route from British Columbia, which was taken only occasionally and then by someone with wanderlust, was that of the fur traders down the Crooked, Pack, and Parsnip rivers to the base of Mount Selwyn where the junction with the Finlay marked the beginning of the Peace [see Map 7].

Jack Pringle, son of Yukon missionary Dr. John Pringle and nephew of First World War and BC coast loggers' Padre George Pringle, spent the winter of 1911-12 working in Vancouver's Hastings Mill. In the spring he travelled by CPR to Ashcroft and from there walked the more than 300 miles to Fort George. At Summit Lake [see Map 7], twenty miles farther on, he built a raft on which he journeyed down the rivers as far as the great Rocky Mountain Canyon through which nothing could pass and live.[2] Hudson's Hope lies at the Canyon's lower end; from here almost to its mouth the Peace deserves its name, for it flows placidly along at four or five miles an hour. On another raft Jack travelled to Dunvegan [see Map 6], there to turn inland and finally settle on a homestead, later to become Spirit River. He had only one neighbour, the operator in the government telegraph cabin who, on August 5, 1914, came running over with a telegram.[3] War had been declared. Half an hour later with his pack on his back, Jack started on the 400-mile walk to Edmonton to enlist. The Peace River saw him no more for he was killed in France.

When farmers in sufficient numbers occupy a region, other developments must follow, even though their arrival may be painfully slow, as they were in the Peace River District. One early proposal was the brainchild of the Welsh coal magnate, D.A. Thomas, later Lord

Rhondda, who planned a railroad to run from Peace River and on to tidewater at Kitimat.⁴ Large sums were spent in surveying and even in purchasing right-of-way in the vicinity of Terrace, but almost the only actual accomplishment was the construction and operation of a stern-wheel steamer, the *D.A. Thomas*.⁵ Even this was only a minor success, for the early policy of the company in providing the same uniformed personnel as required on ships crossing the English Channel played havoc with revenues. Worse, navigation was possible only from the break-up of ice in later April until low water which, in the upper half of the river, came in August.

Another abortive, though interesting, scheme undertaken by Sir Donald Mann, co-builder with Sir William Mackenzie of the Canadian Northern chain of railroads, was the building of a 'Peace to Pacific' railway which would have its western terminus at Stewart. Charters were secured from the federal and British Columbia governments and construction was started with the laying of some sixteen miles of heavy steel up the valley from the Stewart wharf. A depression and the commencement of war combined to stop operations and, when these were over, Sir Donald was in retirement.

Later Mann described this railway as 'the greatest enterprise left in the white man's world' and justified the claim by referring to its grade (the lowest through the Rocky Mountains,); to its millions of tons of coal near Hudson's Hope ('above railroad grade and better than Welsh or Pennsylvania anthracite'); to its being a great mineralized area; and to its having remarkable stands of pulp timber west of the Rockies. His concluding bit of optimism was the conviction that 'at or near the forks of the Peace will arise a greater industrial centre than Detroit and a mightier metallurgical centre than Pittsburgh.'

The one railway which finally reached the Peace after so many years of difficulties was the ED&BCR or Edmonton, Dunvegan, and British Columbia Railway, though its failure to reach either Dunvegan or British Columbia caused exasperated residents to refer to it by less complimentary names.⁶ In 1915, construction of a sort had been completed from the southern terminus a few miles north of Edmonton for 362 miles to Spirit River, with a fifty-mile branch from McLennan to the town of Peace River which had just abandoned the name Peace River Landing by which it had been known for generations. Further plans provided for a sixty-five mile extension from Spirit River to Pouce Coupé in British Columbia but, despite construction of the grade, the plan was abandoned in favour of building through Grande Prairie to Dawson Creek many years later.

Both construction and financial troubles beset the ED&BCR. Much of the country through which it ran was blessed with deep, fertile soil which made gravel for railroad ballast hard to find and also caused most of the streams to be 'cut bank,' which meant heavy expenditures for bridges. The near unanimous opinion of engineers that the Peace River could not be bridged at any point upstream from the town of Peace River – an opinion finally upset by the building of the Alaska Highway Bridge – seemed to mean that a railroad would be required on each side of the river. The insufficient funds were spread so thinly that for years trains were limited to a speed of twenty miles an hour and, on occasion, a train might be held at one divisional point until enough coal could be borrowed to carry it to the next.[7] At last the end came. When the reorganization had been completed, the ED&BCR was replaced by the Northern Alberta Railway under the joint management of the Canadian Pacific and the Canadian National.

British Columbia's Peace River District was contained chiefly within the Block, a square of 3,500,000 acres, almost bisected by the river with its eastern boundary nearly coinciding with the interprovincial boundary [see Map 1]. The Block owed its existence indirectly to the Canadian Pacific Railway whose original contract with the federal government contained provisions for a grant of land 'not to exceed twenty miles on each side' of the completed line throughout western Canada. British Columbia had agreed, as part of the terms of union, to convey the necessary land to the federal government so that the contract with the railway might be carried out. Later, the province found that its side of the bargain could not be entirely kept because many parcels of land within the twenty-mile limit had already been alienated, and in lieu of these, the much more extensive Peace River area was substituted.

In 1880 British Columbia probably considered that a good bargain had been made, but thirty-five years later difficulties had arisen. As federal land, the Block was now administered by federal officials according to federal regulations, meaning that prospective settlers desiring to secure a quarter section of land had to comply with homestead law rather than BC pre-emption requirements, and that disputes or matters in doubt had to be referred to Ottawa, not to Victoria.[8] In addition, revenues chargeable against land holdings were payable to the federal authority, but the province was responsible for the cost of such essential services as education, health, and police and fire protection. Discussions on these matters were held by both jurisdictions, but it was not until many years later that the Block was returned to British Columbia.[9]

Partly for these reasons but more because of long distances from any railroad, developments in the British Columbia portion of the Peace River country were slower than in the Alberta part. Indeed, the most easterly point of the Block was still sixty-five miles from Spirit River, Alberta, by a road which was almost impassable when wet. While transportation on the Peace River was possible, it was infrequent, irregular, and available only from May to August. Such conditions were not likely to attract prospective settlers: in 1915, there were only three schools: at Rolla, Pouce Coupé, and Saskatoon Creek.[10] The only other hamlet, Fort St. John, then sited on the bank of the River, possessed two trading posts and a telegraph cabin on the north side, with the buildings occupied by Chief Constable Harry Taylor and the provincial police on the south. The present prosperous Dawson Creek did not secure its first school until 1919.[11] It required optimism and vision in those days to foresee what lay ahead.

'NO CHILDREN LEFT'

The once-a-week ED&BCR train left its Edmonton station at five o'clock in the afternoon for Peace River points. Three day coaches and one sleeper were crowded, so I counted myself lucky to have secured a berth, even though a brass plate on the sleeper wall carried an inscription: 'Wabash Railway 1891.' Half an hour later I was not so sure when the conductor asked me to move so that dinner might be served. I discovered that the front half of the car doubled as a diner, with the men's dressing room serving as a kitchen. There being a lot of hungry passengers on board, dinner continued until almost midnight, breakfast began at six o'clock, lunch started as soon as breakfast was over, and the holders of those berths were able to use them for six hours of the night.

I was on my way to Fort St. John in response to a request in February for a school there. At once I had made enquiries from every source I could think of as to how one got from Prince Rupert to Fort St. John. The replies were vague and contradictory except on two points: 'Don't attempt it in the winter,' and 'Go to Edmonton.' Now, in mid-May, I had come to Edmonton where I had been told that my best plan would be to travel by the ED&BCR train to McLennan, transfer there to a branch line running to Peace River Landing, and try to secure passage on some craft going upstream.

The 260 miles to McLennan took almost twenty-four hours and we arrived on time. No one at the station knew when the train for the Landing would leave, but they were quite sure that it would not be until the next day, so the half-dozen passengers headed in that direction secured beds at McLennan's stopping place and had an appreciated night's sleep.

It was fifty miles from McLennan to the Landing. The train's regular time to run it was six hours, but this one took almost double that. Shortly after leaving McLennan we saw from the rear platform two priests arrive at the station. After they realized the train had left, they tossed their cassocks over their shoulders and started to run after it. They had no trouble catching up! It was a fine day, and when a car ran off the rails which happened several times, passengers would stroll ahead until the damage had been repaired (experience having made train crews very competent with heavy jacks and logging chains) and the train had caught up with *them*.

This was the first year of operation for the branch line. The grade, which had been built during the previous fall and winter, had to be constructed with due regard to the company's difficult financial position. Local materials contained far too little rock and gravel, but had to be used since long hauls were expensive. Ties were laid in the dirt, rails spiked to them, and the completed line looked attractive enough until the frost came out of the ground in the spring. Then there was trouble as the weight of trains forced miles of track down into the mud, seldom to the same extent for more than a few yards, thus giving the appearance of an endless series of waves as one looked ahead. When one rail was several inches higher than the other which was common, cars were likely to be derailed in spite of careful driving. Bridges were firmly built and because they were, there was an invariable drop at each end to the sunken grade. All in all, travel on the ED&BCR was unusual.[12]

The Landing was in the midst of a minor boom and hotel accommodation was at a premium, but that problem was solved with the assistance of an RCMP officer who had been a fellow passenger. My room overlooked a vacant lot and at ten o'clock that night while watching a baseball game from my window, I realized one of the climatic wonders of the Peace River country: it was still light enough for baseball and for growing wheat.[13] The Peace does not have more frost-free days than areas farther south, but it does have many more hours of sunshine, a major reason for the excellent quality of its grain. This interesting fact was of no help in securing transportation upriver, however. There was no regular service; after exploring several suggestions, the only one which offered any hope was an ancient launch which according to the owner would have to make the trip 'maybe in ten days or so.' The prospect was so bleak that I wired my correspondent in Fort St. John in the faint hope that he might provide a solution. He did within an hour for his reply read: 'Trip needless expense; no children left in district.' At that moment it was welcome news even though it meant that two weeks and a couple of hundred dollars had been spent uselessly.

NOTHING STOPPED THE MODEL T

In their earlier days, Peace River schools followed the practice common in the prairie provinces of remaining open during most of the summer and closing for the long vacation in December and January. The severe cold in the winter and the long distances which some children had to travel to school made it desirable, and the much smaller supply of fuel to be provided was a further advantage. The policy was entirely local and, as schools increased in number, had to be discontinued since most teachers were reluctant to accept positions which placed them out of step with the prevailing provincial pattern. While it lasted, however, it was something of a bonanza for the inspector who had to travel from Prince Rupert to visit the district.

In the summer of 1917 there were only three schools in the Block, but increased settlement had brought requests for more. Immediately following the close of schools in June, inspectors were required to be at departmental headquarters in Victoria for six weeks or more, in connection with examinations and the preparation of the annual Public School Report, so it was almost the middle of August when I left for Edmonton and the ED&BCR. That railway, still 'under construction,' operated a weekly service to Grande Prairie ninety miles by road from Pouce Coupé (pronounced locally without the final accent, and owing its name to a one-time Indian chief who, if legend is correct, had suffered a cut thumb).[14] It was then, if not the capital, at least the best-known settlement in the Block.

The Model T Ford had reached Grande Prairie, and the owner of one agreed to drive me to Pouce Coupé and to return for me in a fortnight or whenever I should send for him, the entire cost to be ninety dollars. With the cars of those days and bone-dry dirt roads, ninety miles was a comfortable, one-day, enjoyable drive. For the first thirty miles, most land we passed was occupied and in crop, though Beaverlodge was the only village; even Wembly, later famous as the home of Herman Trelle, producer of world championship wheat, was scarcely a name.[15] Farther from the railway, settlement gradually diminished and finally ceased almost entirely in the hilly, wooded area near the British Columbia border, only to resume substantially in the excellent Pouce Coupé soil some twenty miles beyond [see Map 6].

Pouce Coupé possessed a store, a government telegraph office, Charlie McLean's stopping place, and three or four other buildings, all made of logs and usually with sod roofs.[16] The only frame structure, the bank, was something of a tribute to the vision of the Canadian Bank of Commerce which had opened the branch a few months before. The bank staff of two were provided with living quarters behind the bank office and, as I can gratefully testify, were generous in placing these at the disposal of occasional wanderers. Pouce Coupé residents took considerable pride in the presence of a bank but much more in the fact that its manager possessed the finest driving team in the Peace River and a magnificent pair of Russian wolfhounds which had developed an unusual ability for chasing and killing coyotes.[17]

Inspection of the three schools and arrangements for the establishment of two more in the vicinity were easily completed with the help of guide Charlie McLean and his team, but the problem of getting to Fort St. John, which also wanted a school, was more difficult.[18] The sensible way, as Charlie saw it, was to borrow one of his saddle horses and just follow the trail, but Charlie's background had few things in common with mine. No horse could throw him, he would never lose his way, and he would enjoy camping overnight (it was a two-day ride), while I was extremely likely to find myself lost, on foot, and forty miles from anywhere. With a good deal of reluctance I agreed to ride but only if he would come too, and I hoped my pleasure was not too obvious when he offered several reasons why he could not and suggested an alternative.

'Herbie Taylor has a launch,' said Charlie.[19] 'You wire him at Fort St. John and he will likely meet you at Cut Bank Landing.' I sent the wire. An hour later came the reply: 'It will cost twenty dollars to deliver the telegram.' My feeling that this was another of the not-unusual attempts to charge a government official on an expense account as much as possible was quite wrong, though, as a better knowledge of the country would have shown me. Herbie Taylor lived some ten miles downstream from Fort St. John, and a telegram could be sent to him in only two ways. The messenger could go by canoe and pole the entire distance back, or by horseback which would mean riding many miles out of the way to ford the deep, cut-bank streams which joined the Peace between Fort St. John and Taylor's. In either case I concluded the charge was reasonable and paid it.

Charlie McLean drove me out to the river and agreed to wait there until my return which I hoped, optimistically, would be in two days. We slept under the trees that night and about noon the next day, Herbie Taylor appeared with the 'launch,' an ancient canoe powered by a no-less-ancient outboard motor. Our progress upstream was slow for the motor could barely make headway against the full current and when we kept close to the bank to avoid this, the propeller would occasionally strike the gravel, drop off, and the canoe would fall back 100 feet before the situation was under control. We were travelling perhaps four miles an hour, however, and I had not given up hope of reaching Fort St. John that night.

Suddenly a black bear appeared directly ahead of us, swimming across the river. Silhouetted against the setting sun it made an almost perfect target. Herbie's first shot from his Ross rifle hit it in the shoulder, but the rifle jammed when he tried to eject the shell for a second shot. He swore, picked up the pole, and with considerable emphasis, ordered me to paddle. When I ventured to ask what he proposed to do, the only reply was 'Paddle!'

The bear had foolishly turned around and started the long way back to shore. Herbie worked the canoe upstream until we were a few yards above and directly in line with it, then let us drift back. His intention was plain enough – far too plain for my peace of mind. But my protests brought only the grunted 'Hang onto that paddle!' Two years before on a trail near the upper Fraser River I had come across two small cubs crying like babies and tugging at the body of their dead mother who, after being shot through, had succeeded in getting far enough away to save her young. The experience had given me a strong dislike for having any part in killing wild animals, but Herbie was in no frame of mind to be deterred by my qualms. As the canoe touched the bear, he first hit it a heavy blow on the head with his camp axe and when this seemed to have no effect, dropped a noose of half-inch rope over its head, and with one foot in the canoe and the other against the bear, pulled.

An hour later we were on shore, our travel over for the day. Herbie was joyfully skinning the bear and I sitting in front of the campfire trying to console my complaining stomach with thoughts of the morrow, for neither of us had brought any food, and fresh bear steak was a last resort which my hunger had not yet reached. Finally I went to sleep, but only until the fire died down and the cold woke me, for there can be a few degrees of frost in the Peace River country even in August. Alternately we stoked the fire until the first rays of light showed in the east, loaded the bear skin into the canoe, and gladly prepared for the last stage of our journey.

Two hours later we were still there. The motor was temperamental at best and the night's frost had reduced it to a state of such stubbornness that it refused to show any sign of life until the sun had warmed it thoroughly. Shortly after it started and we were again moving up river, a further, but welcome delay occurred. A large, flat-bottomed boat came into sight around a bend and when we drew alongside, the occupants turned out to be British Columbia Premier H.C. Brewster, Minister of Lands T.D. Pattullo, Surveyor-General J.E. Umbach, and UBC Dean of Agriculture L.S. Klinck.[20] They had come from Prince

George by the early fur traders' route – the Crooked, Pack, and Parsnip rivers – and were continuing on to Pouce Coupé and Grande Prairie.[21] A stop for lunch was due and the invitation to join them was more welcome than they could possibly have realized.

At Fort St. John we enjoyed the hospitality of an old friend, Chief Constable Harry Taylor.[22] There were two reasons for our enjoyment: good food and interesting conversation. Chief Taylor was a good rough-and-ready cook himself, but was then being served by a chef de luxe. This man had come into the district in 1917 with an Imperial Oil crew who were searching for oil; he had a disagreement with the superintendent, quit his job, and in return for accommodation at the police barracks until he could get transportation downriver, was doing his best to show how good a chef the oil company had lost. The chief's official life had been an interesting one from his early experience with the Nanaimo coal miners' strike until the previous spring when, with all rivers in flood, he had investigated a double murder 100 unmapped miles to the north.[23] The stories we heard that night were epics of courage and hardship but they are his, not mine.

My work was soon completed, and next day the downriver trip proved uneventful. McLean was waiting at Cut Bank Landing, and we were at Pouce Coupé in the early evening. There to my surprise I found my Grande Prairie driver. Eight hours earlier I had wired from Fort St. John that I was ready to return as we had arranged, but my satisfaction at his prompt response was soon removed when he explained with some embarrassment that he had come for a different reason. Premier Brewster's party were still at Pouce Coupé, to be guests of Grande Prairie's Board of Trade at dinner on the following evening and the invitation had included transportation, for which service my driver had been engaged. Four passengers and their baggage would crowd the car uncomfortably, but my query 'What shall I do?' brought only a shrug and the quite unnecessary information that the weekly train to Edmonton left Grande Prairie at five o'clock on Friday afternoon and that this was Wednesday.

The Pouce Coupé telegraph operator was sympathetic and, though telegraph offices were closed for the night, succeeded in locating another Grande Prairie car owner who agreed to come for me and to leave early the following morning.[24] In a state of deep, though as things turned out, misplaced content, I went to the bank to share the accommodation which the manager had offered. There were three rooms – a kitchen, a living room with a davenport convertible to a bed, and a bedroom with two beds. Premier Brewster was there and, since his visit was a major event, so were many of the district's settlers all anxious to explain their problems and to learn how the new government intended to address them. Shortly after midnight the last one departed and Brewster, near exhaustion, said he would like to go to bed. He and the minister of lands occupied the davenport, Dean Klinck and Surveyor-General Umbach shared one bed, and the manager and I had the other. We were all asleep almost immediately but only briefly, for one who must remain anonymous began to snore with a volume and rhythm that must surely have been unique. For the rest of the night, sleep was only possible at intervals.

The Premier's car left at eight o'clock the next morning. At nine o'clock the Beaverlodge operator reported that my driver had just passed through on his way to Pouce Coupé.[25] At noon, a cloud of smoke appeared over the hills twenty miles to the southeast and at four o'clock visibility in Pouce Coupé was less than 100 feet. The telegraph operator learned that a bush fire was burning for fifteen miles on both sides of the road, that the premier had passed through before it had become serious, and that nothing was known of our driver. At last, long before the headlights were visible, we heard the sound of a motor and at midnight the car arrived with a driver who, though red-eyed and tired, asked only for coffee and four hours sleep.

We woke him at five o'clock and started. The fire had almost burnt itself out and affected us only because half-a-dozen bridges had either been destroyed or were impassable. Fortunately, the warm summer had completely dried the creeks and sloughs which they spanned, and it was always possible to get across by cutting down the banks on either side, for nothing seemed to stop that Model T Ford and driver for long. Still, time was fast running out, and it was a few minutes past five when we reached the ED&BCR station in Grande Prairie. The train was still there and, when I asked the station agent what time it would leave, he said, 'You'd better go eat.[26] We've got to borrow enough coal from somewhere to get to Spirit River.'

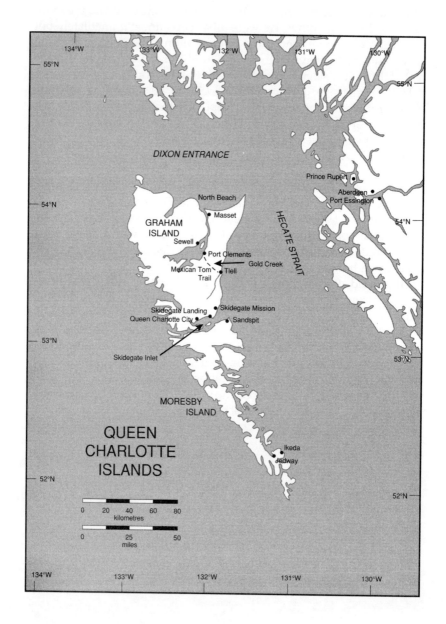

Map 8

CHAPTER SEVEN

Isolation in the Charlottes

WAITING FOR THE BOAT

Thirty-odd years ago, communication with the Queen Charlotte Islands was by Union Steamship Company boat which left Prince Rupert fortnightly, called at Masset and other northern Graham Island points, proceeded in leisurely fashion down the east coast to Jedway and Ikeda, and returned to Prince Rupert. The round trip took twelve to fourteen days and in good weather was pleasant enough while on board for the cabins were comfortable, food was good, and the boat's crews were friendly and companionable.

On shore it was a different story. The Islands in the years prior to the First World War were deep in a depression, with little market for any of their products save fish. Money was scarce and residents had to depend, in the main, on what they could raise or manufacture. Stores gradually reduced their stocks and two of the three hotels left more than a little to be desired.[1] Roads were confined to a few miles along the noted North Beach and a longer stretch on the south and east of Graham Island. Travel anywhere else was by gas boat or by trail.

Inspection of Island schools necessitated making a choice. There were three schools at each end of Graham Island, separated by fifteen miles of muskeg trail followed by thirty miles of sand and pebble beach.[2] One either got off the boat at Masset, rejoined it two weeks later on its next trip and went on to the south end for a second fortnight, thus spending four weeks for six schools, or one walked forty-five miles. The decision was not hard to make: I walked.

'Mexican Tom' Trail was unfortunately wet.[3] Three miles out, Gold Creek had flooded to form a lake 100 yards across. The trail led into it and out on the other side, so perforce had to be followed. Flood water was deep enough to soak the bottom of a pack, with the result that the remaining twelve miles became increasingly uncomfortable. The stopping place on the Tlell River was a welcome sight even though some help was needed to get out of bed the next morning.[4]

A thirty-mile walk down the beach, however, soon revived tired muscles, and a comfortable hotel at Queen Charlotte City with 'Dad' Smith's genial hospitality brightened the prospect of a six-days' wait for the boat. I visited three schools, spent a day at the Haida village of Skidegate Mission watching artists carve slate totems, enjoyed pleasant evenings in hospitable homes, and at length learned that the boat would be in soon after midnight.[5]

Of course, there are pleasanter ways of spending time than waiting for a boat. Twenty-four hours passed before word came that my boat had run onto a rock and could not be refloated until the next high tide a full month later. Island rumour also had it that the mail contract expired with this trip and that the steamship company had refused to renew it.

Two telegrams to the company's Prince Rupert office went unanswered. A third to a towing firm brought the reply that a tug could be sent for $150. This was a staggering sum for a young and very junior civil servant, but the hotel was charging $4 per day, my time was worth something, and the delay seemed likely to be one of several weeks at least. Accordingly, I sent a wire ordering the tug.

Half an hour later, the postmaster appeared and asked whether the mail could be handled on the tug, willingly agreeing that $25 each way would be a reasonable charge.[6] Two merchants whose supplies from the wholesale houses were marooned in the run-aground boat were not long in asking if they too could utilize the tug for transporting duplicate shipments. And, since most of their merchandise consisted of such weighty materials as gasoline, flour, and sugar on which regular freight charges were substantial, they and the postmaster together made up much of the tug's cost. By the time that craft arrived, twelve passengers, each paying $1.25 for the ninety-mile trip to Prince Rupert, had reduced my own commitment to this modest one-way fare.

Three weeks later an expense account item of twenty-five cents for a tip was rejected in a caustic letter from Victoria. No question was ever raised, though, concerning an expenditure of $1.25, surely a bargain fare from Queen Charlotte City to Prince Rupert!

THEY NEVER LOOKED BACK

Kumdis Slough lay near the head of Masset Inlet on the eastern side. It was connected with the nearest village, Port Clements, by four miles of trail, narrow and usually wet, and passable only on horseback or on foot. Like much of Graham Island, the Slough possessed good enough soil, but preparing it for cultivation was a heartbreaking task. Large stands of huge spruce trees had to be cut down and disposed of, stumps removed and, most backbreaking of all, deep drains dug at frequent intervals. The labour involved in clearing three acres could not be justified on any economic grounds, but a certain resident of Kumdis Slough did not know that nor would he have cared if he did. His interests were in other things.

The clearing contained three buildings – a house, a barn, and a school – all built of local materials with the earmarks of unskilled carpentry. For walls, shakes were used and for ceilings and floors spruce planks roughly smoothed with an adze. Labour was the most abundant commodity and money the scarcest, so only those items which were essential were bought. In the school that meant a door and two windows. Even the blackboard was literally that, a rough board painted with a mixture of oil and lamp black.

Everyone connected with the school – the teacher, ten pupils, and trustees – lived in the clearing. The pupils were the teacher's children or his foster children, for he was a rigid observer of the law which said 'six to sixteen years' was school age. At sixteen a natural child was replaced by an orphan secured from an institution; thus there were always ten pupils though, as will develop later, there were eleven on the roll. Two of the three trustees were sons of the teacher; the third was the teacher himself until he found that, too, was illegal and invented an imaginary one.

Francis L. Tonturier was in charge of the school, for that name appeared at the foot of the register and on Department of Education reports. It was also the name on the Quebec teacher's certificate which had enabled him to secure official teacher status in British Columbia. For most interests aside from the school, he used another name – F.L. Donroe – under which he appeared on the voters' list, got most of his mail, and was generally known. A third – Robert Lanahan – was reserved for special purposes, as when a third trustee was required to complete the school board.[7]

'Robert Lanahan' was the father of 'Bridget Lanahan' who was always the eleventh pupil on the school register. Whenever I visited the school her name was there but she was always absent; her attendance had been recorded regularly until the day of my visit when 'she had a cold.' Very rarely in some other school, attendance of one or two children was faked when their absence, if reported, would have caused it to close. No such reason explained 'Bridget,' for there were always more pupils present in Kumdis School than the number required to ensure its operation. Some years later Mary Donroe explained that 'Bridget was another name Father had for me.'

Instruction in Kumdis School resembled what I imagine must have been usual a century ago in Ontario. The only subjects were the three Rs but, for them, perfection was sought and secured, in so far, at least, as Tonturier understood his aims. The pupils' handwriting was copperplate, and their accuracy and speed in using numbers were remarkable. Even the younger ones would have the answer to an addition question of eight columns, twelve figures to a column, in half the time that I could complete it myself. Reading, always oral, was clear and distinct, with every word receiving its full and correct pronunciation and every comma, semicolon, and period its proper pause.

That was all. There was nothing else. All day, each class in turn was drilled in the three Rs, and woe betide the one who made a mistake, for punishment was swift and sure. There was no inattention, for the children's fear was too great. Neither was there any happiness, joy, or fun. Once, for most of a day, I did the teaching and resorted to various kinds of nonsense to bring a smile to some face, but there was no change in any expression. From the first years of understanding they learned one lesson – to obey. The word of their father was law even to the older sons who, when they reached manhood, were forbidden to shave.[8] Nothing was known of the outside world for they went nowhere and the rare visitors to the clearing remained but briefly.

The teacher's salary was $960 a year. That in itself was enough to arouse resentment in those depressed days when few Graham Island wage earners made more than half as much. That Tonturier was paid for teaching his own children made it seem even worse. Criticism was widespread and, when the oldest daughter eloped with a logger, the couple leaving during the night and rowing thirty miles to be married, it did not lessen, though there was much conjecture as to how the courting had been carried on. Things came to a head when the second daughter ran away from home and appealed to the nearest police for protection. An investigation followed. When it was over the children under sixteen were placed first in a hospital and then in an orphanage. They walked away and never looked back.[9]

CHAPTER EIGHT

Chilcotin Country

GREAT CATTLE EMPIRE

Riske Creek and Anahim Lake, Redstone and Kleena Kleene, Cheza-cut and Tatlayoko Lake are unusual names which suggest places that are out of the drab routine of rural villages. Actually they are mere dots on a map of British Columbia, names in a post office directory with populations in two low figures, and to the casual visitor, with nothing about them important enough or interesting enough to justify a drive of fifty miles, but they are part of this province's great cattle empire. These, along with Hanceville and Big Creek, Meldrum Creek and Alexis Creek, Tatla Lake and half-a-dozen others, together with the districts they serve, make up the Chilcotin or, 'Chil-i-cotin,' as the old-timers prefer to call it.[1]

It is a country of considerable distances even for British Columbia. The main road, which runs across from east to west, travels 225 miles from Williams Lake to its current end at Anahim Lake.[2] On the east, the Fraser River separates it from the Cariboo, while the Coast Range forms both the southern and western limits. The Gang Ranch is in the extreme south east, Nazko is in the farthest north, and the mileage of the exceedingly winding road which connects them is close to 140. For that matter, all roads are winding roads or were until very recently, for the Chilcotin is a plateau of ups and downs with little flat land and the early trails laid out to go round the hills rather than over them, a sensible arrangement when horses and cattle provided the only traffic.

The Chilcotin climate often provides extremes. Zero or near-zero [-17°C] temperatures may be expected any time from early September to late April and are certain to come with some frequency during the three months that are officially winter. Once on June the 3rd I drove

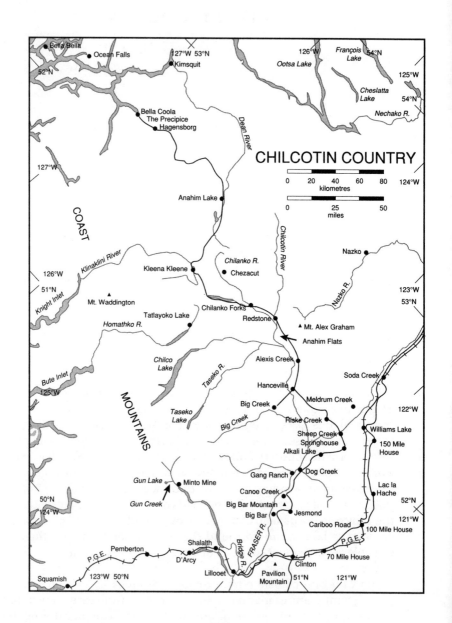

Map 9

from Tatla Lake to Williams Lake, most of the way in a snowstorm, and had the car radiator frozen that night. The following September 20th it again snowed all day but experience had taught me the lesson of always draining the radiator. Local ranchers claimed that twice in July of that year it had been necessary to break the ice in the horse troughs. With due allowances for local pride, which may be a bit extreme even in matters of adversity, frost is a certainty in eleven months of every year and a possibility in July. Summers, however, can be very hot and dry.

Present-day visitors to the Chilcotin, be they coming to hunt, fish, scale Mount Waddington, or just tour, have three choices of entrance. The more travelled and perhaps the easiest follows the Cariboo Road to Williams Lake, then turns west for eighteen miles to cross the Fraser River via the narrow Sheep Creek Bridge reached from either side by an 800-foot switchback descent. It is an interesting and, in places, a spectacular trip which may be a bit dismaying to timorous city motorists, particularly if they find themselves behind a drive of several hundred beef cattle when halfway down the hill.

A second route leaves the Cariboo Road at Clinton and swings west and north through Jesmond and Big Bar Mountain to Canoe Creek where the Fraser River has again been bridged. It passes through the noted Gang Ranch, crosses Big Creek, and connects with the first route at Hanceville. Bella Coola has provided a third gateway though, since 1893, one that has been more hoped-for than real. Some day the present seventy miles of road eastward from the Bella Coola wharf will be extended into the Chilcotin but, as yet, the difficult intervening gap is best suited for pack horses.

For the adventurous, if competent in the woods, there are still other routes. The summit separating Chilcotin's Taseko Lake from Bridge River's several mines has been crossed a number of times, and trails of a sort follow the Dean River from Kimsquit and the Klinaklini from Knight Inlet. Oldest of all is Bute Inlet which Alfred Waddington tried to develop as an alternative road to the Cariboo gold fields and in 1868 proposed (to no avail) as a route for a transcontinental railroad. The trail, which began at the head of the inlet and followed the Homathko River to Tatlayoko Lake, was never completed as a wagon road. It was seldom used after the 'Waddington Massacre' in 1864, though a buffet in Bob Graham's house at Tatla Lake, packed in from Bute Inlet, bears witness that it was still passable many years later.[3]

Throughout the Chilcotin the one great product is cattle – beef cattle – chiefly shorthorn, with here and there a herd of Herefords and very occasionally a few black, polled Aberdeen Angus. It is the country of the cowhands, with chaps, red neckerchief, and rope; of the roundup and the long cattle drive to the railroad; of summer and winter range and hay meadows; of low prices which meet neither the cost of production nor the overdraft at the bank; of high prices when nothing is too good for ranch, family, or district; but never the country which demands or wants government subsidies or price support, for the rancher is a self-reliant and independent person.[4]

Cattle ranching, even on a moderate scale, is a considerable undertaking. The ranch organized to sell 200 three-year-old steers each year must have a herd of over 1,200. In the spring they must often be driven a long way back into the hills for summer range where they will fatten on bunch grass and pea vine. When autumn arrives, they are rounded up; those that will command the best price on the market, usually three-year-olds, are separated, and the rest are turned out on winter range. Even during a mild winter, range grass has to be supplemented by perhaps three-quarters of a ton of hay for each animal. The cutting, hauling, and stacking of 800 tons requires much labour, especially if the hay meadows are twenty miles from the home ranch as is often the case. Because of the slow growing season, haymaking begins in mid-September and is constantly plagued by the threat of early snow. Also costly in both money and labour is irrigation which, since Chilcotin is definitely a dry belt, is essential everywhere. Fortunately, lakes and streams are abundant, so the only problems are those of engineering know-how and of finance.

The only return on this investment comes from the sale of those 200 steers. Before they can be sold they must be driven to the rail connection which, for all of central Chilcotin, means Williams Lake. A cattle drive averages seven miles a day and rests every seventh day, thus allowing such close-in ranches as Moon's and Cotton's to deliver their cattle in four or five days, while Bob Graham's, 150 miles distant at Tatla Lake, will require over three weeks.[5] This costs money, not only for the easily reckoned items of wages and food for cowhands but also for the inevitable shrinkage in weight of the cattle themselves.

Steers are sold by the pound, live weight, and are graded for quality by the buyers who represent the large packing house firms. Alive, a good three-year-old steer will weigh in the neighbourhood of 1,100 pounds and slaughtered, will dress from 50 to 55 per cent. This range may appear narrow but it affects packing house profits as well as the reputation of the buyers whose success depends on the accuracy of their estimates.

The price paid is based on prevailing market prices in western Canada less the cost of transportation by rail to Vancouver. Over the years it has been subject to extreme variations. During the Depression, indeed, for most of 1930 to 1940, the top price was three cents a pound, and grading so severe that it was not unusual for a rancher to find less than 60 per cent of a drive graded No. 1, with the balance selling as low as $5 for a good fat cow. The rancher who sold 200 head would gross not more than about $6,000, which would leave him further in debt than the year before. In those years of high production costs, a price of six cents a pound would have been reasonable.

Conversely, prices went to the other extreme when controls imposed during the Second World War were lifted, particularly when the United States' markets were reopened for Canadian beef. Then, with prices in excess of thirty cents a pound and with generous grading, the same rancher sold his 200 steers for around $65,000. It was a too-familiar story.

Cattle country must be thinly populated because of the very nature of ranching. Even a small ranch must have more land, owned or leased, than would equal a Saskatchewan township, while several Ontario counties, taken together, would find room to spare inside the largest one. Yet the permanent population of both would only be two figures. When I knew the Chilcotin twenty years ago [circa 1930], only five schools could find ten resident children and in at least two of these, the official eye had to be closed to the practice of 'borrowing' the odd youngster.[6] To illustrate, for one year at least, everyone connected with Tatla Lake school, including the teacher, lived at Bob Graham's house though the school register recorded only three Graham children.[7]

They were lucky people to live in that house. I first saw it late one October evening at the end of a long, slow, 150-mile drive from Williams Lake and from the railroad. The mass of the house loomed up, then the front door opened and light streamed out – electric light. My bedroom had running water both hot and cold. The bathroom was next door. If any of the conveniences and comforts of a city dwelling were missing, I never discovered them. Instead, I found a spaciousness, a freshness, and a restfulness that only the remote rural areas can provide.

There was more than that, much more, and all of it common to the Chilcotin; the genial welcome when you arrived, the direct courtesy whereby your acquaintance could differ with you yet make you glad, the blunt expression of opinion which always seemed to get down to essentials and, perhaps most of all, the natural, unobtrusive kindness. On that first visit I was on a diet, mainly of fish, chicken, or eggs. Fish was at times unprocurable while to ask for chicken seemed like an imposition, so I asked for, and was served, eggs. During the next few months Mrs. Margaret Graham discovered my hesitation; thereafter chicken appeared on my plate the evening I arrived and each evening until I left.[8] For all this I paid, with some sense of shame, fifty cents for a meal and fifty cents for a room, the standard Chilcotin and Cariboo charge for fifty years – old-timers resenting change in that as in other things.

Early Chilcotin settlers were unusual men and women. Norman Lee, for example, was born in England and educated there at a good public school and later in Germany. He followed the practice of the time and came to Manitoba to learn farming. In the early 1890s he moved to Hanceville where he developed a ranch, a trading post, and a stopping place, the latter two managed by his wife Agnes, a personality in her own right with a rare ability to sum up her overnight guests in one trenchant phrase be they university professor, commercial traveller, or school inspector. Only by chance did one discover her excellent education and that a brother-in-law was a professor at Oxford.[9]

Another was Fred Becher who in 1885 worked for the Hudson's Bay Company at Dunvegan on the Peace River, then freighted on the Cariboo Road, and finally operated a road house at Riske Creek. The original building was the usual Chilcotin type – one storey, built of logs, and roofed with sod. It burned and was replaced by a thirty-room frame hotel mainly because the provincial liquor act of the day demanded thirty rooms as a first requirement for a licence. Many furnishings were imported from England, and the appointments of Mrs. Florence Becher's private quarters might well have come from a Mayfair drawing room.[10]

This was an expensive and, as it turned out, an unfortunate investment. Prohibition during and after the First World War seriously reduced revenues, but the arrival of the automobile and motor truck almost wiped them out. Nonetheless, the hotel operated for many years, providing full consideration for guests, good meals, and even the annual dance attended by the entire Chilcotin population, most of whom drove home by daylight. Becher's later years were saddened by failing eyesight and by financial difficulties. I last saw him in 1935 in connection with the establishment of Riske Creek's first school.[11] He enquired hopefully, 'I suppose the teacher will board here?' I had to say with regret that the six-mile trip to the school made that impossible. As he turned and walked away, I realized how important that forty dollars a month was to him.[12]

There were many others. Andy Stewart at Redstone who had opened a store and gas station at the outer end of settlement after his return from the First World War and had prospered;[13] Bob Pyper, halfway between Redstone and Tatla Lake, whom everyone stopped to see for his good company and also to use the only telephone in fifty miles;[14] Mrs. Dolly Moore, granddaughter of a British university professor who had her own brand, ran her own herd of cattle, and was said to equal any man with axe, horse, or rope;[15] and Captain David Lloyd, retired British army officer at Tatlayoko, so competent a letter writer that he persuaded the Post Office Department to establish a mail service against its will.[16] His final letter of appeal read: 'Our population has been substantially increased: last night Mrs. X gave birth to a son. Now, may we have our post office?' Alex Graham, justice of the peace, whose ranch just west of Alexis Creek included the fertile Anahim Flats, was yet another individualist.[17] While presiding over one of his first cases he whispered to the constable, 'Is there any law against smoking in court?' Horrified, the constable assured him that such a thing was not done. 'But is there a law against it?' repeated Graham. When the constable admitted that he didn't know of any such law, out came Graham's pipe and justice proceeded on its way.

One part of the Chilcotin, now remote and even more sparsely settled, may, indeed will, become an important and populous community in another decade or two when the district around Tatlayoko Lake becomes the centre of a great power development program. Many problems must first be met, since the diversion of the waters of Chilco Lake from the Fraser River watershed is involved, and Chilco Lake is a major salmon spawning area. When the conflicting interests of power and fisheries have been resolved, a second Kitimat will arise at Tatlayoko Lake.[18] In the meantime, the residents are squatters, for a far-sighted government placed this land under reserve fifty years ago.

AN EDUCATED MAN

I first met Henry Koster one evening in late September.[19] Shortly after I left Williams Lake, there started to fall the kind of snow that is soft, wet, heavy, and difficult to drive in even with chains. There was no change as I passed Springhouse and Alkali Lake. By Dog Creek, the snow was six inches deep. An invitation from the ever-hospitable Places, Charles and Ada, to spend the night was tempting, but I was still thirty-five miles from my destination and if it continued to snow through the night, cars would not leave Dog Creek for several days.[20] I settled for a cup of tea and left for Jesmond immediately.

A mountain separates Dog Creek from Canoe Creek, its top reached from each end by a two-mile switchback road which has to be driven cautiously. When I reached the bottom at Canoe Creek it was dusk. I switched on the lights of the car but nothing happened. Half-an-hour later, my amateur efforts had proved fruitless. I was still twenty miles – twenty empty, untenanted miles – from Jesmond, so I turned west and drove farther down to the Canoe Creek ranch house. An explanation of my trouble and a request for a night's accommodation brought an unexpected reply: 'I suppose we will have to, but it is inconvenient.' Such was doubtless the case for late September is hay making time in the Cariboo when extra workers must be housed and fed, and the snowstorm had caught this ranch half-finished. A few moments later, there were angry words in the kitchen, the meaning of which were clear enough when my host, Koster, returned to say that my dinner would be delayed. When I told him that I had eaten at Dog Creek, he smiled and said, 'That simplifies matters.'

Henry Koster was born in the Cariboo, the son of a German miner who brought him up from babyhood and taught him to read from such classic writers as Thackeray. Of formal education in the sense of schooling he had none, but that evening we sat in front of the fire till long after midnight talking of cattle prices and diseases, of communism, of religion, of trees and placer mining and of the beauty of the Cariboo, always in the language of Thackeray and always in language precise and exact, with sentences and words which, if fortunate, one might hear from a university graduate with a major in English.

These words were the vehicle of his mind, a mind with a clarity and a simplicity rare enough in my experience to be impressive. He seemed to break down any problem to its essentials, to eliminate the less important elements, and to reach a conclusion which fully satisfied him. He was not always right, for no human being can be, but his integrity was solid and sure. Such people are found, when they are found at all, among the hills and the trees and the cattle, where a mind can be free from the multitude of minor things that cannot be avoided in thickly populated areas.

We talked that night about a new tax just imposed by the government of the day – a levy of five mills on the assessed value of all land 'outside school districts.' Naturally enough it was looked upon as a school tax by ranchers who, in most cases, had no school within their land holdings and did not want one, as they had strong feelings against attempting to mix schoolchildren with roundups or cowhands with schoolmarms. Actually, it was not a school tax, merely an impoverished government's effort to secure some additional funds, the proceeds going directly into consolidated revenue. It might have been justified and even accepted with some willingness, but unfortunately was imposed without explanation or warning and at a time – 1932 – when the price of beef was at an all-time low.[21]

Mr. Koster told me how that tax affected him. 'Last year I sold 300 steers at an average price of twenty-one dollars each. They cost me forty-five dollars to raise, and one dollar out of every twenty-one went to pay that extra tax.' 'Did you pay it?' I asked. It was an impertinent question, but I knew that some of the largest outfits had refused to pay. This was his answer. 'As much as anyone else I was responsible for putting this government in office. I am under a moral obligation to comply with any legislation it imposes.'

In the true sense of the word, Henry Koster was an educated man.

PEWTER MONEY

Three dates are important in the history of the Bella Coola Valley: 1793, 1867, and 1894. Insofar as development is concerned, the first, 1793, which marked Alexander Mackenzie's visit; and the second, 1867, the establishment of a Hudson's Bay Company post; are of little importance, for its first substantial settlement began with the third date, 1894, upon the arrival of a group of Norwegians from the United States.

The previous year the forerunners of this group had come to Victoria to interview the government and to present a request which has a familiar sound even today. They wished to secure land for settlement where they could bring up their children 'removed from the evils of modern society.' Their representations were well-received, for Norwegian settlers had, as they still have, a high reputation in British Columbia. Land was made available on generous terms, assistance was promised with roads, bridges, wharves, and schools, and, perhaps the greatest inducement, liquor licences were permanently banned.

It was expected, certainly by the government and probably by the new arrivals, that the district would soon become a prosperous agricultural community. There was an abundance of land even though much of it involved heavy clearing, and John Clayton had already demonstrated that farming, especially stock raising, could be profitable.[22] Markets also existed among the canneries and logging settlements up and down the Coast for which it was assumed that transportation would be provided as soon as a sufficient volume of production justified it. A road up the valley, over 'the precipice,' and across the Chilcotin to connect with the Cariboo Road would provide an economical shipping route for Cariboo and Chilcotin beef cattle, and there were even optimistic dreams of a railroad.

A quarter of a century later the white population of Bella Coola was estimated by the British Columbia *Yearbook* to be about 300 and the amount of cultivated land was probably less than that number of acres. The Valley, far from supplying food for much of the Coast, was producing little more than enough for its own needs. Transportation was confined to the Union Steamship's weekly call, the road to the Cariboo was still far in the future, and a railroad was seldom mentioned. None of this meant frustrated hopes – except in the matter of the roads – nor was it any reflection on the ambition, thrift, and ability of the settlers. It was simply due to the greater attraction of another primary industry: fishing. The waters adjacent to Bella Coola teemed with salmon, there was a ready market, and the annual return compared favourably with the rewards of farming. Since both activities could be carried on only during the summer months, small wonder that agriculture suffered.

Present-day students of monetary reform would find some support for one of their theories in the story of 'Brynildsen money.' Barney Brynildsen, a pioneer Norwegian settler, opened a store and soon developed a considerable business not only with the local residents but also with Indian people who came from the Chilcotin to trade their winter's catch of furs.[23] Unfortunately, with the nearest bank 300 miles away, he found himself almost continuously short of small change in a day when small change meant anything under five dollars. He solved his problem by having his own money made in pewter-like metal on which was stamped 'B. Brynildsen, Bella Coola, will pay to the bearer' twenty-five cents, fifty cents, and so on.

On my first trip along the Cariboo Road I spent a night at 100 Mile House, 300 miles east of Bella Coola. When I settled my account in the morning, my change from a bill included an odd coin which I questioned until the stage driver explained, 'That's Brynildsen money; it's good anywhere north of the 70 Mile.'

It remained good until the federal authorities learned what was going on and summarily stopped any further issue. Years later I asked Brynildsen how much had been issued. He said, 'Perhaps five thousand.' Then I asked, 'How much never came back?' but his only reply was a quiet smile.

CHAPTER NINE

Kelowna Beginnings

SOME LASTING IMPRESSIONS

The year was 1910. British Columbia schools reopened for the autumn term on the third Monday in August. As the just-appointed principal in Kelowna, I arranged to arrive on the previous Friday and so departed from my home in Ontario with my rail ticket and thirty-odd dollars in my pocket. When I reached Sicamous Junction on Thursday evening and found the southbound train left the next morning, my remaining money let me eat or sleep. I ate.

On Friday, a slow train to Okanagan Landing and a delightful sail down Okanagan Lake, together with an excellent meal on the SS *Okanagan*, brought me to Kelowna interested and curious. All day heavy smoke from forest fires had prevented me from seeing more than a few feet.[1] I was also worried as my money was now exhausted and I badly needed a night's sleep in a comfortable bed.

Half an hour later I was convinced that British Columbia was a wonderful province and that Kelowna was the best part of it, opinions which have only been strengthened forty-six years later. Tom Lawson, school board chairman, was on the wharf; he greeted me with 'Are you a Presbyterian?'[2] 'Yes,' I replied. 'Are you a Mason?' 'Yes' again. 'Are you a Grit?' 'Yes,' said I. He beamed his satisfaction and led me up the street to the Palace Hotel (predecessor of the Royal Anne) and introduced me to mine host Arthur Augustus Peabody with the remark: 'We'll find a boarding house for him in a few days.' Then with 'Maybe you'll need this, it's your August salary,' he handed me a cheque and departed. The cheque was for $100. Later I was to learn that in British Columbia salaries were paid for every month and that the August cheque went to the incoming teacher. Both the amount and the method of payment seemed generous, for in my last Ontario

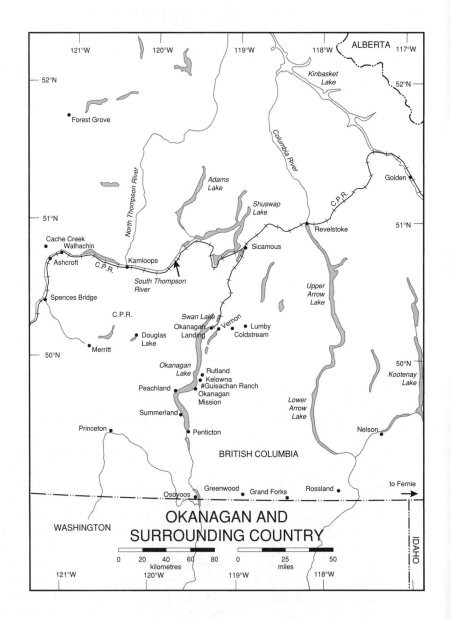

OKANAGAN AND
SURROUNDING COUNTRY

Map 10

school where my wages, to use the local term, were $550 per annum, I was paid $100 in June and the balance in December.

My qualifications for the principalship of what, in those days, was not a small school were meager enough, since they consisted only of a degree from Queen's University and three years experience in Ontario rural schools. My degree did meet BC legal requirements though, for in the absence of a provincial university a graduate of 'a university in the British Dominions' could receive a certificate to teach. I had, however, enclosed with my application a document which turned out to be much more important. Two or three years earlier I had tutored the son of the Dean of Queen's Medical School; when this lad passed into high school, I received an envelope which contained a surprising cheque and a letter, and that letter was the enclosure. Dr. W.J. Knox, a member of the Kelowna School Board, was a graduate of Queen's, knew the dean, and Queen's men, then at least, were clannish.[3]

Kelowna in 1910 had a population of 1,650, as we proved later in the year when pupils of the entrance class and the high school conducted a census. There were perhaps 200 Chinese, of whom two or three were wives, and half-a-dozen were children who would soon attend school. Natives of other parts of Canada were in a majority, especially from Saskatchewan, whose recent boom had enriched many and enabled them to escape from the rigours of Prairie winters to the fabled Okanagan. They brought money, purchased established businesses or opened up new ones, and began such ambitious developments as the Central Okanagan Land Company and Kelowna Irrigation initiated by J.W. Jones and W.H. Gaddes.[4]

The Kelowna district, as distinct from the town itself, was predominantly of Old Country birth. Lord Aberdeen's investments in Coldstream in the 1890s had been widely advertised in Great Britain, and his purchase of the Guisachan Ranch near Kelowna, which gossip still insisted was his refuge from domestic importunities, extended the interest.[5] Many people who came to settle had independent means, not enough to live 'at home' as they might have wished, but ample for a new country. A ten- or twenty-acre fruit ranch planted with many varieties, a couple of hired hands to work it, and no economic worries about fruit prices endued something close to a carefree existence. Cricket, polo, tennis, rowing, the Kelowna Club, the Aquatic Association, along with the more Canadian baseball, lacrosse, and hockey provided, in part at least, for the ranchers' considerable leisure time. So, in winter, did the excellent and successful Music and Dramatic Society which each year produced a Gilbert and Sullivan operetta, a 'Charlie's Aunt', or a music hall performance with a professional touch.

There was another side of the story, though, for this ease of living produced what Archdeacon Thomas Greene of Kelowna's Anglican Church described as 'Okanagan inertia.'⁶ Independent incomes did not tend to strengthen either exertion or initiative, and the fruit industry was to experience deep tribulations when it had to be self-supporting later on. When the First World War erupted, British-born subjects went 'home,' usually at their own expense. Many were not to return, and the incomes of those who did were drastically reduced.⁷

Few children of English-born parents attended Kelowna Elementary School which, from the viewpoint of their fathers, was the equivalent of the 'board school' back home and socially undesirable.⁸ Some went away to boarding schools, but the majority were taught in small, local private schools or occasionally by a governess.⁹ Because of this and because of the considerable proportion of bachelors in the area, I opened school on that August Monday morning in 1910 with *only 235 youngsters divided among five rooms* [editor's emphasis!].

Four rooms were in a wooden building which I believe still stands just behind the United Church at the corner of Glen Avenue and Richter Street. Built in 1904, it was Kelowna's second school; the first, a one-room building, was on Bernard Avenue about where the Post Office now stands. There D.W. Sutherland taught for a good many years before going into business and becoming the city's well-nigh permanent mayor.¹⁰

The fifth room was just across the street in the as-yet-unfinished new school, internally a capacious six-room brick building and externally an architectural monstrosity. The high school was also there occupying one room, fully adequate for its one teacher and twenty-one pupils. It had been established in 1907 with Elizabeth McNaughton in charge, a teacher whose record of consistent success had seldom been excelled in the province's history. For five years single-handed, she taught all subjects in the three-year high school program until 1912, when L.V. Rogers was made her assistant. At her own insistence the two exchanged positions in 1917 and Miss McNaughton continued as assistant until her retirement.¹¹ Throughout those years the standing of her pupils in departmental examinations was always high; of greater meaning, she retained the affection and respect of both pupils and parents.

L.V. Rogers was a Barnardo Home lad who never definitely knew his own age.¹² As a child he was placed in a farmer's home in Ontario's Northumberland County, attended the local little red schoolhouse, and passed the high school entrance examination. His high school course in which he had to support himself was interrupted by two years of service in the South African [Boer] War and was followed by teaching in rural schools in Ontario and Saskatchewan. In 1911, he graduated from Queen's University and came to Kelowna. When he left nine years later he was president of the Board of Trade, a ranking officer of the provincial Masonic Lodge, and had twice been a Liberal candidate for the provincial legislature. The rest of his life was spent as principal of Nelson High School and the Leslie V. Rogers High School in that city honors his memory.

During my four years in Kelowna, the growth of the school was regular and, for those days, rapid. The new six-room school was soon filled and the wooden building divided its four rooms between the high school and elementary classes. In the summer of 1913, a twelve-room school and auditorium building was opened by the local minister of the Crown, the Honourable Price Ellison, with his optimistic assurance that 'This structure will meet Kelowna's needs for all time.'[13] Yet school opened in the autumn with twelve classes enrolled, and thirteen teachers, an additional teacher solely for music and art[14] – a daring innovation in 1913.

The problem of new arrivals was not one of classroom space, but very much more of absorbing a variety of backgrounds into our classes as they were constituted. Hardly a week passed without the arrival of a father or a mother to enrol their children – from Ontario, from Scotland, from Tasmania, from Nova Scotia, from Northern Rhodesia, from Seattle, from dozens of different parts of the world. Few brought report cards and, even when these were presented, they referred to 'forms' or 'grades' which were not easily translated into 'second primer' or 'junior third reader.'[15]

For a few months we applied a rough-and-ready formula. 'How old are you?' 'How long have you been in school?' Then we placed them one term behind our own pupils of the same age and experience. Occasionally we had to accede to an indignant parent, such as the mother from London's Shoreditch who refused to allow her 'almost seven-year-old' to enter first primer because he had been three years in school already. In general, however, we stood firm, confident that these newcomers must secure the rudiments of arithmetic, language, or history which the British Columbia course of study provided and their own did not. It seemed logical and it was the general practice in the province; in fact, as we were sadly aware, our own pupils were usually 'put back' if they transferred, say, to Vancouver.

Then I learned a lesson. Early in January a father and his son came to the school. 'We have just arrived from Fort William,' said the father, 'and my boy will go in the entrance class.' I was starting to explain why the child would have to enter the junior fourth when he added 'Here is his report card.' Ordinarily, a report showing a rank of fourth in a class of forty in an Ontario school would have had no influence but the name of the teacher who signed this one did. William Southon had taught me for three years in my two-room Ontario school and was my ideal of a teacher.[16] When Southon said a boy was good, he was good whether in British Columbia or in Ontario; nor could I face the possibility that Will Southon might some day learn that I had questioned the proficiency of one of his pupils.

The lad from Fort William joined the entrance class in January, halfway through the school year. He had taken no nature study and little art; his knowledge of British Columbia history and geography was as fragmentary as ours was of Ontario; the Ontario texts in literature were different, yet in June he passed the entrance examination near the top of his class. Thereafter newcomers entered the school with the standing they brought with them; only rarely was a change necessary and, when one did occur, it was as likely to be forward as back.

So came my first doubt of the perfection of a course of study or, for that matter, of the infallibility of any educational authority. Thirty-five years later I was to find almost the other extreme in England when London's Chief Education Officer, Sir Graham Savage, introduced me to two of his schools.[17] In one, mathematics permeated the curriculum from top to bottom; in the other, English was all important. I asked: 'What happens to the pupil who transfers from one school to the other?' Sir Graham's reply was 'Transfers are common, but pupils adjust readily. Teachers are much more important than what they teach.'

They are indeed! Two Okanagan pioneers stand out in my memory: Paul Murray and Clarence Fulton.[18]

Paul Murray was more than an Okanagan pioneer. He once told me that he had taught in Maple Ridge [see Map 11, bottom] from before 1892 until 1906 when the school board decided he was too old and suggested he resign. The next six years he spent in Peachland [see Map 10] and was the wise and kindly mentor of novice teachers as they arrived; his advice saved me from several troubles during my first two years in Kelowna. Next he went to Union Bay, [see Map 1] and in 1915 to Pitt Meadows [see Map 11, bottom] where he ultimately retired, only to be elected reeve of the municipality.

Thousands of pupils passed through his hands; hundreds made their mark in the professions, in business, and in public service. Perhaps the one to win most distinction was his son and only child Gladstone Murray who matriculated from Vancouver's King Edward High School to McGill University, won a Rhodes scholarship, finished the First World War as an air force major, and spent several years with the British Broadcasting Corporation before being enticed to the management of the Canadian Broadcasting Corporation by Prime Minister R.B. Bennett. It is an indication of Paul Murray's wisdom that he was strongly opposed to his son's acceptance of the Canadian proposal.[19]

In 1902 Clarence Fulton came from Nova Scotia with a Dalhousie University degree to be principal and sole teacher of Vernon High School. Ten years later, he was dismissed after considerable school board debate fully reported in both the local and coast papers. With the quick decision characteristic of him he retired to his fruit ranch. Six months later he came to Kelowna to apply for a vacant position on our staff. I told him: 'It is a junior third class and the salary is sixty-five dollars a month.' His reply was, 'I don't care what it is. I want to show them I can make good.'

He was with us for a year and a half to our interest, satisfaction, and occasional amazement. To illustrate, once the janitor was called away suddenly. For a week Clarence took charge, stoking the furnace, sweeping, and dusting. He saw a job to be done and he did it.

Another time in early spring, for some special reason, perhaps his wife's birthday, he wished to spend a weekend at home. His family continued to live in Vernon, thirty-seven miles away over a rough road, and in 1913 there was only one way to go. Fortified with two hard-boiled eggs in his pocket, he left the school at four o'clock on Friday afternoon and walked home in ten hours. On Sunday night he made the return trip and Monday found him as enthusiastic and energetic as after any other weekend.

'Closing day' in June meant many visitors – members of the school board, civic dignitaries, and scores of parents. This time Mayor J.W. Jones – the province's minister of finance twenty years later – whispered to me that he had promised one dollar to each pupil in his daughter's class who would make 90 per cent in spelling. 'How many dollars will I need?' he asked. The girl was in Clarence Fulton's class and I thought I knew, but it seemed wiser to ask. Fortunately we did, for the mayor had to go to the bank for thirty one-dollar bills.

Satisfying himself and 'them' that he had made good, Clarence Fulton returned to his ranch at the end of June, but his yen for teaching remained strong. In September he was appointed to the Vernon Elementary School, a few years later was made principal, and finally rejoined the high school staff where I last saw him one day in the late 1940s. Ernest Lee, then director of physical education, was with me when we met Clarence in the main hall.[20] 'Ernie,' I said, 'I want you to meet a man who can teach physical education at sixty-five.' 'Sixty-five, nothing!' Clarence declared, 'I'm seventy and I taught physical education every day this week.'

Clarence Fulton was never a conformist. His methods of teaching were his own and if they were in accord with the pedagogical theory of the moment, it was accidental. Timetables to him were a convenient reminder, nothing more. His pupils' examination results were fair enough, but never startling. Yet, for me, he was one of the half-dozen best teachers I have ever known. Some anonymous genius wrote of Mark Hopkins that 'he sat on one end of a log, a farm boy sat on the other' and together they made a university, for 'education is making men.'[21] Today the faces of Clarence Fulton's old pupils light up when they hear his name: He made them what they are today.

THAT FIRST MORNING

On that first morning in 1910 when I came to the door of the Kelowna Elementary School, a Chinese man was waiting for me with three children: a girl, a boy, and a babe in arms. He said, 'You schoolmaster? You tak' 'em children school?' Learning the girl was eight and the boy was five and a half, I said we would be glad to have them. Then the father smiled broadly and said, 'You keep 'em boy three year, I get five hundred dollar. I give you big present.'

Chinese were a novelty to me, just arrived from Ontario where the only representative of the race was an occasional launderer. Here in Kelowna there were not only about 200 men, mostly market gardeners and labourers on farms, but also a number of wives, though the boy and girl were the first Chinese children to come to school. My curiosity changed to interest which led to visits to homes in the Chinese community and to some acquaintances which were more than casual, particularly with the father of the two pupils, Wu Yuén.

In the spring of 1913 Wu Yuén died. A few days later his widow came to the school and, with some difficulty (for she had little English), I found she wanted 'a paper' to say that her boy had been in school three years. I gave her a statement to that effect, and she left with a broad smile and many words of thanks.

Three weeks later she came back, handed me a letter addressed to her from the federal Department of Immigration, and said, 'You fix 'em.' The letter simply said that her letter to them had been received but was unintelligible. That evening, with the help of another Chinese whose English was excellent, I learned the boy, now nearly nine years old, was actually Wu Yuén's nephew, not his son. Wu Yuén had gone back to China for a visit, found his brother had died leaving an orphan son, and had adopted the lad. On their return to British Columbia, Canadian immigration authorities had required payment of the five-hundred-dollar head tax but, as Wu Yuén understood, had promised it would be refunded if the boy attended school in Canada for three years.[22]

I wrote to the Department of Immigration outlining the situation as it had been explained to me and in reply received a courteous letter asking for further and more specific details, particularly concerning Wu Yuén's departure from and return to Canada. Since Wu Yuén was dead and the boy, then less than five years old, could obviously not remember, we could supply only approximate information. Several more letters were exchanged, but the final one stated that refunds were intended only for adult Chinese entering Canada to secure advanced education and, while refunds had been granted upon occasion for children, there was no documentary evidence available in this case, hence nothing could be done.

From Mrs. Yuén's viewpoint this ruling meant that the five hundred dollars promised her by the Government of Canada and which she desperately needed, would not be paid. For several months she was bitter and resentful. Then one evening she came once more to enquire, 'What you do get married this country?' When I replied that the first step was to find a husband, she said, 'I catch 'em man, Sing Lee; he work in sawmill. What we do next?' I explained the need for a marriage licence and where to get it and also that it was usual to have a minister perform the ceremony. 'You get minister?' she asked. I promised to try and found that the Presbyterian church's brilliant, sympathetic, and unconventional Reverend Alexander Dunn was perfectly willing to act.*

A few evenings later Mrs. Yuén called by again. 'Sing Lee have wife in China; that make any difference?' I had to tell her that it did.

CHAPTER TEN

The View from Headquarters

CURRICULUM IN 1910

In 1910, British Columbia schools were very much like those in Ontario, which was just as well since I knew nothing else. Each province had a seven-year elementary school program using the same divisions and names: first primer and second primer, each requiring one term; and first reader, second reader, junior and senior third reader, junior and senior fourth reader, each for one year. The prescribed subjects were also the same, save for two in British Columbia of which I had never heard and of which I knew nothing – nature study and plane and solid geometrical drawing. I found, too, as I was to find many times, that my cherished university degree was not, in itself, an adequate preparation for a teaching career.

There was nothing accidental about the resemblance between the two systems. Seventy years earlier Egerton Ryerson had founded Ontario's public schools which, at a Chicago World's Fair in 1893, were declared to be the world's best and in 1910 were considered, among BC proponents at least, beyond reproach.[1] In 1872 British Columbia accepted such schools as models, as did the prairie provinces when their time came. Changes did not occur in British Columbia until they were brought about in the mildly revolutionary atmosphere which followed the First World War; even then, they came more rapidly in western Canada than in Ontario and were more in imitation of United States schools than original.

The British Columbia 'Course of Study Prescribed for Graded and Common Schools' was prepared by the Department of Education and distributed to all schools. The section devoted to elementary schools required slightly less than three pages and was followed by half a page which dealt with promotion and the final high school entrance examination. The program was divided into three sections – junior, intermediate, and senior – and eight subjects were listed, so it must be plain to the reader that only essentials were given. Below are examples from the senior section:

> *Reading and Literature* – Fourth Reader. Scott's *Lay of the Last Minstrel*. (The paper in English Literature will test the pupil's knowledge not only of the *Lay*, but also of the prose and poetical sections of the Fourth Reader.) *Universal Spelling Book.*[2]
>
> *Arithmetic* – Milne's *Arithmetic*, Book II, Part II, and Book III (except pp. 116-34, pp. 268-97, and pp. 319-30.)[3]
>
> *History* – British and Canadian as in prescribed texts.

The regulations required that 'there must be, in all graded schools, a general classification at least twice a year for the intermediate and senior grades, and three times a year for the junior grades' and also that 'examinations shall be oral for classes below the senior grade.'

The final examination, high school entrance, was prepared and conducted by the Department of Education. It was held twice a year in December and June until 1910 and was an illustration of an apparently logical idea becoming absurd. The School Act allowed youngsters to enter school whenever they were six years old and, in practice, many beginners arrived in August and in January. Those who progressed at the normal rate completed senior fourth in both December and June, so logic demanded that they enter high school at both times. However, logic was unable to graduate them from high school twice a year, and the added burden on high school teachers was so considerable that the Christmas examination was discontinued in 1910, thus throwing the burden back on the elementary school. Almost thirty years were to pass before the solution of admitting to grade one in September only was in general use.

The examination covered ten subjects: literature, grammar and composition, spelling and dictation, Canadian history, British history, geography, arithmetic, drawing, nature study and hygiene, and oral reading. The maximum mark for each was 100; the passing mark, 34, with an average in all papers of 50. In practice any pupil who received a total of 500 passed, the occasional low paper being raised to 34 without the formality of rereading.

Each paper was set by an inspector of schools who forwarded it to the Department of Education where the entire series, together with record sheets and circulars of instruction, were printed. Thereafter inspectors (in 1910, George Deane, Victoria; Thomas Leith and J.D. Gillis, Vancouver; Albert Sullivan, New Westminster; J.T. Pollock,

Kamloops; A.E. Miller, Revelstoke; D.L. McLaurin, Nelson) were responsible for their own districts. Examinations were written on the last three school days in June, after which the papers were shipped to Victoria where they were marked, still by inspectors, tabulated, and copies of the results mailed to school boards and principals as well as to the press.

The day 'the exams came out' was a notable one for the pupils and for the teachers, a time for considerable celebration or quiet grief. Comparisons among schools were inevitable, but sometimes went to extremes; for instance, one valley newspaper, in publishing 'number writing' and 'number passed' throughout the Okanagan, listed for its own centre only pupils of the central school, but for each other centre included rural school candidates as well.

The term 'high school entrance' was, of course, a misnomer. It was actually a 'public school leaving' test both in purpose and result.[4] It covered all of the subjects and most of the content of the elementary school course, even though these included many phases which the secondary school did not require, but this did not seem unreasonable when fourteen years of age was the end of school for many, and an 'entrance certificate' carried at least the prestige of university matriculation now.

I doubt that the discontinuance of an entrance examination has had any considerable influence on British Columbia schools. It disappeared slowly and in stages, until the junior high school had been fully incorporated into the educational structure; then, clearly, an examination at the end of grade eight was meaningless.[5]

Usually, within my experience, the entrance examination was a good, though not an exact, measuring device, which it did not need to be. Among several hundred pupils whom I taught or, in the following years, have examined as inspector, only two good pupils failed to pass that examination, though at least a score passed whom I would have failed. Further, it was a good standard for judging a competent teacher.[6] True, successful teachers, from time to time, had poor examination results; newcomers to the province unfamiliar with our program, an influx of new pupils, difficult local conditions, personal troubles, all have occurred genuinely enough. Yet, when a teacher had inferior entrance results for several successive years, he – rarely she – was incompetent or lazy. I regret to use a bit of objectionable educational jargon – the word 'motivation.' External examinations were just that. Human nature being what it is, all of us require some form of external evaluation which will be just, reasonable, but inevitable.

The high school program required three years to matriculation, with a department of education examination at the end of each year. Matriculation for most students meant admission to McGill University which had affiliated branches attached to Victoria and Vancouver high schools, with the Victoria branch providing two years in arts, and the Vancouver branch, two years in both arts and applied science; for a degree, the remaining years had to be taken in Montreal.[7]

High school junior grade was divided into preliminary course and advanced course. All preliminary course subjects were compulsory: reading and orthoepy [pronunciation], English grammar, English literature, composition; arithmetic, algebra, geometry; Latin; drawing. The advanced course subjects were the same, with the addition of botany, physics, chemistry, and an option of physiology, Greek, or French.

The third year was intermediate grade. Here, English, mathematics, botany, chemistry, and Latin were continued, and British history, Grecian history, and geography were introduced. Again, one option was permitted: Greek, French, or German.

Students who passed both junior grade examinations were eligible to enter normal school for one term of training and, when that was completed successfully, to receive a third-class teacher's certificate valid for three years. Those who passed the intermediate grade might go to university or, if they wished, attend normal school for the full session and secure a permanent second-class certificate. Actually, not many did either for, while in 1910 there were 37,629 pupils in elementary schools and a rather meagre 2,041 in high schools, only 152 attended McGill's two branches and the normal school enrolled 96.[8]

The course of study also provided for a senior grade and a senior academic grade. The subjects for senior grade were much the same as for the intermediate grade with trigonometry added, Roman history replacing Grecian history, and science limited to physical science. The senior academic grade required additional English, Latin, and either Greek, French, or German. Almost the only purpose of these courses was to enable teachers to secure higher certificates, and they were available only in an occasional school and taken by few students.

Finally, a two-year commercial course was available. It included the English and mathematics of the junior grade course, as well as bookkeeping, stenography, typewriting, business forms, and business law. The slight demand for such training in 1910 is indicated by the fact that only two high schools – Victoria High School and Vancouver's King Edward High School – presented candidates for the advanced or final examination and only thirteen of them at that.

High-school examinations began on the first Monday in July (unless that happened to be Dominion [Canada] Day) and continued for six days. Since they were held in only twenty-six centres scattered from Fernie to Cumberland, all arrangements were made by the Department of Education. In the smaller towns a local person of repute, frequently a cleric, presided, but in large centres members of the board of examiners were in charge.

This board was made up of the superintendent of education, the inspector of high schools, members of the staffs of the McGill colleges in Victoria and Vancouver, and an occasional high-school principal of long service. It was responsible for the preparation of examination papers and for everything connected with marking, tabulating, and releasing results to the press. The University of British Columbia brought heavy faculty representation to the board of examiners, but its duties remained unchanged until the late 1940s with one unimportant but, to some board members, regrettable omission. For many years members were assigned to each major section of the province to 'supervise' examinations. Duties were far from onerous, merely to visit five or six high schools and ask 'Is everything in order?' The weather was usually good, expenses were paid, and the whole affair was a pleasant, but unnecessary holiday.

The brevity of the 1910 course of study shows a considerable contrast to the several hundred pages of curricula which provide for the same school grades in 1956. In the intervening years a number of alterations occurred which, until the mid-1930s, were comparatively minor revisions made by two or three inspectors or normal school instructors working for a week or two in their spare time. These alterations were brought about by dissatisfaction with the division of material, by developments in the world or, on occasion, by the introduction of a new textbook. The only cost was for printing, as it was unthinkable that department of education employees should be paid in addition to their annual salaries.

In 1934 Liberal Education Minister George M. Weir appointed Dr. H.B. King as his technical adviser and shortly afterwards as director of curriculum. On loan from Vancouver's Kitsilano Junior-Senior High School, King was a prominent and controversial figure in British Columbia education, with pronounced opinions on practically all matters having to do with schools and not the least on curricula. He attacked his new responsibility with zest. King knew what he wanted and intended to get it.[9] Subject-matter committees were set up composed of teachers with an occasional inspector or normal school instructor added; publishing houses were invited to supply their recent textbooks or to prepare new ones; meetings were held, and progress reports demanded.

The completed curricula were in three sections: one for the elementary school, one for junior high school, and one for senior high school. Each section required several hundred pages and began with a lengthy, detailed statement of educational aims. Time allotments were provided for each subject and, for the secondary schools, these were converted to 'credits,' with one period per week throughout the year equalling one credit. Each subject was divided into a number of units and a complete teaching procedure was provided for many of these. Various types of evaluating procedures were also recommended and complete, cumulative records required.

A full analysis of this program would be lengthy; it would likewise be fruitless for, following King's retirement in 1945 and the appointment of H.L. Campbell as director of curriculum, a revision was undertaken which, when completed, bore little resemblance to its predecessor.[10] However, some phases merit attention because they were both important and controversial.

Accredited high schools, a major aim of King's, were supported by many high-school teachers and opposed by a few as well as (unofficially) by the university faculty. Two strong arguments were advanced by those who favoured the proposal: (1) education was a continuous process from grade one to university graduation and no arbitrary barriers should be permitted at any point; and (2) the judgments of the teachers who had worked with students were a more valid measure of their fitness than external examinations. The opposition felt and said that accrediting would result in a general lowering of standards and that teachers would be subjected to undesirable pressure by the parents of weaker students.

The powerful support of the Department of Education brought the measure into operation, an accrediting board was established, and a set of standards devised. Initially, the semi-official position was that very few students would be recommended in all subjects and that at least one-third would be required to write departmental examinations, predictions which quickly proved to be unreliable. It would be futile to guess what proportion of university entrants would fail if rigorous external examinations were required, but certainly the number would be considerable. It may or may not be the ethical responsibility of a university to accept students as they come and provide for them, but with accrediting in force, a state-run university has little choice.

General science replaced special sciences up to and including matriculation, the argument being that physics, botany, and chemistry were of value only to a minority of students who would enter university, whereas general science, 'a life situation subject,' was of value to all. Ten years later, the validity of the argument was in considerable doubt, but there was no doubt at all that general science did not prepare a student for university science. The university did institute preparatory courses in botany and physics but regrettably first-year students in chemistry failed in large numbers until the revised curriculum came into operation some ten years later.[11]

The situation was both unfortunate and unnecessary. The curriculum allowed French to commence in grade seven and Latin in grade eight in those districts where junior high schools existed. It followed that at the end of grade eleven, students would have completed a considerable part of the matriculation requirement and would have much less than a normal year's work in grade twelve. It would have been simple and reasonable to have taken one or two of the special sciences, but regulations prohibited this. Instead, such subjects as music, art, or typing were required.

Evaluation of any curriculum is difficult for the compelling reason that well-nigh a generation must pass before its influence on the students who were developed under it can be examined. That, after all, is the only real test. Even then, any conclusions reached must be largely subjective, since the task of locating several thousand persons who were students twenty years ago, interviewing them, and weighing the effect of other educational influences would be a considerable deterrent in securing the facts.[12] I myself, have some personal opinions which I hold strongly and which I know are shared by some and firmly opposed by others.

A curriculum is one of several necessary elements in a school system. It is certainly not the most important nor is it, in itself, an end to be accomplished, but merely an instrument which, together with equipment, textbooks, an auditorium or, indeed, a building, helps teachers develop pupils into good citizens. Styles in buildings change – quite rapidly in recent years – and for a time are popular; so do styles in curricula. However, change for the sake of change is not necessarily improvement. Unless change provides greater help to teachers, it is of no value whatsoever.

It is a moot question whether there should or should not be a complete, detailed curriculum covering an entire province. Such a practice does permit the central education authorities to exercise a close check on classroom procedures, in terms of credits to maintain exact records of pupil performance, and to grant graduation diplomas on the same footing everywhere. Teachers with one or two years of experience and most mediocre teachers of whatever length of service find it comforting; in fact, many have used the printed curriculum as a textbook and even dictated it to their students. To be sure, this assembly-line method of management has proved efficient in manufacturing automobiles, but its application to education raises many disturbing educational concerns. With the regrettable creation of very large schools, however, some of its phases may be unavoidable. Perhaps its most unfortunate effect is that it is a considerable deterrent to that most valuable of all teacher traits: initiative.

There is much to be said for a program which broadly states essentials and allows schools and even teachers within those schools to develop those essentials in accordance with their own intelligent conception of what is best for the pupils in the local district. It would be helpful if such teachers had considerable freedom in the selection of textbooks to be used. A one-time minister of education who, like a certain English king of old 'never said a foolish thing and seldom did a wise one,' once remarked, 'I can think of nothing which would annoy me more than to be told to sit in a certain place at a certain time and read something I had already read half-a-dozen times.' Could not the central authority list a number of recommended texts for each subject and permit each school to select the one best suited to its particular needs, with the implications that an annual per capita grant to school boards would be supplied?

Since 1910 the schools of this province have had four different curricula and anyone who would venture to say which of them was the best or the worst would be rash or foolish. The social attitude toward secondary school has changed markedly, and the right of every child to attend has been accepted, along with the age basis for promotion.[13] The 'holding power' of the high school has become a fetish, even though the number of compulsory courses must be reduced and the content of all subjects tailored to fit the abilities and even the inclinations of the average half of the class. Unfortunately, alternative courses have been introduced for the weaker pupils, not for the superior ones who continue with work designed for the average.[14] It may well be, however, that this curriculum meets the present complex and difficult situation as well as its 1910 equivalent satisfied a much simpler society.

ALEXANDER ROBINSON

A faculty of education dean, after occasional visits to Vancouver during the 1940s, made an interesting comment.[15] 'In your province,' he said, 'education has been cursed by personalities.'

Whether those he had in mind were a curse, a blessing, or something of both, will have to remain a matter of opinion or for the judgment of some future historian, but the extent of their influence is not open to doubt. During the forty-odd years following 1900, education in British Columbia was developed largely according to the ideas and opinions of half-a-dozen men who usually held office at different times and for terms ranging from five to twenty years.[16] Each had strong convictions about the kind of eduction this province should have, and each had substantial success in securing authorization for the changes which he advocated even though this meant discarding much that a predecessor had accomplished. They differed in many ways – in physical characteristics, in moral traits, and in their concept of social amenities – but were alike in mental arrogance, in flaming energy, and in unassailable confidence in their own judgment.

The earliest and, in at least some respects, the most notable was one who is today a vivid memory to a few, but scarcely a name to most. Alexander Robinson, superintendent of education from April 1899 until September 1919, has been described by one associate as 'the most dynamic personality who ever stood in a British Columbia classroom,' while another who knew him long and well said: 'He came close to being a really great man; only the animal in him prevented it.'[17]

Robinson was born in New Brunswick, taught school there briefly, secured his BA from Dalhousie, and moved to British Columbia in 1890 to become principal of Vancouver's Central School and, the following year, of its young, ambitious high school. Eight years later, still in his early thirties despite graying hair, he was appointed provincial superintendent of education. A fine mind, organizing ability, energy, and self-confidence may well have justified so rapid a promotion, but it had a political angle as well.

In the federal election of 1896 W.J. Bowser ran as an Independent Conservative against the party's official candidate George H. Cowan. The result was the election of a Liberal, the Reverend George Maxwell of First Presbyterian Church, and a permanent cleavage in Conservative ranks. In that campaign high school principal Robinson gave Bowser strong support, but in a provincial election two years later transferred his allegiance to the stormy petrel of British Columbia politics, Liberal 'Fighting Joe' Martin.[18] Martin was elected and became [acting] minister of education for eleven months, long enough to dismiss Superintendent S.D. Pope and install Robinson in his place. Politics, however, had no place in the Department of Education during Robinson's term of office or, indeed, for ten years after his retirement. Policies were determined and carried out, local difficulties were adjusted, and appointments were made on their merits or, at any rate, as Robinson saw their merits, without consideration of political ramifications.

Robinson *was* the Department of Education. There was never any doubt about that. Ministers of education came and went, but they had the additional portfolio of provincial secretary, and were content to allow a man considered to be both competent and economical to carry on, wishing only to be kept informed. As the years passed, Robinson came to know every detail of the education system; he might delegate responsibility to a subordinate but the final authority was his. He determined changes in policy and, where these affected the School Act, drafted the necessary amendments and briefed the minister who had to present them to the legislature for approval. Changes in curriculum, major review of textbooks, and requirements for teacher certification were made on his initiative. Even the marking of departmental examination papers came under his watchful eye through the practice of taking home for study a random sampling of completed ones, and woe betide the unfortunate marker who had been careless. Certainly, Robinson was an autocrat, but a competent one.

The election of 1916 brought a change. The Liberal party had come to power, and J.D. MacLean, a physician from Greenwood, became minister of education.[19] MacLean had a personal knowledge of schools for he had taught for several years at Mission and Rossland before studying medicine at McGill University. This experience, coupled with shrewd common sense, had produced definite ideas on what education should be and should do, and these ideas spelled changes to the existing pattern. Robinson was informed of MacLean's views and, when not in agreement, kept his own counsel and continued as he had always done, making decisions and informing MacLean when expedient. Such a situation could not long be endured by a responsible minister, saying much for the patience and sense of justice of MacLean that it lasted three years.

Late one September afternoon in 1919, a letter from MacLean was laid on Robinson's desk. Brief and to the point, it dismissed him from office that day with three months' salary in lieu of notice and a retirement allowance of $140 per month. Ten days later Robinson replied through an open letter to the press in which he damned his successor with faint praise, referred to three 'much abler men' who had been overlooked, accepted three months' salary as his right, and refused the retirement allowance as 'a bribe.'[20]

The half-dozen years which followed were unpleasant ones. Appointed principal of Victoria High School in 1920, he remained for only one year when the refusal of the staff to work under him resulted in a second dismissal and retirement to his small farm in Saanich, behind Mount Tolmie.[21] MacLean renewed his offer of a retirement allowance, but Robinson curtly rejected it. Heavy family responsibilities, a steadily climbing cost-of-living index, some expensive tastes, and no income combined to make his circumstances more and more difficult until finally these, with some mellowing of the bitterness which burned in his soul, prevailed. He asked for and received the twice-spurned allowance, then applied for, and was appointed to, the staff of Oak Bay High School where he remained until the introduction of an age limit for teachers compelled his final retirement.

The Oak Bay years were his happiest and, perhaps, even his most useful ones. Scores of Oak Bay pupils have testified to his amazing gifts as a teacher, often saying Robinson was 'the best teacher I ever had.' His financial position was secure, for Oak Bay salaries were high, and the retirement allowance was granted for life. Most of all, the rancour and the hatred which had been his greatest weakness were replaced by something not far removed from serenity and peace.

By those who still recollect him, Robinson is remembered for many things, good and bad, great and petty. His massive head with its piercing eyes and abundant snow-white hair come first to mind and with them his voice, ordinarily clear, vibrant, and mellow but bitter and harsh when, as often happened, his temper took over. His correspondence, public addresses, and private conversations reflected his training as a classical scholar and his love of good books as an English scholar, even though his more personal observations could be thickly sprinkled with favourite expletives neither cultured nor classical.

His rages, usually over small matters, while brief, were forceful. Once, having arranged to exchange roosters with a neighbour, he delivered his bird by dropping it over the fence of the chicken run where it was attacked by the home rooster and promptly ran for shelter. Robinson jumped the fence, caught his bird, wrung its neck, and hurled it fifty feet away.

In 1915 for the first time since 1896, Robinson came into official conflict with W.J. Bowser (who had inherited the premiership when Sir Richard McBride departed for England), showing in his wrath he respected neither persons nor office. The city of Victoria, well into an uncomfortable depression, had elected a school board pledged to economy which had promptly imposed a substantial fee on non-resident pupils attending their high school, most of whom came from Esquimalt, Oak Bay, and Saanich where no high schools existed. Some parents affected by the changes were property owners and taxpayers in Victoria and, under the School Act, were entitled to send their children to school in whichever district they preferred. They appealed to Robinson, who wrote a letter to the Victoria School Board supporting their position.

A few days later the Executive Council was in session with President William Manson in the chair. Bowser brought the matter up and asked that Robinson be sent for. When he appeared Bowser read his letter to the school board and asked, 'You sent that letter?' 'I did,' replied Robinson. 'You will retract that letter,' Bowser declared. 'Your duties are to carry out the orders given to you by this government, not to interpret the law.' Robinson's answer is unprintable, but it consisted of eight, short, ugly words followed by 'Go straight to hell!' It is compelling evidence of an unusual personality that such language from a civil servant to the premier of the province had no sequel.

When angry over something which to him seemed important, Robinson acted differently, became very quiet, and said little, but in tones of ice. Few could risk a repetition of 'You have been guilty of an unpardonable indiscretion, sir. I have no confidence in you.'

He took strong dislikes, often for little reason. He might say, 'I do not like that man.' 'I don't like the way he walks,' or 'He has an evil eye; he cannot be trusted,' and he seldom changed his opinion.

Some of his most bitter resentments went back to his days as a Vancouver principal and to the objects of these he could be merciless. An example was a teacher institute at King Edward High School with a crowded auditorium and [then-Superintendent] Robinson in the chair for, in 1913, teachers' gatherings were largely Department of Education affairs.[22] The morning's agenda contained three addresses. The first was by the Reverend Eber Crummy, able and silver-tongued minister of Wesley Methodist Church, and the third by the first and greatest president of the University of Saskatchewan, Walter Murray. Sandwiched in between these intellectual giants was one of Robinson's special aversions, a Vancouver principal whose address was entitled 'Problems in City Grading.'[23] When the principal had finished, Robinson rose and said, 'The next item on the agenda is discussion of the address we have just heard. As there is nothing to discuss, we shall proceed with the next item.' The principal's later comment of 'Ajax trying to defy the lightning' suggests that the aversion may not have been misplaced.[24]

Robinson was often kind, especially to old-timers.[25] When a Fraser Valley school board dismissed its principal of long standing and wrote asking that a successor be recommended, his reply was 'I have pleasure in recommending the best teacher in British Columbia whom you have just dismissed.' For that not inconsiderable group of middle-aged male teachers whose existence was well-nigh nomadic, he had a warm spot in his heart. Every summer and often in December, some would climb the three flights of stairs to his office in the Government Building and enter the open door. 'Well, Jones,' might be the greeting, 'what is the trouble this time? Drunk again?' The lecture which followed was incisive and to the point, but the twinkle in his eye betrayed the fact that when it was finished the delinquent would leave with an appointment to another school.

Such sympathy came not only from a deep-seated compassion for the underdog, who would never have achieved success as that mirage is often understood, but also in part from his own fondness for what he termed 'alcohol,' of which he was something of a connoisseur. His capacity was remarkable: an evening which began with two or three cocktails, several whiskies during dinner, a liqueur afterwards, concluding with his favorite 'Velvet' – a mixture of champagne and porter – apparently left him quite unaffected. In fact, he greatly enjoyed taking the last of the party home or putting the reveller to bed and being the only one able to appear for work the following morning.

In spite of all this, or perhaps because of some of it, Robinson did much for British Columbia: much that has never been and could not have been publicly recognized because of the circumstances surrounding his retirement. He had a major share in establishing the University of British Columbia in 1915. Even more importantly, he gave affectionate and understanding support to the province's rural schools. His 'assisted' schools, without parallel elsewhere in Canada, meant that, wherever ten pupils could be brought together, a school would be provided at no local cost. Some of our leading citizens in industry, the professions, and government, who had their early, and even their entire education in these schools, owe much to Alexander Robinson. Whether he was a great man, whether his virtues exceeded his faults, he was the only educational leader in our history who was always 'The Chief' to his staff and 'Sandy' to the rest of the province.

SAMUEL J. WILLIS

One evening in mid-September 1919, Lemuel Robertson, UBC professor of classics, received a messenger from Education Minister J.D. MacLean with a terse letter which read: 'Which one of these three would be best as Superintendent of Education?'[26] At the foot of the letter Robertson wrote 'S.J. Willis,' sealed it in an envelope, and the messenger returned with it to Victoria. A few days later the press announced that Alexander Robinson had retired and that S.J. Willis had been appointed in his place.

Professor Robertson, Dr. MacLean, and Mr. Willis had much in common: they had all been born in Prince Edward Island, were graduates of McGill University, and had taught in British Columbia schools. Along the way Robertson had come to know MacLean and Willis intimately, with the result that MacLean had complete confidence in Robertson's judgment and he, in turn, was satisfied that

Willis had no superiors as a teacher and administrator. Nor was their common background a negligible factor at a time when most of British Columbia's leaders in education had their origins in the maritime provinces.

After graduation from McGill in 1900 with honours in classics, Willis came to British Columbia where he was granted a first-class, grade A teacher's certificate and was appointed to the Victoria staff. His first assignment was division six in the Boys' Central School at a salary of $55 per month. One year later he was transferred to Victoria High School, and his salary went up 50 per cent to $1,000 for the year. In 1908 he became principal. Under his wise and able leadership over the next five years, no school in the province was more highly regarded, then trouble came.

For a year or more before the outbreak of the First World War the British Columbia coast underwent a depression chiefly because of the collapse of the real estate boom which struck Victoria early and hard. Money was scarce, tax collections were poor and, following the acceptable policy of the day, the Victoria school board cut salaries, also early and hard. Teachers with good reputations – and there were many at Victoria High School – experienced little trouble finding positions elsewhere and had to be replaced with those willing to come. Each term Willis saw the standing and tone of his school drop a little lower until, in something approaching despair, he accepted a position which he had declined a year or two earlier, becoming in September 1916 [associate] professor of classics at UBC under his old friend Lemuel Robertson.[27]

He remained at UBC for two years. In 1918 Vancouver's King Edward High School urgently needed a principal who was a proven teacher, administrator, and disciplinarian. Willis was appointed, but again his tenure was to be short; one year and three weeks later and nineteen years after he began teaching, he became superintendent of education, a position he was to fill for twenty-six years.

Dr. Willis – he was to receive an honorary degree from his alma mater a year later – was not a personality in the sense that his predecessor was.[28]

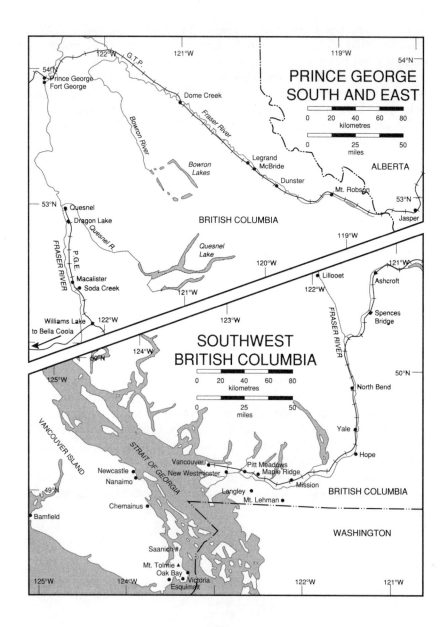

Map II

CHAPTER ELEVEN

Losers and Winners

CERTAIN COMMUNITIES

In a certain community better unidentified, a prominent merchant had his own standards, not always in accord with usual business practice or with the laws of the province. He resented competition and showed it so openly that, when the other village store was set on fire one night, little wonder that he was suspected. A charge of arson was laid, but the defending lawyer imported from Prince George succeeded in having it reduced to mischief with a $200 fine rather than a jail sentence. The lawyer felt that his fee of $500 was reasonable but the merchant disagreed.

A few months later he was again charged, this time for 'blind pigging.'[1] Unfortunately, it was his second offence which, in those days of prohibition, meant a jail sentence with no option of a fine if convicted. Knowing that the local police had a good deal of evidence, he wired Prince George's other lawyer to come to his rescue. The reply: 'My fee is $500, and I won't leave Prince George till I get it.' The money was sent, the lawyer came, heard his client's story, advised him to plead guilty, and returned to Prince George.

On his release from jail six months later, the 'prominent citizen' was elected to the school board and at its first meeting appointed to the chair.

Sam X was the leading merchant in another anonymous village. A widower of sixty, he lived alone in a comfortable house and divided his time among his general store and the half-dozen other local industries in which he had acquired an interest. He was also something of a political power in the community, all the more so because his party now held office in Victoria where he did not hesitate to forward requests, complaints and, more commonly, orders.

The local constable of the British Columbia provincial police was aware – painfully aware – of this for, on several occasions, his sense of duty had conflicted with the wishes or conduct of Sam X and he had lost. True, these were minor matters, such as driving a car with expired licence plates or fishing without a licence, but the law was clear, so when the constable's recommendations were rejected, he was annoyed and worried. Then his sergeant had said quietly, 'Better watch your step with Sam X or you'll find yourself transferred.'

An angry, disturbed father came to the constable one evening, reporting that Sam X was bothering his teenaged daughter and others as well. Often he would buy ice cream for a girl in the village café, then make suggestive remarks and sometimes show her pictures that she should not see. The constable listened, deeply concerned. It was awkward. Such actions had to be stopped yet, if handled through official channels, they could result in publicity for the girls and much trouble for himself. At last he said, 'I'll have it stopped, but don't mention it to anyone.'

On Saturday evening after supper, the constable went for his customary stroll down the main street where Sam X was standing on the sidewalk in front of his store. They chatted for a few minutes, then the constable said, 'Come up to the house and have a drink, Sam.' As they entered the office attached to the house, the constable closed and locked the door. Surprised, Sam X said, 'What's the idea? Is this a pinch?' 'It could be,' he replied, 'unless you do as you're told. Empty your pockets onto that desk.' Sam X flushed, swore, and turned to the door. It was still locked and one glance at the constable's face convinced him that it would remain locked. He walked back to the desk and slowly, reluctantly, drew from his pockets keys, money, letters, a notebook, and finally an assortment of pornographic material. The constable took a large manilla envelope from a drawer and across its face wrote 'Property of Sam X' and the date, inserted all the questionable evidence, sealed it and placed it in the safe saying, 'That stays here until I hear of you talking to a girl again,' then with a smile, 'Well, Sam, suppose we have that drink?'

THE GETAWAY LOG BOOM

Sunday afternoon in June at Dome Creek [see Map II, top], a point about 100 miles up the Fraser River from Prince George, the sky was without a cloud and there was no wind. Sunday being treated with some respect, the only sound came from the river in full flood, rolling along twenty feet below the bank where my host and I were seated.

He was the local manager of an Ottawa lumber company with

extensive timber limits along the upper Fraser. All through the winter his workers had been cutting logs and now the entire season's cut lay before us; 'Close to two million feet' was his estimate. They filled the river from side to side and upstream for a full half-mile until the river's bend took them from our view. Strong boom sticks held them in place, massive logs joined together with heavy logging chains and, at each end, anchored with wire rope to a huge fir tree. It was a picture of strength and power such as one seldom sees, the three-foot diameter logs, the powerful boom sticks, the vast fir trees, and the throbbing, pulsating river.

Suddenly, noiselessly, and for no visible reason, those boom sticks parted in the middle and slowly, inexorably, swung over to the river's sides. Slowly at first and then faster, the logs shot away until, in half an hour, none were left except where one had been caught here and there against the bank. They were gone and nothing could be done. Some would be washed ashore in the next 400 miles, some would be chewed to pulp in the canyons, and some perhaps would reach the Strait of Georgia. For my host it was almost a tragedy; for me it was the power of a mighty river.

THE GATES OF HELL

A front-page headline in the *Toronto Globe* read 'Walked 300 miles from the Gates of Hell.' The general assembly of the Presbyterian Church was in session in that city, with ministers in attendance from most Presbyterian churches in Canada, thanks to the generosity of a wealthy layperson. The representative from Fort George spoke of his work in that community and, according to *Globe* reporters, used emphatic language in describing the social conditions which included a 100-foot bar that, according to reports, 'never closed its doors, day or night,' and many red-light houses.[2] The minister also left the impression, presumably inadvertently, that the 300 mile journey to Ashcroft had been made on foot rather than by the well-organized, though expensive riverboat and stage services of the BC Express Company.

Even in those times Toronto papers reached Fort George in a few days, and this issue of the *Globe* was no exception. Its arrival created interest, which varied from cynical amusement among the patrons of the Northern Hotel to righteous indignation in the real estate offices where, it was felt, such unfortunate publicity might negate the effects of their tremendous advertising campaign in eastern Canadian newspapers. Dire vengeance was promised for the outspoken minister on his return.

When that day arrived, wiser heads were in control. As the boat on which he arrived from Soda Creek reached the Fort George dock, it was greeted by a banner which read: 'Welcome Back to the Gates of Hell!'

A LITTLE RICHER, A LITTLE HAPPIER

Most of the time Bill Sykes was a good teacher.[3] Born in England, he went to a board school and a training college, taught school for a few years, and came to Canada. He liked country people and country schools and they liked him, for he was the last to give offence and quick to show appreciation. Bill taught most things well enough; after two or three months the writing of his class was copperplate, and their spelling was perfect, but it was in music that he really excelled. His pupils loved to sing, and to hear them in three-part harmony was like listening to surpliced choristers.

Yes, most of the time!

Once in a while Bill took a drink, preferably of rum though, if that were not available, anything else would do. It didn't happen often, never more than once a year but, when he wanted that drink, he had to have it right away. The first was just the beginning; the last came when the local supply was exhausted. He wasn't noisy or trouble-some, tried not to disturb anyone, and always seemed to remember when he had to go back to work. When he did so, however, there could be unhappy results.

In September, Bill went to a new school in a village located along the Canadian Pacific Railway.[4] All fall the youngsters read, wrote, and sang, and the district congratulated itself and its teacher. Then came the Christmas vacation. Bill packed his bags, walked to the station, bought a return ticket to Victoria, and asked, 'How is the train?' Told it was four hours late, and would come about two o'clock in the morn-ing, he debated what to do, for it was two miles to his room and a cold, blustery night. Finally, he went over to the bench in the waiting room, sat down in a comfortable position, and began to snooze. An hour later a noise wakened him and, in a moment, an odour assailed his nostrils. Bill needed but one look before he walked across the waiting room and joined the logger with a bottle.

Forty-eight hours later he caught the westbound train which was on time that night. The next morning, sober, dishevelled, and badly hungover, he left the CPR station and found his way to the pier for Victoria, his destination. Bill Sykes loved Victoria for the English accents he heard in the shops and on the streets, the retired colonels in plus fours, honey and crumpets in the tea rooms, but most of all, for its being the official home of the superintendent of education, everywhere known with half-concealed affection as 'Sandy' Robinson.

Sandy Robinson's office door was always open, facing the landing at the top of the three flights of stairs which led to the Education Office in a wing of the Government Building. This morning he was seated at his desk reading a telegram from a school board informing him that its teacher had been drunk for two days in the railroad station. When Robinson glanced up, there in the doorway stood the culprit! It was a nervous moment for Bill. Ten minutes later he was shaken to the depths of his soul when he was told that 'You can't go back.' But Robinson had a fondness for country schools and for their teachers so he mellowed enough to add: 'I will send you to a school on the Cariboo Road, but if you get drunk there you'll lose your certificate.'[5]

From January until October Sykes went his pleasant, cheerful way. Then he got unexpected news which came as a shock; province-wide prohibition was coming into force in a few weeks. He had not had a drink for months, nor did he want one now, but he would have to be prepared, so he ordered a dozen bottles of rum. These arrived by stage and were waiting at the door of his cabin when he got home from school on Friday evening. The happenings of the next two days can only be surmised, but on Monday morning Bill went to school on a road deep in mud. The frightened youngsters ran to their parents who wired the superintendent who replied, 'Put him out and keep him out.'

Two years later Bill Sykes returned from Alberta because he loved British Columbia. His certificate was still valid and, strangely enough, the only reputation he had was for good teaching. During the next dozen years spent in two schools, he continued in his kindly, genial way giving to his pupils some desires and some abilities that would make their lives a little richer and a little happier. One day on his way back home from school, he dropped dead. I think he would have had it so.

THE TRAIN TO DUNSTER STATION

Since it was a November evening, it was dark when the train reached Dunster Station shortly after six o'clock. There was no one on the station platform and no light to be seen in any direction. Nor was there any trace of a road. However, a few minutes before, through the train window, I had seen a momentary gleam which might have come from a house. For lack of alternative, I walked back along the track.

Indeed it was a house. My knock on the door brought an immediate response and, when my identity was known, a warm invitation to come in. There were two rooms, one downstairs which met all living requirements during the day, and the other, upstairs and reached by a ladder, for sleeping quarters. The building itself, like most pioneer houses, was made of logs and differed from others only in having a second storey and some unusual furniture. Most was home-made from local lumber hand-sawn and smoothed with an adze, while several chairs were fashioned from sections of logs which had been peeled, dried, and roughly evened. Other furnishings stood out in contrast: two large mirrors with ornate gold frames hung on the wall; two huge, deep-seated leather-covered chairs had places of honour; and a small piano stood in one corner. Later I learned that these were all that remained of a full complement of furniture which had graced their former home in a fashionable suburb of an Atlantic seaboard city half-a-dozen years earlier.

The head of the house had held a government position of some responsibility in the maritime provinces where he had been born. Life had been moderately good to him, for he had a congenial, capable wife and bright, active children, a comfortable house, and a better-than-average salary. He was not satisfied, however. The call of the west attracted him, as it had so many other Maritimers who believed a fortune waited there for the taking and they were fools to work for a government. So he resigned his position, sold his house, loaded his furniture in a freight car, and started west with his family, his first destination being Edmonton.

For the next few years, he and his family had one piece of bad luck after another. Most of their capital had been sunk in a down payment on wheat acreage northeast of Edmonton, heavy additional payments for several years being assumed in full confidence that these could be met from the profits of farming. The family's optimism seemed to be justified by the experiences of many others who had been able to do just what they had hoped for, becoming comfortably situated within a few years. In this family's case, however, the weather had been against them for, in three years, their crops were ruined by drought, hail, and frost respectively. Broke, they moved to Edmonton, rented a small house on the outskirts, and father began the discouraging task of looking for work during a depression.

Failing to find any permanent job in Edmonton and still hoping to live the independent life of a farmer, he set out on foot along the track of the Grand Trunk Pacific Railway in search of land available for homesteading. He travelled almost 500 miles before returning to Dunster, the finest place he had ever seen, settling at length on a quarter section of government land. Perhaps his own high estimate of the place might not have been justified, but there were plenty of trees which furnished not only logs for a house but also fence posts which meant cash on a prairie market willing to take all available.

The family was still in Edmonton when the house was far enough advanced to assure shelter and trains were at least running, but there still was no money for rail fares. Then fortune smiled upon them, even if at first in a black enough guise. An older son employed in an industrial plant fell down an open elevator shaft and broke a leg. The money paid by the plant as compensation was sufficient to bring them and the few relics of their furniture to Dunster.

Life was not easy during their first two or three years. The 'farm' produced water and firewood in abundance, but little else of the essentials of life except rabbits, which tend to become monotonous as a staple food. Everything else needed money and it was hard to come by. There was no demand for casual labour in Dunster since the half-dozen settlers were all poor and the only permanent employment – working as a section hand for the railroad – seldom had a vacancy. Cutting fence posts could be profitable as a long-range activity for the raw material was almost unlimited, but markets had to be developed and shipments of less-than-carload lots were difficult to dispose of. In the early stages the cash returns were small and very slow in arriving. Perhaps it was just as well that the nearest store was thirty miles away and that supplies had to be ordered by mail, for only necessities were likely to be bought.

Those necessities were few, for it was surprising how little a family could get along with when it had to. Once, in another district, having left the train at five o'clock in the morning, I was invited for breakfast by the section boss, a French Canadian, and shared with his family of eleven children a huge iron pot of oatmeal porridge with plenty of milk. I knew his salary was sixty-three dollars a month, and I asked him how he managed. His answer: 'We have de cow, we have de hens, lots of fish in de river, but de boots, they are de devil!' There was no cow in Dunster, at least for the first two years, but a moose shot in the fall furnished meat for most of the winter and flour or sugar sacks made children's clothing of a sort. Boots were indeed 'de devil,' and smaller children were scarcely able to go out of the house until spring for lack of them.

Each time I returned to Dunster conditions were better for this family. More land was cleared, and they were able to raise more vegetables for the winter; they bought a cow and a horse, and eventually a team. The children were growing up and one by one found work, became self-supporting, and were able to help out at home. Two of the older boys were employed on the rail section crew, and the oldest daughter went to clerk in a store in the village thirty miles distant. The market for fence posts became steadier and more profitable while their improved skill, more hands, and the team significantly raised productivity. All in all, the family was truly on its way to comfort and security.[6]

I well remember my last visit. Previously I had slept in the station waiting room or in the pump house, for Dunster had not reached the status which justified a recognized stopping place, but this time I was the guest of the teacher and shared with him the two-room 'teacherage' at the back of the school.[7] This young man had arrived in September full of fears and hopes, to teach his first school without any idea that more immediate and personal challenges awaited him. Back in his city home food arrived on the table cooked and ready to eat without a thought on his part. If he wished to take a bath, he went to the bathroom and turned a tap; light came by pressing a switch. Laundry was his mother's responsibility, not his. In Dunster he found two rooms containing a stove, two chairs, a table, a bed, a frying pan, a saucepan, a coffee pot, and a few dishes; plenty of trees outside for firewood, a creek flowing cheerfully by a hundred yards away, and the nearest store thirty miles distant.

That young man was a good teacher and did much for the youngsters of Dunster, but Dunster did even more for him. I was there for three days, sleeping between spotless sheets he himself had washed and in a bed which he had made. We ate good food which he cooked, including a mulligan of moose meat (which he had canned himself) and vegetables. He was proud of these accomplishments, as he had every right to be, for he had mastered all in a few months and had learned the thrill of tackling a hard task and carrying it through.

Notes

Owing to editorial constraints, there are those who helped whose contributions are no longer reflected in the annotations which follow. I am nonetheless grateful to Ted Girdler, Hallvard Dahlie, Irene Bliss, Tim Bayliff, Marjorie Wrinch, J.A. Shelford, Hans C. Larsen, Alton Myers, Albert Leonard, Reverend James A.E. Hoskin, Norman Wade, Keith Miller, A.L. Leach, Dave Owen, Neil Peterson, R.G. Carter, Susan Marsden, L.L. Bongie, David Thomas, John Stager, Kenneth M.Leighton, and Dennis Milburn for their assistance.

INTRODUCTION

1 Helen Colls to D.M. Henshaw, Vancouver, BC, 1 September 1982.
2 Biographical note from Lord to Dr. A.P. Brown, transcript supplied by Janet McLeod (nee Brown).
3 Ibid. See also Mary Inman to the editor, West Vancouver, BC, 16 October 1990.
4 Superintendent of Education, *Annual Report of the Public Schools of the Province of British Columbia* [hereafter ARPS] (Victoria, BC: King's Printer 1917), A43.
5 Ibid.
6 Ibid., 1922, C35.
7 Ibid., 1925, M50.
8 See J.H. Putman and G.M. Weir, *Survey of the School System* (Victoria, BC: King's Printer 1925). For a brief appreciation of the main reproof contained in this report, see John Calam, 'Teaching the Teachers: Establishment and Early Years of the BC Provincial Normal Schools,' *BC Studies* 61 (Spring 1984), 45-8.
9 Irene Howard, 'First Memories of Vancouver,' *Vancouver Historical Society Newsletter* (October 1973), 3, cited in Joan Adams and Becky Thomas, *Floating Schools and Frozen Inkwells: The One-Room Schools of British Columbia* (Madeira Park, BC: Harbour Publishing 1985), 47.
10 A.R. Lord and George A. Cornish, *Canadian Geography for Juniors*, British Columbia edition rev. and enl. by A.R. Lord and V.L. Denton (London and Toronto: J.M. Dent 1934).

11 See, for example, ARPS, 1937, 134. Hall succeeded Lord as principal at the Vancouver Provincial Normal School, serving from 1950 to 1952.

12 *Statutes of British Columbia*, An Act to Amend the 'Public Schools Act,' 1929, 309-10.

13 H.B. King, *School Finance in British Columbia* (Victoria, BC: King's Printer 1935).

14 For instance, A.R. Lord to Major H.B. King, Technical Adviser, Educational Finance Survey, Vancouver, BC, 28 August 1934.

15 Ibid.

16 Ibid., 14 January 1935.

17 S.J. Willis to A.R. Lord, Victoria, BC, 12 April 1935.

18 G.M. Weir to A.R. Lord, Victoria, BC, 31 July 1936.

19 See David C. Jones, 'Creating Rural-Minded Teachers: The British Columbia Experience,' in David C. Jones, Nancy M. Sheehan, and Robert M. Stamp (eds.), *Shaping the Schools of the Canadian West* (Calgary, Alberta: Detselig Enterprises 1979), 155-76.

20 ARPS, 1943, B32; ibid., 1945, Y43; ibid., Y44.

21 Interview with Edith Chamberlayne, Qualicum Beach, BC, 21 September 1986.

22 Provincial Normal School, Report of Principal [hereafter PNSRP], in ARPS, 1943, B38.

23 Ibid., 1937, 134; ibid., 1941, D44; ibid., 1942, B43-44; ibid, 1943, B38; ibid., 1944, B39-40; ibid., 1946, MM39; ibid., 1949, N32, etc.

24 Brief exchanges with Frank C. Hardwick and LeRoi B. Daniels, Vancouver, BC, 15 April 1987.

25 Chamberlayne interview.

26 *Province*, 29 June 1950, 7.

27 Note that in Lord's day, the superintendent of education was the senior civil servant of the Department of Education answerable to the minister of education. The term 'inspector of schools' no longer applies and, to a marked degree, neither does the job. The newer 'superintendents' are local boards' chief education officers, unlike provincial inspectors who reported to the superintendent. For a close analysis of shifting emphases within the inspectorate/superintendency, see Thomas Fleming, 'Our Boys in the Field: School Inspectors, Superintendents, and the Changing Character of School Leadership in British Columbia,' in Nancy M. Sheehan, J. Donald Wilson, and David C. Jones (eds.), *Schools in the West: Essays in Canadian Educational History* (Calgary, Alberta: Detselig Enterprises 1986), 285-303, and 'In the Imperial Age and After: Patterns of British Columbia School Leadership and the Institution of the Superintendency, 1849-1988,' in *BC Studies* 81 (Spring 1989), 49-76.

28 For elaboration, see A.L. Farley, *Atlas of British Columbia: People, Environment, and Resource Use* (Vancouver, BC: University of British Columbia Press

1979), 2-3; *Seventh Census of Canada*, 1931, Vol. II (Ottawa: King's Printer 1933), Table 8, p. 9.

29 *Canada: Every Day Scenes and How to Reach Them by Canada's Grand Trunk Pacific Railway System* (Winnipeg, Manitoba: General Passenger Department 1913). For similar propaganda as it applied to the Fort Fraser area, see Lenore Rudland, *Fort Fraser (Where the Hell's That?)* (Cloverdale, BC: D.W. Friesen and Sons 1988), 34-56.

30 See 'The Zeitgeist of Western Settlement: Education and the Myth of the Land,' in J. Donald Wilson and David C. Jones (eds.), *Schooling and Society in Twentieth Century British Columbia* (Calgary, Alberta: Detselig Enterprises 1980), 71-89.

31 See Margaret A. Ormsby, *British Columbia: A History* (Toronto: Macmillan of Canada 1958), 355, 359, 365, 407; 'Agricultural Development in British Columbia,' in Dickson M. Falconer (ed.), *British Columbia: Patterns in Economic, Political and Cultural Development* (Victoria, BC: Camosun College 1982), 160; Patricia E. Roy, 'Progress, Prosperity and Politics: The Railway Policies of Richard McBride,' ibid., 233. For a Canada-wide analysis of the First World War economy, see Robert Craig Brown and Ramsay Cook, *Canada 1896-1921: A Nation Transformed*, Canadian Centenary Series (Toronto: McClelland and Stewart 1974), 234, 239-40. The authors indicate the winter of 1914-5 as particularly difficult for Canadian labour, but refer to their period in general as 'the triumph of enterprise.'

32 Ormsby, *British Columbia*, 438, 441. For a Canada-wide account, see John Herd Thompson with Allen Seager, *Canada, 1922-1939: Decades of Discord*, Canadian Centenary Series (Toronto: McClelland and Stewart 1985), 76-7, 193, 195, and passim. For a treatment of the economy of the Upper Skeena and Bulkley Valley during Lord's tenure in that inspectorate, see Paul James Stortz, 'The Rural School Problem in British Columbia in the 1920s,' MA thesis, Vancouver, BC, University of British Columbia, 1988, 64, 65, and passim.

33 *Revised Statutes of British Columbia* [hereafter RSBC], 1911, Vol. III (Victoria, BC: King's Printer 1911), Ch.206, 2566; ibid., Art.96, 2583. Qualified voters were householders and 'wives of same,' twenty-one years of age or more, and district residents for at least six months prior to a given board meeting. The stipulation 'Chinese, Japanese, Hindoos, and Indians shall not vote' gives some sense of ethnic prejudice of the day, ibid., Art. 88, 2581.

34 Ibid., Art.116, 2589; ibid., Art. 109, 2586; Art. 110, 2589; ibid., 1936, Vol. III, Ch. 253, Art. 135, (1),(b), 3752; ibid., (2), 3754; ibid., (1),(i), 3752; ibid., Art. 82,(e), 3724; ibid., (j), 3724; ibid., (h), 3724; ibid., Art. 137, (4), 3757. Norah Lewis points to the Canadian Red Cross, British Columbia Women's Institutes, and parent associations as examples of voluntary groups taking much earlier initiatives in the health and welfare of schoolchildren. Meanwhile, systematic medical inspections in provincial rural and assisted

schools began in 1911 under the School Health Inspection Act passed in 1910. Interview with Norah Lewis, Vancouver, BC, 5 January 1990; Norah Lewis to the editor, Vancouver, BC, 8 January, 1990; Norah Lewis, 'Physical Perfection for Spiritual Welfare: Health Care for the Urban Child 1900–1939,' in Patricia T. Rooke and R.L. Schnell (eds.), *Studies in Childhood History: A Canadian Perspective* (Calgary, Alberta: Detselig Enterprises 1982), 139, 142; 'Advising the Parents: Child Rearing in British Columbia During the Inter-War Years,' PhD thesis, Vancouver, BC, University of British Columbia 1980, 17, 19, 123–5.

35 Putman and Weir, *Survey*, 196.

36 S.J. Willis, ARPS, 1929, R11. Note that in 1929, a year was added to the high school program extending the total years in school from 11 to 12.

37 RSBC, 1911, Vol. III, Ch. 206, Art. 11, (a), 2562; ibid., (g), 2563; ibid., (b), (e), 2562, (i), 2563; ibid., (c), (d), (f), 2562, (h), (j), 2563; ibid., 1936, Vol. III, Ch. 253, Art. 155, (k), 3765.

38 Ibid., 1911, Vol. III, Ch. 206, Art. 9, (g), and passim, 2561; ibid., (h), 2561.

39 Putman and Weir, *Survey*, 244.

40 British Columbia Department of Education, *School Inspectors' Reports* [hereafter SIR], 1918–57, British Columbia Archives and Records Service [hereafter BCARS] Microfilms, GR 122, Reel 6667, Meldrum Creek, 6 June 1933; Dog Creek, 12 May 1933.

41 H.B. King, *School Finance in British Columbia* (Victoria, BC: King's Printer 1935), 128–9.

42 Maxwell A. Cameron, *Report of the Commission of Inquiry into Educational Finance* (Victoria, BC: King's Printer 1945), 15, 28.

43 The controversial question of teacher financial status is discussed in William A. Bruneau, 'Teachers in Five Decades: The BCTF, 1917–1968,' unpublished ms., n.d., 16–17; Timothy A. Dunn, 'The Rise of Mass Public Schooling in British Columbia, 1900–1929,' in Wilson and Jones, *Schooling and Society, 41*; J. Donald Wilson, '"I am Here to Help If You Need Me": British Columbia's Rural Teachers' Officer, 1928–1934,' *Journal of Canadian Studies* 25:2 (Summer, 1990), 98. Note that Wilson's comparative figures lead him to conclude that 'in terms of disposable income, rural female teachers, especially if single, were not badly off compared with other female occupations such as domestic servants, stenographers and typists.'

44 For an admirable review of 'schools usual and unusual,' see Adams and Thomas, *Floating Schools*, 23–35. An earlier work, John C. Charyk's *The Little White Schoolhouse* (Saskatoon: Prairie Books 1968), Vol. 1 and 2, styles each such school as 'the bulwark of civilization in a new and primitive land,' and stresses the educational importance to its students of enduring difficulties for the sake of sound instruction, 1: 2; 2: 339 and passim.

45 Wilson, '"I am Here to Help"'; ibid., 105.

46 For instance, Adams and Thomas, *Floating Schools*; Jean Cochrane, *The One*

Room School in Canada (Toronto: Fitzhenry and Whiteside 1981); Neil Sutherland to the editor, Vancouver, BC, 23 May 1989.

47 ARPS, 1922, C34-5.

48 Adams and Thomas, *Floating Schools*, 76.

49 Thomas Fleming, 'Our Boys in the Field,' 291; ibid., 289.

50 Putman and Weir, *Survey*, 235, 238-9.

51 Adams and Thomas, *Floating Schools*, 78.

52 With certain exceptions, this view of BC society inferred from Lord's manuscript squares fairly well with provincial teachers' views as presented in J. Donald Wilson, 'The Vision of Ordinary Participants: Teachers' Views of Rural Schooling in British Columbia in the 1920s,' in Patricia E. Roy (ed.), *A History of British Columbia: Selected Readings* (Toronto: Copp Clark Pitman 1989), 239-55. The major exception, in Wilson's opinion, is that British Columbia teachers of the time 'held their Japanese-Canadian students in high regard,' ibid., 243.

53 Lord quotes Sir Graham Savage, City of London chief education officer in 1948, with whom he was discussing the problem of pupil transfer among schools with different curricular emphases.

54 A.R. Lord, 'A Canadian Looks at Teacher Training,' *The Elementary School Journal* (January 1937), 356; 'Changes in Vancouver Normal School,' *The School* 26 (February 1938), 478.

55 This is not to say that Lord shunned United States educational contacts. As his correspondence testifies, he took particular interest in teacher education south of the Canadian-American border, exchanging views with such American educators as C.H. Fisher, President, Washington State Normal School; Linda Lee Tall, President, State Teachers College, Maryland; and Professor Charles H. Judd, University of Chicago.

56 See MacLaurin, 'The History of Education in the Crown Colonies of Vancouver Island and British Columbia and in the Province of British Columbia,' Ph.D. thesis, Seattle, University of Washington, 1936; F. Henry Johnson, *A History of Education in British Columbia* (Vancouver, BC: Publications Centre, UBC 1964); J. Donald Wilson, 'The Historiography of British Columbia Educational History,' in Wilson and Jones, *Schooling and Society*, 8 and passim; Dunn, 'The Rise of Mass Public Schooling . . . ,' ibid., 23-51; Jane S. Gaskell and Marvin Lazerson, 'Between School and Work: Perspectives of Working Class Youth,' in J. Donald Wilson (ed.), *Canadian Education in the 1980s* (Calgary, Alberta: Detselig Enterprises 1981), 197-211; Harro Van Brummelen, 'Shifting Perspectives: Early British Columbia Textbooks from 1872 to 1925,' *BC Studies* 60 (Winter 1983-4), 3-27; Jean Barman, *Growing Up British in British Columbia: Boys in Private School* (Vancouver, BC: University of British Columbia Press 1984); Adams and Thomas, *Floating Schools*; F. Henry Johnson, *John Jessop: Gold Seeker and Educator* (Vancouver, BC: Mitchell Press 1971); Alan H. Child, 'The Historical Development of the

Large Administrative Unit in British Columbia Prior to 1947, with Special Reference to the Introductory Phase, 1933-1937,' PhD thesis, Edmonton, University of Alberta 1971; Fleming, 'Our Boys in the Field'; 'In the Imperial Age . . .' Out-of-province studies include Donald P. Leinster-Mackay, *Cross-Pollinators of English Education: Case Studies of Three Victorian School Inspectors* (Leeds: University of Leeds 1986); R.J.W. Selleck, *Frank Tate: A Biography* (Carlton, Victoria: Melbourne University Press 1982); and B. Anne Wood, *Idealism Subverted: The Making of a Progressive Educator* (Montreal: McGill-Queen's Press 1985). Light hearted pieces include Maurice Gibbons, 'The Inspector Cometh,' *The BC Teacher* 37: 3 (December 1957), 135-7, and Cyril F. Poole, *The Time of My Life* (St. John's, Newfoundland: Harry Cuff Publications 1983), 7-15.

57 British Columbia Department of Education, *One Hundred Years: Education in British Columbia* (Victoria, BC: Queen's Printer 1972), 97; *Province*, 21 April 1952, 4.

58 Two sources known to Lord, but which he did not exploit, are the superintendent of education *Letterbooks* and the provincial newspapers, indexed and filed in the British Columbia Archives and Records Service.

59 For an auspicious start, see Thomas Fleming and Madge Craig, 'The Anatomy of a Resignation: Margaret Strong and the New Westminster School Board 1913-15,' *Educational Administration and Foundations Journal* 5:1 (1990), 7-23.

60 Fleming, 'Our Boys in the Field.'

61 British Columbia Department of Education, ibid., 106-7.

62 Ibid.

63 Dunn, 'The Rise of Mass Public Schooling,' 47 and passim.

64 David C. Jones, 'Agriculture, the Land, and Education: British Columbia, 1914-1922,' PhD thesis, Vancouver, BC, University of British Columbia 1978, 417; James Collins Miller, *Rural Schools in Canada: Their Organization, Administration and Supervision* (New York: Teachers College 1913), 151-3, cited in Neil Sutherland, *Children in English-Canadian Society: Framing the Twentieth-Century Consensus* (Toronto: University of Toronto Press 1976) 169-70; Michael B. Katz, *Class, Bureaucracy, and Schools: The Illusion of Educational Change in America* (New York: Praeger 1971), 103. Dunn believes his own work 'buttresses' that of Katz; Jones adopts the opposite stance.

65 Jean S. Mann, 'G.M. Weir and H.B. King: Progressive Education or Education for the Progressive State?' in Wilson and Jones, *Schooling and Society*, 91-118.

66 Ibid., 92-3, 104, 115.

67 George S. Tomkins, *A Common Countenance: Stability and Change in the Canadian Curriculum* (Scarborough, Ontario: Prentice-Hall Canada 1986), 199. Tomkins draws here on Robert S. Patterson, 'Progressive Education:

The Experience of English Speaking Canadians 1930-1945,' an unpublished paper recently appearing as 'The Implementation of Progressive Education in Canada, 1930-1945,' in Nick Koch, Kas Mazurek, Robert S. Patterson, and Ivan De Faveri (eds.), *Essays on Canadian Education* (Calgary, Alberta: Detselig Enterprises 1986), 79-96. Patterson concludes that, despite attempts to 'merge the new with the old,' Canadian teachers experienced 'ambivalence, confusion and reluctance' regarding progressive education throughout the Depression and the Second World War (see 93).

68 Neil Sutherland, 'The Triumph of "Formalism": Elementary Schooling in Vancouver from the 1920s to the 1960s,' in Robert A.J. McDonald and Jean Barman (eds.), *Vancouver Past: Essays in Social History* (Vancouver, BC: University of British Columbia Press 1986), 176; Hilda Neatby, *So Little for the Mind* (Toronto: Clarke Irwin 1953); Neil Sutherland, '"Everyone seemed happy in those days": the culture of childhood in Vancouver between the 1920s and the 1960s,' *History of Education Review* 15: 2 (1986), 38, 49, and passim.

69 J. Donald Wilson and Paul Stortz, '"May the Lord Have Mercy on You": The Rural School Problem in British Columbia in the 1920s,' *BC Studies* 79 (Autumn 1988), 24-58. The authors offer as tentative explanation of why rural teachers' cries for help were largely ignored the probabilities that (a) the Teachers' Bureau records were rarely seen by educational policymakers; (b) inspectors had too little time to familiarize themselves with local problems; (c) inspectors gave 'overly positive' accounts of their districts; and (d) policymakers were preoccupied with other aspects of education such as urban schools, increased enrolment, and an expanding bureaucracy. Wilson, 'The Visions of Ordinary Participants,' 3, 7-8.

70 Selleck, *Frank Tate,* xi, 45, 84, 86. Among many comparative studies in frontier culture, a thoughtful example remains Louis Hartz, *The Founding of New Societies* (New York: Harcourt, Brace and World 1964).

71 See *East Charlton Tribune,* 9 September 1899, 2-3; ibid., 13 September 1899, 2, cited in Selleck, *Frank Tate,* 105, 272.

72 Though he wrote between 1953 and 1956, Lord has little to say about international understanding, focusing instead on empire/commonwealth concerns in the two world wars that punctuated his professional career.

73 See 'Schedule, Education in BC Schools, Inquiry Terms of Reference,' unpublished, 1, which briefly lays out for Commissioner Sullivan those educational issues the British Columbia government of the day wished to undergo scrutiny. They include objectives, quality, accountability, teaching methods and curriculum, and educational structures. Comprehensive responses to this mandate may be found in Barry Martin Sullivan, QC, *A Legacy for Learners: The Report of the Royal Commission on Education,* 1988 (Victoria, BC: Queen's Printer 1988).

CHAPTER ONE: NORTH OF FIFTY THREE

1 Among many renditions of Duncan's missionary endeavours, excellent
points of departure are Jean Usher's 'Duncan of Metlakatla: The Victorian
Origins of a Model Indian Community,' in W. Peter Ward and Robert A.J.
McDonald (eds.), *British Columbia: Historical Readings* (Vancouver, BC:
Douglas and McIntyre 1981), 127–53. Other sources include R. Geddes
Large, *The Skeena: River of Destiny* (Vancouver, BC: Mitchell Press 1957), 18–
22; and a recent work of wide interest, Peter Murray, *The Devil and Mr.
Duncan: A History of the Two Metlakatlas* (Victoria, BC: Sono Nis Press 1985).

2 This was an enormous craft some 55.5 feet long, 4 feet wide, and hewn from
a single cottonwood trunk. For a succinct story of its astonishing capabili-
ties and eventual demise, see E.M. Cotton, 'Last Voyage of Interior BC's
Largest Canoe,' in Art Downs (ed.), *Pioneer Days in British Columbia*, Vol.2
(Surrey, BC: Heritage House Publishing [1977]), 22–5.

3 Back in the 1870s, William Houseman ran a boarding house in Barkerville.
For an illuminating account of litigation with his Chinese cook, see *Cariboo
Sentinal*, 3 June 1871, 3.

4 An excellent reference on Cariboo passenger and freight transportation
with which Lord's estimates generally agree is Art Downs, *Paddlewheels on
the Frontier: The Story of British Columbia and Yukon Sternwheel Steamers*
(Sidney, BC: Gray's Publishing 1972), 54 and passim.

5 For a dramatically illustrated complementary account of this radical
change, see Guy Lawrence, 'Memories of the Cariboo and Central BC:
1908–1914,' in Downs, *Pioneer Days*, Vol. 4, 6–15.

6 Pre-emption was a form of land acquisition based upon a combination of
residence, land improvement, and nominal purchase or certification fees.
For details and early regulation changes, see Margaret A. Ormsby, 'Agri-
cultural Development in British Columbia,' in Dickson M. Falconer (ed.),
British Columbia: Patterns in Economic, Political and Cultural Development
(Victoria, BC: Camosun College 1982), 155–6; F.S. Wright, *Northern British
Columbia Index and Guide* (Prince Rupert, BC: F.S. Wright 1916), 28; *Wrigley's
British Columbia Index, 1918* (Vancouver, BC: Wrigley's Directories 1918), 32.

7 Robinson's official title was Superintendent of Education, a post he held
from 1899 to 1919.

8 When in 1910 Lord was appointed principal at Kelowna, matriculation
occurred at the end of grade eleven following success on the provincial
examination. In 1929 a year was added to the high school program thus
establishing grade twelve as the matriculation year. In either case, the
qualification was referred to as 'junior matriculation.' 'Senior matriculation' was used to denote a year of university-level studies taken at high
school.

9 Here, Lord expresses an ideal. As with varying standards of school accom-

modation, so community pride also suffered wide variation, as Lord himself noted at the time. To illustrate, one of his schools enjoyed enthusiastic parent support and residents surrounding a second took 'justifiable pride in their school...' Conversely, a third was situated in the uninspiring corner of a farmyard, the teacher of a fourth was not 'receiving from the parents the co-operation to which she is entitled,' and a fifth flew no flag 'through lack of a rope.' See respectively SIR, GR 122, Reel B 6648, Noosatsum, 2 May 1919; Reel B 6667, Dog Creek, 12 May 1933; Meldrum Creek, 6 June 1933; Tatlayoko, 9 June 1933; Pemberton, 23 November 1932.

CHAPTER TWO: NORTHERN INTERIOR EPISODES

1 Probably the judge was the Honourable F. McB. Young, Supreme and County Court Judge, see F.S. Wright, *Northern British Columbia Index and Guide* (Prince Rupert, BC: F.S. Wright 1916), 33. The official name of the 'Old Men's Home' was 'The Provincial Home for Old Men,' opened in 1895. Charles Barnes got his wish, arriving at the Kamloops facility on 29 December 1916. See Hugh McLean to A. Campbell Reddie, Kamloops, BC, 29 December 1916. Documentation regarding Barnes and many other cases may be found in GR 624, BC Provincial Secretary, Provincial Home (Kamloops), 1895-1917, Box 6, BCARS.

2 Sperry Cline nicknamed 'Dutch' joined the British Columbia Provincial Police at Hazelton in 1914 and retired thirty-two years later with the rank of sergeant from the Victoria Police Training School. For appreciations, see Cecil Clark, 'Sergeant Sperry Cline: Frontier Policeman,' in Art Downs (ed.), *Pioneer Days in British Columbia*, Vol. 4 (Surrey, BC: Heritage House Publishing 1979), 38-43; Province of British Columbia, Department of the Attorney General, *Report of the Superintendent of Provincial Police for the Year Ended December 31, 1924* (Victoria, BC: King's Printer 1925), x8.

3 Loutet recalls May as 'over 6 feet and ... straight as a bean pole. He spent all his life prospecting and could tell great tales of Barkerville. When I left Hazelton, Jim was 84 and still looking fit. I believe he was over 90 when he died.' See J.C. Loutet, 'Pioneer Days in Hazelton,' in Downs, ibid., Vol. 1, 12.

4 Large describes Wrinch as a 'powerful man physically and his character and mental development were in keeping ... He was a leader in all community activities, particularly in things horticultural, and eventually in 1924 was elected to the Provincial Legislature as a Liberal member' serving until 1933. Hazelton's Wrinch Memorial Hospital honours his name. See R. Geddes Large, *The Skeena: River of Destiny* (Vancouver, BC: Mitchell Press 1957), 53.

5 The 'conditions' had to do with girls frequenting the boys' dormitory in 1877. But the school did not close until 1890 when, because of day schools by then established in the Cariboo, Okanagan, and Nicola Valley, it was no

longer required. For a brief history, see John Calam, 'The Cache Creek Experiment: An Early Boarding School in a Public System,' in 'An Historical Survey of Boarding Schools and Public School Dormitories in Canada,' MA thesis, Vancouver, University of British Columbia, 1962, 74–94.

6 'Rancherie' is western Canadian usage for Indian reservation stemming from the Spanish *rancheria*.

7 The first ferry was owned by Bob Gerow of Burns Lake. In 1915, Wiggs O'Neill 'brought his launch to Burns Lake,' skidded it to François Lake, and had it lashed to a barge which he himself skippered from 1916 to 1917. See Pat Turkki, *Burns Lake and District* (Burns Lake, BC: Burns Lake Historical Society 1973), 204–5.

8 John Bostrom was born in Sweden in 1869, went to the US in 1886, married in 1905 and, after a sojourn in Ontario, moved to British Columbia. For details of his life as a railway contractor, cattle rancher, seed cultivator, housebuilder, and school trustee, see ibid., 258; Betty Hart to the editor, Burns Lake, BC, 23 March 1987; Lukin Johnston, *Beyond the Rockies: Three Thousand Miles by Trail and Canoe Through Little-Known British Columbia* (London: J.M. Dent and Sons 1929), 134. Bostrom died in 1941. His wife Olga carried on with the farm until 1945. Eventually the farmhouse, 'a [Grassy Plains] landmark, and considered one of the finest ranch buildings in the Central Interior, burned to the ground,' Hart, ibid.

9 According to Shelford, Harry Morgan and two companions were the first permanent white settlers on Ootsa Lake. In 1904 they left Kemano, climbed the Coast Mountains, descended to Tahtsa Lake, and followed the Tahtsa River to Ootsa where 'they staked land.' Morgan 'remained to his death in 1936.' Swamped by high water, as of 1953 backed up behind Alcan's Kenney Dam, Morgan's cabin and land now lie drowned, casualties of industrial expansion. Arthur Shelford, 'We Pioneered,' in Downs, *Pioneer Days*, Vol.2; 9, 11; Turkki, ibid., 268–9.

10 This school, John Michelson's unused cabin, was located at Wistaria, some 15 miles from the community of Ootsa Lake. Its teacher, Florence A. Hinton, earned $75.00 per month. She was 'a graduate of the Conservatory of Music in England and an accomplished violinist and singer ...' See Arthur Shelford, *We Pioneered* (Vancouver, BC: Mitchell Press, n.d.), private publication, Vol. 26 of 100, 17 (3); ARPS, 1916, Alxxxiv; Turkki, ibid., 282.

11 For a discursive biographical note, see *Who's Who and Why, 1917–1918* (Toronto: International Press, Ltd. 1918), 1002–3.

12 There is little doubt that one of these schools was at Braeside. On 5 June 1918, Peter Neufeld, a young Mennonite settler there, wrote in his diary: 'Thursday after dinner Mr. Smith and the School Inspector for the division, a Mr. Lord, came to see father about building a school here.' Cited in Velma Johnson to the editor, Vanderhoof, BC, 26 October 1987. I am grateful to Mrs. Johnson and Mr. J.V. Neufeld of Surrey, BC, for confirmation.

13 Lord was a determined walker. Other evidence points to the probability that he got off the train at Engen, spent a couple of hours at the local school, walked north some 2.5 miles to the Nechako River's south bank, crossed on deteriorating ice to the north bank, continued about 5 miles to Braeside, spent the afternoon at the school there, then struck out, mostly in the dark and along a difficult route, walking roughly 9 miles to Redmond's house, near the Nechako school and 6 miles northwest of Vanderhoof. See *Map of the Central Section of British Columbia Shewing the Country Served by the Grand Trunk Pacific Railway* (Chicago: Poole Brothers 1911) courtesy H. Kruisselbrink, Smithers, BC; Lyn Hancock (ed.), *Vanderhoof: The Town that Wouldn't Wait* (Vanderhoof: The Nechako Valley Historical Society 1979), 'Homesteading,' by Lil McIntosh, Jake Friesen, and Bill McLeod, 39, and 'The Mennonite Churches,' by Jake Friesen, 115; ;Bill McLeod, *Nechako Valley Settlement Circa 1915-1925* (map), Hancock, ibid., 6; *Fort Fraser, British Columbia* (map), Sheet 93K (Ottawa: Department of Mines and Technical Surveys 1952); Dorothy MacKinlay, 'The Little Log School House,' in Hancock, ibid., 125; Audrey L'Heureux to the editor, Vanderhoof, BC, 26 March 1987; Velma Johnson to the editor, Vanderhoof, BC, 26 October 1987.

14 All evidence points to this having been Robert Joseph Redmond locally known as Joe Redmond. I am obligated to his son James (Jimmy) Redmond for confirming this and for adding interesting details about his father's boyhood in Ireland's Dublin and Wexford areas, his experiences in Australia as a Melbourne cable-car operator, his expertise with horses and ponies, and the adventures and yarns of his brother, James Redmond's Uncle Bill. Telephone interview with James Redmond, Penticton, BC, 30 October 1988. For coverage of James Redmond's and others' contributions to the restoration, relocation, and official opening of the Redmond home in the Vanderhoof Heritage Village, see 'Historic home opens,' *Omineca Express*, 10 August 1988, 11.

15 'Mother' was Florence Elizabeth Redmond, nee Lett. She was born in Ireland and came to Canada in 1914. Again, I am indebted to James Redmond for this information.

16 Most probably the Nechako school, see ARPS, 1917, Alxxxiv.

17 Such was the nickname of Jean Jacques Caux, held by Sperry Cline to be 'the best packer British Columbia – and possibly North America – ever produced.' Among scores of references, articles, and photographs, Cline's sympathetic 'Cataline,' in Downs, *Pioneer Days*, Vol. 1, 98-103, provides a most interesting portrait.

18 Here Lord's version diverges from Cline's. Cline describes the burning hotel, but declares Cataline dashed back into the building to retrieve a favourite knife, an errand he in fact survived. Cline adds that 'one day in the spring of 1922 he became ill and I was sent for . . . A few weeks later he

submitted to entering the hospital and died within a few days.' Ibid., 103.

19 George Ogston recalls Dr. W. Ross Stone as 'a man of fine personal character, keenly alive to the thoughts and trends of the world and always intensively interested in what makes it tick.' For this and other perspectives regarding early health care in the Vanderhoof area, see Hancock, ibid., 17, 76, 77, 101, 105-7.

20 On 24 October 1918, the ss *Princess Sophia* ran aground on Vanderbilt Reef in Lynn Canal, recognized for its treacherous Alaskan waters. High seas and blizzards prevented rescue, and all 353 souls on board perished. For dramatic accounts see Louise McFadden, 'BC's Worst Marine Disaster,' in Downs, *Pioneer Days*, Vol. 1, 104-11; see also Ken Coates and Bill Morrison, *The Sinking of the Princess Sophia* (Toronto: Oxford University Press 1990).

21 Father Coccola 'succeeded Father Morice in the mission at Fort St. James . . . Eventually he was appointed principal at Lejac [Indian Residential] School . . . and in 1934 became chaplain to the new Catholic hospital in Smithers . . . until his death on 1st March 1943 at the age of eighty-nine.' Large, ibid., 77. As Orchard notes, 'these pioneer priests of the Order of Mary Immaculate . . . were men of unusual culture and ability. Father Coccola, the forceful Corsican, was no exception.' For a brief appraisal and striking photograph, see Imbert Orchard, *Martin: The Story of a Young Fur Trader* (Victoria, BC: Sound and Moving Image Division, BCARS 1981), 53-4. For a full, absorbing account of and by this remarkable man, see Margaret Whitehead (ed.), *'They Call Me Father': Memoirs of Father Nicolas Coccola* (Vancouver, BC: University of British Columbia Press 1988).

22 Turki explains that Fathers Nicolas Coccola, Joseph Francis Allard, and Charles Wolf all stationed at Fort St. James, and Father Godfrey (surname Eichelsbacher) at Hagwilget had each received a year's medical training in preparation for their mission in the field and 'one of them came through the [Lakes District] area several times a year. Father Cocola [Coccola] later came to Babine and Burns Lake more often and was better known in the district.' Turkki, ibid., 12. For Father Coccola's own dramatic account of his 1918 Cheslatta visit, see Whitehead, ibid., 173-4. I am obliged to Reverend Thomas A. Lascelles, OMI, for verifying Father Godfrey's surname.

CHAPTER THREE: POLITICS AND PERSONALITIES

1 Chilco was then a small community school about 10 miles east and slightly north of Vanderhoof.

2 Ellwood Rice, sometime teacher at Hulatt, a GTP station seventeen miles east of Vanderhoof, relates much the same story of 'two school boards each . . . claiming to be the legal one.' Joan Adams and Becky Thomas, *Floating Schools and Frozen Inkwells: The One-Room Schools of British Columbia* (Madeira Park, BC: Harbour Publishing 1985), 128.

3 The records show a Miss Norma B. Hoy who taught seven boys and seven girls for a salary of eighty dollars a month during 1915-16, ARPS, 1916, Aclxxvi. She probably attended Vancouver Provincial Normal School, British Columbia's only training centre for public elementary school teachers prior to 1915.

4 Documents indicate a W.S. Moore succeeded Miss Hoy. He held a temporary permit and taught eleven boys and eight girls for eighty dollars a month. ARPS, 1917, Aclxxvii, Alxxiii.

5 This man was Bishop Frederick Herbert du Vernet who, in 1904, succeeded Bishop William Ridley in the Diocese of Caledonia.

6 Most likely the Reverend William Sweetnam.

7 McBride had resigned as premier on 9 December 1915.

8 Bowser was sworn in as premier upon McBride's resignation, but the Conservatives lost the 1916 election, and W.J. Brewster formed a Liberal ministry on 23 November 1916.

9 First elected to the provincial legislature in 1906, Thomson had been chosen by Bowser to be minister of finance. But, with the Conservative defeat in 1916, he never assumed that portfolio nor, according to some, was he eager to do so. See *The Daily News*, Prince Rupert, 19 July 1916, 2.

10 Newton took over as editor from John Houston who had established *The Empire* as Prince Rupert's first newspaper. Newton's pithy, one-column editorials appeared in an asterisked frame as quickly identifiable features among his newspaper's First World War news.

11 Ormsby points out that *The Crisis in British Columbia* was actually generated by the Ministerial Union of the Lower Mainland, published under the name of its secretary, the Reverend A.E. Cooke, but 'prepared by Moses B. Cotsworthy, an accountant, statistician and actuary.' Margaret A. Ormsby, *British Columbia: A History* (Toronto: Macmillan of Canada 1958), 387.

12 William Roderick Ross was elected member for Fernie in 1903 and reelected in 1907. In 1910 he was appointed minister of lands in the McBride cabinet. John McInnes was MLA for Grand Forks, 1907-9, and for Fort George (CCF), 1945-9.

13 This was the Nechako school. Grace Pebernot (nee McIntosh) recalls that 'as soon as there were ten children living nearby to make up the legal number ... my father arranged with Inspector Gower [Lord's predecessor] to open one in a tiny cabin donated by Joe Murray ... The teacher [Beatrice Smith] rode out on horseback from Vanderhoof, a distance of about seven miles.' Dorothy MacKinlay writes that 'when the ... children moved into their new building ... in 1917, the oldest boy acted as janitor.' Bessie Bailey (nee Redmond) remembers 'we didn't have the equipment they have nowadays. We had to make do with what we had, but we played all the games, had a girls' baseball team and got along very well.' See

Dorothy MacKinlay, 'The Little Log School House,' in Lyn Hancock (ed.), *Vanderhoof: The Town that Wouldn't Wait* (Vanderhoof: Nechako Valley Historical Society 1979), 125.

14 The Nechako school, situated east of Prairiedale and west of Chilco, was opened for the 1916-17 school year. Teacher Beatrice Smith held a temporary permit, taught six boys and six girls, and earned $75.00 a month. ARPS, 1917, Alxxxiv; Hancock, ibid., map, 6.

15 Compare Ormsby's figures of 37 Liberals, 9 Conservatives, and 1 Socialist – Parker Williams, Ormsby, ibid., 394, and the official report showing 36 Liberals, 9 Conservatives, 1 Independent and 1 Independent Socialist, 'Elections British Columbia,' *Election History of British Columbia 1871-1986* (Victoria, BC: Queen's Printer 1988), 123.

16 Thomas Dufferin Pattullo was first elected as Liberal member for Prince Rupert in 1916 and re-elected in 1920, 1924, and 1928. He joined H.C. Brewster's cabinet in 1916 as minister of lands and continued in this capacity in the John Oliver administration. Following the Liberal defeat in 1928, he became leader of the opposition, assuming the premiership following the Liberal victory in the provincial election of 1933 and serving until 1941. Alexander Malcolm Manson was first elected in 1916 as Liberal member for Omineca. In 1918 he became deputy speaker and was promoted to speaker in 1921. In 1922 he assumed responsibilities as attorney general and minister of labour, eventually becoming a Supreme Court judge.

CHAPTER FOUR: DIG YOURSELVES OUT

1 The Rocher de Boule mine located on its namesake mountain yielded 'high-grade chalcopyrite [$CuFeS_2$] with good gold values.' It was developed to production stage in 1914, but the First World War curtailed its activities. Silver Standard Mine exploited the silver/lead ore of the Babine Range and was a consistent producer. See R. Geddes Large, *The Skeena: River of Destiny* (Vancouver, BC: Mitchell Press 1957), 160. Despite their reputations, Leonard argues that the GTP actually discouraged 'the operation of the mines in the Hazelton district,' through preoccupation with townsite land sales. See Frank Leonard, 'The Limits of Spite: Grand Trunk Pacific and the Blighting of a Northern British Columbia Mining District, 1910-1918,' paper presented at the Conference on Boom and Bust Cycles in Communities in the Canadian and American West, University of Victoria, August 1987, 7, 22, 34, and passim.

2 With Frank Warren and Frank Rowell, 'Big Bill' Moxley formed the 'first train crew set up in Prince Rupert' following completion of the GTP north-central/north coast section. Frank Parker, Sr., 'For Railroaders Only,' in Tina Hetherington, Marjory Rosberg, and Winnie Robinson (eds.), *Bulkley Valley Stories* (Smithers, BC: Heritage Club, nd), 160.

3 Something of the sweep of scholarship generated through academic interest in Kitwanga, Kitwankool, and other Indian settlements within the general area may be derived from such comprehensive works as Franz Boaz, *Tsimshian Mythology*, Based on Texts Recorded by Henry W. Tate, Thirty-First Annual Report of the Bureau of American Ethnology to the Secretary of the Smithsonian Institution, 1909-10, Washington, DC, Government Printing Office, 1916, 29-1037. Current interests are no less intense, particularly the ethical question of collection and study of aboriginal artifacts, a topic Professor Cole has recently explored. See Douglas Cole, *Captured Heritage: The Scramble for Northwest Coast Artifacts* (Vancouver/ Toronto: Douglas and McIntyre 1985), an argument strongly supporting 'the museum and its collectors,' 311 and passim.

4 This is St. Paul's Church, 'one of the finest Anglican Mission churches still standing.' It was raised by the Reverend Alfred E. Price in 1893 using spruce and cedar lumber which Price manufactured in a sawmill he built at Minskinish [Meanskinisht, etc.], now called Cedarvale. As Veillette and White remark, 'building a church of the refinement and size of St. Paul's (thirty by sixty-seven feet) was a considerable undertaking . . .' which took several years and attracted the talent of Joe Williams and other local artisans. For excellent photographic and descriptive data, see 'Kitwanga (Skeena R.),' photograph 90813, BCARS. I thank Barbara McLennan, Leni Hoover, and Carolyn Smyly for alerting me to this and many other relevant photographs. See also Large, ibid., 81-3; Barry Downs, *Sacred Places: British Columbia's Early Churches* (Vancouver, BC: Douglas and McIntyre 1980), frontispiece and 153-4; John Veillette and Gary White, *Early Indian Village Churches* (Vancouver, BC: University of British Columbia Press 1977), 69-71; *Diocese of Caledonia 1879-1950* (Prince Rupert, BC: See City, nd), unpaginated, second page (photograph). Lord's description of a small, unadorned building may reflect both temporal aberration and urban comparison on his part.

5 The twinkle-eyed cleric was Dr. Vernon Ardagh who was born in Aurangabad, India, trained as a medical doctor at Edinburgh University, and took up missionary service in French Equatorial Africa in 1887. Following further missionary work in India, he commenced medical practice at Metlakatla in 1889 before returning to England in 1901. Ten years later he came back to British Columbia, was ordained a minister of the Church of England in Canada, and 'sent to take charge of the mission at Kitwanga . . .' Large, ibid., 87. I am indebted to Doreen Stephens, Archivist, Anglican Provincial Synod of British Columbia Archives, for helping identify Dr. Ardagh.

6 Started in 1880, the Hazelton post constituted a firm link in the chain of HBC forts extending from Fort Simpson to Bear Lake, Babine Lake, Stuart Lake, and Fraser Lake. Large, ibid., 45.

7 Port Essington is a small community in the Skeena River estuary near the mouth of the Ecstall River. Blaine Boyd testifies to the culinary surprises of the New Hazelton Hotel, circa 1906, including 'a bottle of whiskey between every two men, a bottle of beer at each plate,' and spiced wine to come. Martin Stevens Starret refers to proprietor 'Macdonell' offering a $150 bonus to a HBC riverboat captain to ignore the regular Hazelton supplies and 'take a cargo of booze' instead. Blaine Boyd, 'The Coming of the Steel,' in Downs, *Pioneer Days*, 2: 99; Imbert Orchard, *Martin: The Story of a Young Fur Trader* (Victoria, BC: Sound and Moving Image Division, BCARS 1981), 38.

8 The second Union Bank robbery at New Hazelton in 1914 is a favourite, often-told, and richly varied story. For a wide sample, see Hetherington et al., ibid., 100; J.C. Loutet, 'Pioneer Days in Hazelton,' in Downs, ibid., 1: 11; Cecil Clark, 'Sergeant Sperry Cline: Frontier Policeman,' ibid., 4: 43; Cecil Clark, 'When Guns Blazed at New Hazelton,' in *Tales of the British Columbia Provincial Police* (Sidney, BC: Gray's Publishing 1971), 122; Large, ibid., 131-2; Mark Hamilton, 'Shoot Out at New Hazelton,' in Downs, ibid., 3: 128-9.

9 For a close examination of the three-Hazelton syndrome, see Leonard, ibid., 7-24 and passim, and Figure 2, 'Townsites, District Lots, and Mines in District of Hazelton,' 4. As Leonard shows, by March 1913, the GTP 'had designated South Hazelton as "Hazelton" on its timetables and maps over the objections of the residents of New Hazelton,' ibid., 24. See also 'Hazelton Buildings – Railway Stations,' Photograph 76951, BCARS; the station sign at South Hazelton reads 'Hazelton.' Moreover, as early as 1911, the Poole Bros. map of the region already reflected this fact. See *Map of the Central Section of British Columbia Shewing the Country Served by the Grand Trunk Pacific Railway* (Chicago: Poole Bros. 1911).

10 Probably the agent was W.A. Gow.

11 The Hazelton teacher at the time was Minnie B. Wentzel who held classes in a 'comfortable building.' Lord reported that her control and teaching were good, as was class tone. Students made good progress, performing well in arithmetic. At roughly the same period (1917-19), New Hazelton was served successively by three teachers – Mr. T.A. Martin, BA, Miss E.J. Mutch, and Miss S. Gladstone. See SIR, GR 122, Reel B6648, Hazelton, 9 December 1918; 14 April 1919; ARPS, 1917, Aclxxx; ibid., 1918, Dlxvi; ibid., 1919, Alxx.

12 During Lord's inaugural inspectorate the teacher at Fort Fraser was J.S. Ross, BA. He held the academic certificate and in 1915-16 taught five boys and ten girls at a salary of $100 a month; see ARPS, 1916, Aclxxviii, Alxxvi.

13 Initially seven stops from the GTP western terminus, Kwinitsa was 46.4 miles east of Prince Rupert. The Kwinitsa tunnel was one of many difficult construction projects on the lower sixty miles of the GTP Skeena River section. The old railway station at Kwinitsa has been moved to the Prince

Rupert waterfront where it now serves as a railway museum. For a graphic account of the January 1962 avalanche, see Phylis Bowman, *The Last Little Station* (Port Edward, BC: P. Bowman 1989), 11.

14 Allan Kilpatrick, superintendent of the GTP western section, lived in Smithers from 1917 to 1920 and took an active part in local volunteer work. See R. Lynn Shervill, *Smithers from Swamp to Village* (Smithers, BC: Town of Smithers 1981), 44-5, 65, 68.

15 In 1916, the Smithers Citizens' Association elaborated on this point, directing its complaint to Superintendent Kilpatrick. 'On Tuesday, Dec. 26th last,' the SCA secretary wrote, 'three of our citizens who had been spending the Xmas holidays at the Barrett Ranch, were returning to Smithers and arrived at Barrett Station about 5 AM in order to take the west-bound train ... The train did not arrive on schedule and there being no telephone or telegraph communication ... the three travellers had no means of finding out when the train was likely to arrive, consequently they had to remain at the station all day and until 5 PM when the train arrived.' Ibid., 37. I am grateful to Nancy Leighton for drawing the Shervill volume to my attention, relating many anecdotes about growing up at Evelyn (near Smithers) in the 1930s, and enduring endless ramblings of my own about the editorial work at hand.

CHAPTER FIVE: BY RIVER TO QUESNEL

1 Lord refers here to John Collins who lived at Soda Creek. His *Circle W* made the working trip from Quesnel to Fort George in about a day and a half compared with the *Rounder's* one day. H. Joan Huxley to the editor, Quesnel, BC, 14 January 1989, citing Albert Leonard of Quesnel.

2 The engineer in question was Bill Collins, son of Captain John (Jake) Collins. Huxley, ibid.

3 Known as the 'Queen of Northern Waters,' the *BX* was launched against her shipyard workers' better judgment on Friday, 13 May 1910, at Soda Creek. The 'most up-to-date riverboat that engineers and builders could provide,' she was designed to carry loads upstream, drawing a maximum of 30" of water 'when loaded with 100 tons dead weight.' In service until October 1915, she ceased the Fort George-Soda Creek run because of reduced business during the First World War. Restored in 1918, she resumed previous schedules until late August 1919, when she 'struck a reef, smashing a hole in her bottom.' She was salvaged with some difficulty 'but never sailed again.' For a fascinating biography of the *BX*, see Willis J. West, *Stagecoach and Sternwheel Days in the Cariboo and Central* BC (Surrey, BC: Heritage House Publishing 1985), 41-52; Art Downs, *Paddlewheels on the Frontier: The Story of British Columbia and Yukon Sternwheel Steamers* (Sidney, BC: Gray's Publishing Co. 1972), 50-1. The

disaster which struck the vessel on 29 August 1919 is dramatically described in the *Prince George Citizen*, 3 September 1919, 1.

4 Outlying schools would have included Beaverley, South Fort George, Chief Lake, Giscome, and Willow River, all within a 20-mile radius of Prince George. See 'The Schools in the Fort George Electoral District, 1918-19,' ARPS, 1919, Alxxxii. On a prior trip, Lord had visited the log school at Beaverley and commented favourably on Olive M. Clarke's pupils who closed school each day 'by singing the national anthem and repeating the oath of allegiance.' SIR, Beaverley, 20 February 1919. Fairservice writes that 'John Henderson and wife Mary arrived with son Martin in Prince George during 1917 from Saskatchewan. John pre-empted a ¼ section and his son . . . a ½ section [160 and 320 acres respectively]. In 1919 John Henderson was a dairy farmer with 8-10 cattle. He was also a butcher and had a cottage industry butcher shop in town. He sold milk and cream to a list of customers.' Barbara Fairservice to the editor, Prince George, BC, 29 April 1987. I am grateful to Mrs. Fairservice for acquiring this information and to Clark Henderson, John Henderson's grandson, for supplying it.

5 The purser would have been John Arnold Davis of South Fort George, shown in occupational retrospect in the 1920s voters' list as 'Purser, BX boat.' See *List of Persons Entitled to Vote in the Fort George Electoral District, September 13, 1920* (Victoria, BC: King's Printer 1920), 19, No. 1,164; telephone interview with Mrs. Arlene Wilson, Prince George, BC, 24 March 1989. Mrs. Wilson is J.A. Davis's granddaughter.

6 West describes this facility as having 'a large double brass bed with fine springs and mattress, down pillows, and specially fine linen and blankets, with a silk eiderdown costing $150.00.' West, ibid., 44.

7 The reference pinpoints Lord's *BX* voyage to mid-May 1919, the time of the Winnipeg general strike.

8 The master of the *BX* would have been Captain O.F. Browne, previously in command of the *Charlotte* and famous for his sternwheeler exploits. Perhaps his most memorable adventure (other than its sinking!) on board the *BX* was a Mississippi-style race with the *Conveyor* - Captain Jack Shannon – which the *BX* crew claimed they won. See West, ibid., 86-91, 93-4.

CHAPTER SIX: PEACE RIVER MEMOIRS

1 Born Henry Fuller Davis, 'Twelve-Foot' Davis left Vermont for the California gold rush, later arriving in the Cariboo where the legal claim limit was 100 feet. Macdonald writes that a clandestine night survey of Williams Creek convinced Davis that two adjoining claims 'measured a total of two hundred and twelve feet. He moved in between them and staked his own claim, thereby earning himself a small fortune and a new name.' In the

1870s he 'found pay dirt' on the Peace River not far from Fort St. John. See David L. Macdonald, *Peace River Past: A Canadian Adventure* (Toronto: Venture Press 1981), 26–7.

2 The route took Jack Pringle from Summit Lake down the Crooked River, McLeod Lake, and the Pack and Parsnip rivers to Finlay Forks, then down the Peace River. Since 1964, this waterway has been substantially altered by the Peace River hydroelectric project.

3 The telegrapher must have been W.R. Holden, appointed to the Spirit River post in July 1912 at a salary of $900 per annum. Operators' salaries were a little lower than $100 per month for ten-months, the rate generally paid teachers in the area. See 'Report of the Minister of Public Works on the Work under His Control for the Year Ended March 31, 1914,' *Sessional Papers, Volume 13, Fifth Session of the Twelfth Parliament of the Dominion of Canada, Session 1915* [hereafter DSP], 48.

4 Thomas (Baron Rhondda) typifies the early-century boom-time entrepreneur. Among his other schemes was the Peace River Development Company aimed at oil exploration and exploitation of Hudson's Hope coal deposits, projects terminally interrupted by the First World War. See R. Geddes Large, *The Skeena: River of Destiny* (Vancouver, BC: Mitchell Press 1957), 63, 68, 120–5.

5 Though in Fryer's opinion 'too big and a hard luck vessel besides,' the *D.A. Thomas* was a 'magnificent twin-stacker' sternwheeler plying the Peace River between Fort Vermilion, Alberta, and Hudson's Hope, British Columbia. Her 167-foot length and 40-foot beam made her the biggest riverboat then afloat in Canada. Like the *BX* of Lord's memoirs, she was elegantly appointed; and like the *BX* she suffered ignominious demise, stuck in the mud at Fort Fitzgerald in 1930 following a hair-raising encounter with rocks in the Vermilion Chutes. Despite the vessel's sticky end, Hansen terms the *D.A. Thomas* a 'floating fairyland, the stuff that dreams are made of.' Harold Fryer, 'Sternwheel Days on the Peace River,' in Art Downs, *Pioneer Days in British Columbia*, Vol. 1 (Surrey, BC: Heritage House Publishing 1973), 124–7; Evelyn Hanson, *Where Go The Boats: Navigation on the Peace 1792–1952* (Peace River, Alberta: Peace River Centennial Museum 1977), 12–13.

6 For instance, 'Extremely Dangerous and Badly Constructed!'

7 Of the ED&BCR in 1924, Stacey writes 'it never mattered whether northern trains arrived or departed on time. Some years later, the porter on the Waterways Branch was said to carry a calendar instead of a timetable and was usually able to predict the day on which the train would arrive at its destination.' F.C. Stacey, *Peace Country Heritage* (Saskatoon: Western Producer Book Service 1974), 61.

8 The federal policy of homestead settlement, copied from the American Homestead Law of 1862, was embodied in the Free Land Homestead Act of

1872 and subsequent revised statutes. Comparison with British Columbia pre-emption legislation shows federal land acquisition laws more demanding in their cultivated acreage requirements. Further, not all land was available on homesteading terms. Only even-numbered sections were open, odd-numbered ones being reserved for schools, railway or other grants, or direct purchase. See *Encyclopedia Canadiana* (Ottawa: Canadiana Company Ltd. 1958), 145; *Encyclopedia Canadiana* (Toronto: Grolier of Canada 1970), Vol. 5, 145, Column 1; Edgar McInnis, *Canada: A Political and Social History* (New York and Toronto: Rinehart 1959), 334.

9 The Block was conveyed to the federal government following passage of the Settlement Act of the British Columbia Provincial Legislature on 19 December 1883 and of the Dominion House of Commons on 21 March 1884. It was restored to British Columbia as one of the last acts of negotiation Liberal Premier John Oliver carried out with Ottawa before his death on 17 August 1927. The agreement restoring 10,976,000 acres to provincial jurisdiction was sealed on 20 February 1930. For a clear description, see Dorothea Calverly, 'Peace River Block,' in Lillian York (ed.), *Lure of the South Peace: Tales of the Early Pioneers to 1945* (Fort St. John; Dawson Creek: Alaska Highway Daily News; Peace River Block News 1981), 7–8.

10 Rolla is said to have derived its name from Rolla, Missouri which, in turn, 'is a corruption of Raleigh, North Carolina . . .' The school was referred to as Pouce Coupé North until 1923. See *B.C. Centennial 1958, Dawson Creek and District*, prepared by M.E. Coutts (Edmonton, Alberta: Dawson Creek Historical Society 1958), 27; ARPS, 1924, T100; Bruce Ramsay and Dan Murray, *The Big Dam Country* (Fort St. John, BC: Dan Murray Ltd. 1969), unpaginated. In 1915 Rolla School (Pouce Coupé North) was first taught by A.W. Cameron who earned $100 a month on an academic certificate, ARPS, 1916, Aclxxxiii. The same year, Winifred Fairman started up the Pouce Coupé Central School, teaching there for two years on a temporary certificate for $100 a month, ibid., Aclxxxiii, Alxxxv; ibid., 1917, Aclxxxv, Alxxxvi. At Saskatoon Creek, Annie Ligertwood taught from 1915 to 1917 on an academic certificate for $100 a month, ibid., 1916, Aclxxxiv, Alxxxvi; ibid., 1917, Aclxxxvi, Alxxxvii. At the end of his first year, Cameron joined the Canadian army; he was killed in action overseas. Ligertwood and Fairman survived an arduous journey to the district, leaving Vancouver for Edmonton, thence north to the end of steel, by mail carrier to Peace River Crossing, back by wagon (unbeknown to them, upriver service was suspended for the season) to Grande Prairie, then ninety miles by wagon trail to Pouce Coupé. Ligertwood set up class at Saskatoon Creek 'in Slim Ford's shack, but soon removed to a new log, sod-roofed building, erected by joint effort of the settlers.' Her successor in 1917, Dorothy Oliver, described the building as '16' x 20', with a sod roof, topped by another roof of local spruce shakes. The logs were unhewn and there were two small windows, 24" x

24″. The eleven desks were the standard type sent in by the Department of Education from Victoria. The blackboard was homemade and about a yard square.' Coutts adds that 'the building would have been warmed by a wood-burning airtight heater. Water for drinking would be melted snow in winter, dam water in summer.' Coutts, ibid., 27.

11 The first teacher was J. McDairmid, with an academic certificate, at a salary of $1,320 per annum, teaching thirteen boys and fourteen girls, ARPS, 1920, C70.

12 By 1917 things were not much better. Walker reported that the ED&BCR was 'graded from Spirit River for a distance of sixty miles to the British Columbia boundary, but the steel is not laid. The contract was let for the said steel twelve months ago, but it was requisitioned by the Government and it would appear that there is no possibility of steel being laid until after the war.' H.E. Walker, 'A District Agriculturalist Reports,' in Gordon E. Bowes (ed.), *Peace River Chronicles* (Vancouver, BC: Prescot Publishing 1963), 351.

13 At 56°15′ N, Peace River Landing and Fort St. John are the most northerly communities Lord visited among the many places he mentions.

14 An alternative derivation relates to a Beaver Indian called Pooscapee, a name whose sound to French-speaking voyageurs was close enough to Pouce Coupé for their use. See Ramsay and Murray, ibid., unnumbered; James G. MacGregor, *The Land of Twelve Foot Davis: A History of the Peace River Country* (Edmonton, Alberta: Applied Arts Products 1952), 160; 'The Pouce Coupé Story,' in York, ibid., 848.

15 Stacey speaks of a man whose 'success and showmanship brought literally thousands of settlers to the Peace.' MacGregor sees Trelle as 'an inspiration to others . . .' Fryer calls him a 'hot headed farm genius' who 'found it difficult to work with others' but 'left a record that likely will not be duplicated.' See Stacey, ibid., 114–15; James G. MacGregor, *Grande Prairie* (Edmonton, Alberta: Reidmore Books 1983), 24, 83; Fryer, ibid., 172.

16 By 1919, the McLean brothers had established a hotel. See Esme Tuck, *A Brief History of Pouce Coupé Village and District, British Columbia, Canada* (Pouce Coupé: Pouce Coupé Women's Institute [1954]), 3.

17 The bank was Pouce Coupé's branch of the Bank of Commerce and its manager a [William Grant] Cruickshank whom District Agriculturalist H.E. Walker consulted regarding land usage during his 1917 visit to the region, see Walker, ibid., 350. The reference dates Lord's visit as September 1917.

18 Official reports yield the following about these schools: Pouce Coupé, teacher D. Clarke, 3rd class certificate, $100 per month, 25 children; Pouce Coupé Centre, teacher A. Simpson, 1st class certificate, $100 per month, 14 children; Pouce Coupé North, teacher C.E. Braden, temporary certificate, $100 per month, 16 children. ARPS, 1918, Dlxx. The common salaries indicate a tendency for teachers in the region to be paid not for years of experience,

level of certification, or class size, but rather for doing a particular job.

19 Donald Herbert Taylor was born in Manitoba in 1866 and as a young man was firefighter with a North Dakota railway. At age 30 he moved to Edmonton, then Grouard, homesteaded at Peace River Crossing, and five years later joined the Hudson's Bay Company at Hudson's Hope. By 1912 he had left the Company and settled at Taylor Flat 'in the area which is now the south side of the road from the refinery,' and where he was ferry operator for many years. A skilled boater he sometimes fetched supplies by drifting downstream to Peace River Crossing and poling back upstream. His exploits as farmer, trapper, sled dog handler, hunter, and road builder are well-remembered in the Peace River country. York, ibid., 273; Sandy Taylor, 'The Herbie Taylors,' in Cora Ventress, Marguerite Davies, and Ethel Kyllo (author-editors), *The Peacemakers of North Peace* (n.p.: Davies, Ventress, and Kyllo 1973), 38.

20 Recounting the same story of Premier Brewster's river voyage, Gordon E. Bowes described the vessel as a '35-foot-long scow de luxe, equipped with an Evinrude motor.' Bowes, ibid., 349.

21 Bowes wrote that 'it was a standing joke among settlers that Victoria officials had never heard of Rolla or Pouce Coupé,' and that the voyage in question was calculated to allay further charges of neglect. Another motive, he believed, was that of identifying land suitable for a university endowment. Bowes, ibid., 349; Harry T. Logan, *Tuum Est: A History of the University of British Columbia* (Vancouver, BC: University of British Columbia 1958), 80-1.

22 From headquarters in a tightly constructed log building, Taylor functioned as 'the one administrator of law and order in the community,' his duties ranging from mediating minor disputes to investigating homicides. See Ventress et al., ibid., H36, 165.

23 'Dan' (Donald) MacDonald mentions this event. Returning from the First World War to his homestead near Farrell Creek, the first job he had 'was to accompany Constable [Harry] Taylor of Fort St. John and Jim Beattie to investigate a murder that an Indian, Moses, had reported as "Two White men shot dead. At Lake up Sikanni. Crazy white men!" When they arrived at the scene they found that two prospectors had dutifully buried the bodies. That infuriated the police, as much of the evidence was destroyed.' The eventual verdict was mutual homicide, a rarity! Ventress et al. ibid., H36.

24 This obliging soul was J.J. Dever, first appointed 1 July 1914 at a salary of $900 per annum. His willingness and ability to arrange alternative transportation is an indication of the importance of telegraph operators to the social cohesiveness of a pioneer area, DSP, 1917, 578; Coutts, ibid., 29.

25 This operator was B.L. Burnett, hired 19 October 1915, at a salary of $900 per annum, DSP, ibid., 48.

26 The agent in question was Ben F. Harmer who took up the job in 1916 following completion of the ED&BCR line as far as Grande Prairie. Alice Fortier to the editor, Grande Prairie, Alberta, 28 August 1987; Evelyn Hansen to the editor, Grimshaw, Alberta, 2 August 1987.

CHAPTER SEVEN: ISOLATION IN THE CHARLOTTES

1 In fact there may have been six hotels operating in Lord's time. For details see Kathleen E. Dalzell, *The Queen Charlotte Islands 1774-1966*, Vol. 1 (Queen Charlotte City: Bill Ellis 1968, 1981), 155, 251, 254, 259, 263, and passim.

2 The schools included Massett, Port Clements, and Kumdis Slough at the north end, Queen Charlotte City and Skidegate Landing at the south, and Sandspit on Moresby Island. As Lord explained, irregularities at Kumdis Slough led to its closure in 1917, but elsewhere there was reason for modest satisfaction. In their frame school house at Massett, Bridget Hutchinson's children were 'attentive and interested.' Though weak in spelling, they were fair at arithmetic and good in reading and language. At Port Clements, Beryl A. Nillis, a 'young and inexperienced teacher,' had 'made a good beginning' with creditable results in number work. Vera B. Hurst at Queen Charlotte City Lord characterized as 'a capable and sympathetic teacher' whose pupils had 'made good progress.' Although he worked in 'a small and undesirable building' at Skidegate Landing, Lesley Barraclough had achieved 'a noticeable improvement in the tone of the school.' His pupils had 'made distinct progress and results in general' were satisfactory. And Vivian A. Davis who taught at Sandspit on a temporary certificate, in 'a small frame building not satisfactory for school purposes,' nonetheless was 'doing as good a job as can be expected in view of her lack of training.' See SIR, GR 122, Reel B 6648, BCARS, Masset, 8 February 1919; Reel B 6649, Port Clements, 7 February 1919; Queen Charlotte, 10 May 1919; Skidegate, 10 May 1919; Sandspit, 12 May 1919.

3 'Mexican Tom' was the nickname of William Thomas Hodges, perhaps on account of his early experience working as a Texas ranch hand near the Mexican border. The trail linked Port Clements with Tlell. For details, see Dalzell, ibid., Vol. 1, 231, 233; ibid., Vol. 2, 345.

4 It is likely that Lord refers here to the Neil and Jake Walsh house. At one time 'Mexican Tom' Hodge's property, it 'became a home ranch in the best western tradition. Guests were always welcome.' Ibid., Vol. 1, 282-3.

5 This would have been W.J. 'Hotel' Smith's Premier Hotel. Dalzell makes no mention of a 'Dad' Smith, but admits 'nicknames were the order of the day.' Ibid., 252. The schools would have been Queen Charlotte City, Skidegate Landing, and Sandspit. Technically, the material the Skidegate carvers used was argillite – softer than slate and with no well-defined plane of cleavage.

6 This was George D. Beattie, pharmacist, who served as the community's
first postmaster from 1909 to 1940, see Dalzell, ibid., 263. I am much obliged
to Edna Picket, postmistress, 1958-81, and to Dr. Betty Calam for helping
establish Beattie's precedence in the job and his dates of service.

7 Dalzell gives as the full name Frank Lennie Le Tonturier Donroe, and
indicates that local people preferred 'Dunroe.' A headstone in the old Port
Clements cemetery reading 'DUNROE IN LOVING MEMORY . . .' bears out the
latter usage. In Lord's account, Tonturier comes through as a sinister
figure. Dalzell is similarly critical, depicting him as self-serving, demanding of family and acquaintances, and 'wily' in dealing with educational
authorities. In his multiple identity as teacher, parent, trustee, and even
board secretary, he appears successfully to have manipulated the community to his own interests. Note, for instance, that official reports for 1915-17
show Tonturier as *teacher*. Yet the 1915 report *also* indicates an F.J. Dunroe as
secretary, the 1916 report as trustee, and the 1917 report as secretary once
more. Dalzell, ibid., 141, 149, 151-2, 170, 174, 193, 223, 262-3; ARPS, 1915,
Aclxxvii; ibid., 1916, Aclxxxi; ibid.' 1917, clxxxii.

8 For a family photograph which renders this last statement questionable,
see 'Frank Lennie Tonturier and his wife with seven . . . children,' in
Kathleen E. Dalzell, *The Beloved Island* (Madeira Park, BC: Harbour Publishing 1989), preceding 91.

9 Dalzell, however, disagrees with the impression Lord leaves that the
younger children parted for good. She confirms that the oldest boy – Jim –
established a sizeable house of his own and took in the family, leaving the
father to take his meals in and otherwise occupy the old house. The
Tonturier episode reflects, moreover, the stratagems a desperate man
might knowingly adopt to support a numerous family during severe economic depression. Interview with Kathleen Dalzell, Port Clements, BC, 13
October 1988; Dalzell to the editor, Port Clements, BC, 8 February 1989.

CHAPTER EIGHT: CHILCOTIN COUNTRY

1 Note that the setting for forthcoming sections headed 'An Educated Man'
and 'Pewter Money' fall just outside Lord's definition of the Chilcotin.
They are included in Chapter 8 for editorial convenience.

2 This statement dates Lord's writing of the 'Chilcotin Country' no later than
August 1953. The British Columbia Travel Bureau soon thereafter advised
that the road link from Williams Lake to Bella Coola was completed. See
Reginald Eyre Watters (ed.), *British Columbia: A Centennial Anthology*
(Toronto: McClelland and Stewart 1958), 66.

3 The 'Waddington Massacre' was the name an exploitative society gave to
the 1864 killings by Chilcotin Indians of a ferry operator and nineteen
workers connected with Waddington's road construction party. A full-

blown insurrection was at length avoided. See Margaret A. Ormsby, *British Columbia: A History* (Toronto: Macmillan of Canada, 1958, 1971), 204-8.

Bob Graham had come out from Ireland and 'in 1880 started a sheep ranch one mile above the present Meldrum Creek Road ...' He also pre-empted 160 acres in the Alexis Creek area, sold it to his older brother Alex, and eventually moved to Tatla Lake to start a flourishing cattle ranch, establish a store and stopping house, and serve as local magistrate. I am indebted to Cariboo-Chilcotin archivist Dr. John Roberts, Joyce Graham of Tatla Lake, and Alexina Renshaw (Graham's stepdaughter), North Vancouver, for background information.

Lord's reference to the buffet is doubtless intended to testify not only to the continued existence of the Waddington Trail in Graham's time but also to the cultural priorities of European immigrants. Though she declares the buffet was actually 'purchased in Ashcroft and ... hauled by covered wagon, 300 miles to Tatla Lake in 1914 ...,' Mrs. Renshaw describes a lovely piece of medium light oak furniture with 'knurled supports for lamps at either end, a mirror full width with knurled trim at the top, two single drawers at the top and two larger drawers at the bottom ...' Alexina Renshaw to the editor, North Vancouver, BC, 7 April 1987.

4 Though Lord sees this rancher aloofness from government support as a function of self-reliance, contemporaries in the cattle business at times attributed it to lack of co-ordination. Later observers document the intro-duction of government subsidies and their effects upon cattle ranches of varying size. See, for instance, Harry Marriott, *Cariboo Cowboy* (Sidney, BC: Gray's Publishing 1966), 181; Nina G. Wooliams, *Cattle Ranch: The Story of the Douglas Lake Cattle Company* (Vancouver, BC: Douglas and McIntyre 1979), 234-5.

5 Charlie Moon was born in England in 1872. At age sixteen he came to the Chilcotin, and in 1896 married Jessie Frances Collard. Having worked on the Drummond, Beaumont, and Cotton ranches, he purchased the Deer Park ranch 'a few miles off the Chilcotin highway, alongside the Fraser River,' later acquiring land at Meldrum Creek and Sheep Creek. As Collier concludes, from modest beginnings 'he lived to carve himself a miniature cattle empire that in 1931 ran some three thousand head of Hereford cattle, and had thousands of acres of deeded land under fence.' John Roberts to the editor, Williams Lake, BC, 9 March 1987; Kathleen A. Telford, 'Pioneer Days in the Chilcotin,' in Art Downs (ed.), *Pioneer Days in British Columbia*, Vol. 3 (Surrey, BC: Heritage House Publishing 1977), 11; Eric Collier, *Three Against the Wilderness* (London: The Companion Book Club 1959), 61.

Robert Cecil Cotton, a well-to-do Englishman, took up ranching at Riske Creek in 1886 on a site 'still one of the best situated ... in the Cariboo, sloping down to the edge of the Fraser River ...' The Cotton ranch 'held many long weekend polo matches' and 'had a full-sized English billiard table upstairs' in the two-storey, squared log ranch house. Cotton's wife, Maude Walker, 'came from Tasmania, and was governess for Yollands of the 150-Mile House.' Roberts, ibid.; Donovan Clemson, 'Pioneers of the Jackpine Forest,' in Downs, ibid., 1: 82.

6 The records show eight schools, notably Alexis Creek (12 children present), Big Creek (eight), Chezacut (eight), Meldrum Creek (nine), Tatla Lake (eight), and Tatlayoko (seven). Lord describes Big Creek as 'one of the best schools in my inspectorate,' Chezacut as 'creditable,' Meldrum Creek as obtaining 'pleasing results,' Tatla Lake as 'very satisfactory,' Tatlayoko showing in 1933 'distinct improvement' over the previous year, and Alexis Creek, with some exceptions, 'making satisfactory progress.' SIR, 21 September 1932; 7 June 1933; 6 June 1933; 23 September 1932; 9 June 1933; and 7 June 1933 respectively.

Two ex-teachers remember the Meldrum Creek school. Mary Cullum of the 'pleasing results' states the inspector said it was the worst school in British Columbia (what Lord actually wrote was that it was 'the poorest building in my inspectorate.' See SIR, Meldrum Creek, 6 June 1933). She remembers it 'looked like a root house' and was very 'gloomy and dirty.' See Joan Adams and Becky Thomas, *Floating Schools and Frozen Inkwells: The One-Room Schools of British Columbia* (Madeira Park, BC: Harbour Publishing 1985), 30. Sylvia McKay speaks of the roof which was layered with 'poles, then straw, then sod, and dirt and grass.' But rodents made the most lasting impression. 'There were mice galore in that building,' she recalls. Ibid.

7 For a story which corroborates Lord's high opinion of Chilcotin hospitality, see Mary Cullum's memories of living at the Mulvahill ranch, Chezacut, ibid., 56. Upon arrival in the area she was driven from Williams Lake as far as Hanceville by rancher Norman Lee.

8 Margaret Graham's kindness, not to mention her splendid cooking, are recalled with gratitude by Phyllis C. Bryant who, with her husband, 'had starved out of our pre-emption near Soda Creek after a two-years' struggle,' and was pushing on to Tatla Lake through December snow to start afresh. Near exhaustion, they spotted 'the lamps in the ranch house window' and 'the Grahams fed us hot soup the like of which I never expect to eat again – and lemon pie.' Phyllis C. Bryant, 'December 13, 1921: Sawmill Creek,' in Watters, ibid., 101.

9 Norman Lee was born in Westmorland, England, on 18 October 1862, 'the son of Matthew Henry Lee, a graduate of Oxford, vicar of the Parish of Morland and Canon of the Diocese.' Lee was educated for Marlborough at Hartford House where his uncle, the Reverend Thomas William Lee, taught a classical curriculum. Then 'he entered Haileybury and later was apprenticed to an architect,' a profession he found dull. His brother Robert Warden Lee was 'a Fellow of All Souls, Oxford, and was once Dean of Law at McGill

University.' Lee sought adventure in British Columbia in 1882 and a dozen years later purchased a cabin at Hanceville, from which modest base he launched a stimulating career. By 1912 he presided over 1,700 fenced acres, a complex and skilfully-engineered irrigation system, 600 shorthorns and Herefords, 50 horses, rich soil, and a home ranch including a 'building with 11 rooms, stabling for 10 horses, a stopping house, fencing machinery, and a well-stocked store which supplie[d] the country over a radius of about 20 miles.' His ill-starred attempt in 1898 to drive 200 beef steers 1,500 miles from Hanceville to Dawson City has become a classic in western lore. See Gordon R. Elliot (ed.), *Klondike Cattle Drive: The Journal of Norman Lee* (Vancouver, BC: Mitchell Press 1960, 1964), xvii, xviii; Ashley G. Brown, *British Columbia: Its History, People, Commerce, Industries and Resources* (London: Sells 1912), 390, 394. I am indebted to Dr. John Roberts of Williams Lake for drawing these references to my attention.

Norman Lee married his second cousin Agnes Lee in 1902. She describes her arrival at Hanceville in 1903. 'Having come from an English drawing room, I was soon homesick ... Well, gradually I settled into my new life and learned how to deal with its many problems,' which included sub-zero temperatures, searing wood stoves, piles of dishes which 'I'd never washed ... before in my life,' sleeping on floors, seven-day sleigh rides, and episodes of secret tears in 'this strange new world.' Bryant, ibid., 99–100.

10 An English expatriate and sometime HBC clerk, Frederick Methewan Becher (the name is often spelled and pronounced Beecher) quit his job in 1880 and took up freighting from Soda Creek to Hanceville. Later he started ranching near Riske Creek and by 1912 had '1,500 acres in two sections, one at Rickey [Riske] Creek ... and the other at Meldrum Creek.' Stock then included 500 shorthorns and Herefords and 30-40 horses, and personal innovations included a telephone and an automobile (a Cadillac) each the first in the Chilcotin. Becher was well-known for his hotel and trading post, facilities he lost by fire in 1915 but replaced on an even grander scale, the new hotel featuring six rooms 'furnished to the last piece of wallpaper, by Maple's of London.' Fred and Florence Becher (a good friend of Mrs. Cotton) were married in 1917. She helped arrange the 'spacious sitting room of the trading post' where Eric and Lillian Collier of Meldrum Creek were married. Telford, ibid., 10; Brown, ibid., 394; John Roberts to the editor, Williams Lake, BC, 20 February 1987; Collier, ibid., 16, 26, 69.

11 The first teacher, 1934-35, was I.W. Armstrong who held a first-class certificate, received $780 per annum, and taught 8 boys and 3 girls. ARPS, 1935, S98.

12 Within a year, Fred Becher had died and was buried above the Becher house 'on a knoll overlooking the peaceful valley that had been his home for over fifty years,' Telford, ibid., Roberts, ibid. His wife Florence died in England in 1957.

13 First World War veteran Andrew Lorne Stewart of Nelson left the newspaper business in 1919 and came to Redstone 'to take over the store his elder brother Peter, had started in 1916.' Raised in Kent, England, his wife-to-be joined Stewart at Redstone where 'they spent the rest of their lives ...' Together they developed the store, garage, and machine repair shop to a high reputation still enjoyed today. John Roberts to the editor, Williams Lake, BC, 20 February 1987.

14 Constable Robert Pyper, British Columbia Provincial Police, was based at Soda Creek and later at Alexis Creek. For an account of his enthusiasm for community events see Telford, ibid., 11.

15 Dolly Moore was brought up on a pioneer settlement at Big Creek. She married Ken Moore of Tatlayoko where they continued ranching, but also specialized in outfitting prospecting and survey crews and guiding hunting and fishing parties. See Clemson, ibid., 81; interview, Graham/ Renshaw, 21 February 1987. Vera Bonner of Big Creek adds that Dolly projected a convincing 'cowgirl' image tackling hard outdoor jobs, riding steers at rodeos, and later engaging in packing to the Minto Mines from headquarters at her small place on Gun Creek. She ended her strenuous working days ranching in the Kamloops area. John Roberts to the editor, Williams Lake, BC, 19 March 1987.

16 Pioneers recall Captain David Lloyd as a British expatriate much respected for his initiatives in community affairs. His daughter, Sophy Whittaker, furnishes a touching biography. Born near Birmingham, England in 1895, Lloyd was educated at Oundle preparatory school and Royal Military College, Sandhurst. He served in France during the First World War, was wounded, and stayed in the army until 1924 when at age 29, 'untrained for any work in civilian life,' he was discharged. In the wake of an unsuccessful business post in India leading to personal bankruptcy and divorce in 1929, he came to British Columbia on a remittance of £5 a month. Initially he worked as a surveyor near Victoria and later as helper at a resort on Seaton Lake, but at length settled at Tatlayoko where he was a guide and justice of the peace. In 1954 he sold out, moved to Kleena Kleene, and worked at a lodge, also cooking for fire camps. He retired to his daughter and son-in-law's farm at Cowichan Station, Vancouver Island, in 1963, and died in February 1970. He was a tremendous letter writer, Mrs. Whittaker remembers, particularly to her for whom 'a letter from Daddy was an event ...' Given an active existence, she continues, 'he was able to wear the same old tweed jacket all his life. Upright military bearing and always his moustache.' Interview, Graham/Renshaw, 21 February 1987; interview with Sophy Whittaker, Cowichan Station, BC, 7 May 1987; Sophy Whittaker to the editor, 20 April 1987. Barbara Gilmour corresponded with Lloyd 'when I was at the Book Dept. of the Hudson's Bay Co.' She recalls his

smart, neat handwriting and his interest in adolescent development. Meeting him just once, she recollects 'he reminded me of David Niven, the late actor. Witty, polished and dapper. You could tell that he'd been in the services.' Barbara Gilmour to the editor, Toronto, 4 June 1987; Barbara Gilmour to the editor, Toronto, 13 August 1987.

17 Thanks to his daughter Kathleen, Alex Graham also enjoys ample documentation. She outlines his birth in County Antrim, Ireland, in 1868; his arrival in the Chilcotin in 1887; and his efforts to develop the CI ranch at Alexis Creek from 25 young cows owned in partnership to 1,000 head of cattle run over 4,000 acres. Graham's marriage to 'childhood sweetheart' Anna Scott Harvey following her trip from Ireland via New York and Ashcroft to Soda Creek, their journey into the Chilcotin, and their daughters' (Kathleen's and Frances's) childhoods in a hard-working ranching community provide both a charming romance and a striking glimpse at their emigrant experience and eventual existence facing the rigours of British Columbia's Interior Plateau in the early 20th century. As student (his parents had hoped he would enter the ministry), traveller, railway worker, ranch hand, cattle driver, community leader, employer, merchant, justice of the peace, husband, and father, Graham emerges as the quintessential Chilcotin cattle rancher. Like the 1,665-m mountain named to honour him, he remains a true Chilcotin landmark. Telford (nee Graham), ibid., passim; John Roberts to the editor, Williams Lake, BC, 20 February 1987.

18 Lord's prediction is yet to be realized. For a summary of the Chilcotin's hydroelectric potential, see A.L. Farley, *Atlas of British Columbia: People, Environment, and Resource Use* (Vancouver, BC: University of British Columbia Press 1979), 96-8.

19 Since Lord's character sketch of the thoughtful rancher, several corroborating accounts have come to light. Marriott relates he was 'a man of great ability . . . Not only was he a good cattleman, but he was what the experts call "a man of good executive ability."' His first ranch at Alkali Lake 'was just a stepping stone from which in after years he built up and owned the Canoe Creek Company's ranch and the Empire Valley holdings.' Other perspectives come from Henry Koster's sons. Henry Koster, Jr. confirms that his father was a very well-informed, well-read, self-educated man who loved to engage in the sorts of discussions Lord describes. Jack Koster concurs with Lord's appraisal of his father. Henry Koster, Sr. married Evelyn Hirst of Manchester, England. In the 1900s at Alkali Lake he sustained a severe leg injury, moving to Vancouver where special medical care was available and where he entered the real estate business for a time, succeeding with customary initiative. Marriott, ibid., 62; John Roberts to the editor, Williams Lake, BC, 26 February 1987; Jack Koster to the editor, Canoe Creek, BC, 13 January 1988; telephone interview with Henry Koster,

Jr., Surrey, BC, 2 November 1988; telephone interview with Hilary Place, Vancouver, BC, 1 November 1988.

20 Joseph Smith Place from Bury, Lancashire, settled at Dog Creek in the late 1880s, bought ranches and stores from neighbours, and consolidated them. In 1875 Joseph married Jane Beaumont of Huddersfield, Yorkshire. Together they developed a domain which in 1912 Brown described as '7,500 acres under Crown grant and 2,000 acres on lease, 37 miles of fencing, an irrigation system allowing 600 acres under "dense cultivation" (hay, oats, wheat, barley, vegetables, and small fruits), 800 head of shorthorn cattle, 200 horses, store, stopping house, stabling for 25 horses, and a small lumber and flour mill, each water-driven.' Artist A.Y. Jackson remembers staying at the Place's hotel (then operated by Charles and Ada Place) in 'a large bedroom, painted white and immaculately clean.' Hilary Place, grandson of Joseph and Jane Place, speaks with warmth of Lord's visits to the Dog Creek School and the encouragement afforded him by this 'quiet, delicate man.' Brown, ibid., 404; Robin Skelton, *They Call It the Cariboo* (Victoria, BC: Sono Nis Press 1980), 176; Roberts, ibid.; A.Y. Jackson, *A Painter's Country: The Autobiography of A.Y. Jackson* (Toronto: Clarke, Irwin 1958, 1967),128; telephone interview with Hilary Place, Vancouver, BC, 1 November 1988; Hilary Place to the editor, Vancouver, BC, 30 July 1990; telephone interview with Betty Place, Williams Lake BC, 1 November 1988.

21 School taxes or tax legislation merely mentioning schools could provoke bitterness among ranchers. This prevailing point of view underscores the delicacy with which Lord and his counterparts in other cattle-raising areas had to go about their business of helping and maintaining assisted schools as well as recruiting and holding qualified teachers. For an interesting case in point, see Marriott, ibid., 163, 181.

22 John Clayton, an 'adventurous Englishman,' became a figure central to settlers who farmed the vicinity. After working for the HBC in Bella Coola, he purchased the HBC premises, ran his own store, set up a second store at Bella Bella and in 1900, in partnership with Thomas Draney, built and operated a fish cannery. Roberts, ibid. For comments on Clayton's local dominance combined with innate openness – a subtle blend of independence and interdependence within an essentially utopian settlement – see Gordon Fish (ed.), *Dreams of Freedom: Bella Coola, Cape Scott, Sointula* (Victoria, BC: BCARS, Sound and Moving Image Division 1982), 14, 42; Cliff Kopas, *Bella Coola* (Vancouver, BC: Mitchell Press 1970), 257. This general question of independence/interdependence as an aspect of immigrant history is elegantly examined in Jorgen Dahlie, 'Learning on the Frontier: Scandinavian Immigrants and Education in Western Canada,' in W. Peter Ward and Robert A.J. McDonald (eds.), *British Columbia: Historical Readings* (Vancouver, BC: Douglas and McIntyre 1981), 628-30 and passim.

23 Barney Brynildsen arrived in Bella Coola on board the steamer *Danube* on 6 May 1895. In competition with Clayton, he built his first store at the southeast corner of Clayton's property and, after a period of time elsewhere, returned in 1929 to erect a new store 'only a few yards' from the original on a site to become known as Brynildsen's Corner. Fish, ibid., 42; Kopas, ibid., 255, 257, 267.

CHAPTER NINE: KELOWNA BEGINNINGS

1 The *Okanagan* was launched in 1907 to help handle increased passenger and supply traffic generated by growing settlement along Lake Okanagan. A Canadian Pacific Railway vessel, she carried 250 passengers and, like the *BX* and the *D.A. Thomas*, was 'elaborately fitted out.' But in 1916 when 'the fruit boom collapsed,' she was laid up and finally scrapped in 1937. Art Downs, *Paddlewheels on the Frontier*, Vol. 2 (Surrey, BC: Foremast Publishing 1971), 21, 24.

2 Thomas Lawson who was chairman of the Kelowna School Board for many years and vice-president – later, president – of the British Columbia School Trustees Association, was manager of the town's largest retail store, Thomas Lawson and Co. Ltd. Art Gray, *Kelowna: Tales of Bygone Days* (Kelowna: Kelowna Print 1968), 63-4.

3 Dr. William J. Knox was beloved of Kelowna contemporaries, witness the banquet in his honour on 12 November 1963 at Kelowna's Aquatic Ballroom. His major contributions were in public education, medicine, voluntary associations, and provincial politics. Primrose Upton, 'A Testimonial,' *Twenty-eighth Report of the Okanagan Historical Society* (1964), 90.

4 A prominent realtor, James William Jones served three aldermanic years and five full terms as Kelowna's mayor. Successful in four provincial elections as Conservative candidate for South Okanagan, he was at length appointed minister of finance in the Tolmie administration. In this capacity, his levying a 1 per cent surtax on income over $25.00 a week for married men and $15.00 a week for others earned him the sobriquet 'One Per Cent Jones.' Gray, ibid., 100-2; Margaret A. Ormsby, *British Columbia: A History* (Toronto: Macmillan of Canada 1958), 444.

Dr. W.H. Gaddes was a veterinary surgeon, fruit grower, realtor, and mortgage and insurance broker. In 1906 he, along with Jones and others, bought 1,665 acres of Price Ellison land near Rutland. Together with 6,000 acres in the Dry Valley region and irrigation delivered by flume and syphon from Mill Creek, these assets gave rise to the Central Okanagan Land Company which sold 10-20 acre lots at $150 to $200 an acre. Principal investors are said to have done comfortably well, but lot purchasers experienced uneven results. See, for example, Art Gray, 'Central Okanagan Land Company,' *Twenty-ninth Report of the Okanagan Historical Society* (1957), 83,

101; Patrick A. Dunae, *Gentlemen Emigrants: From British Public Schools to the Canadian Frontier* (Vancouver, BC: Douglas and McIntyre 1981), 114.

5 The investor was John Campbell Gordon, seventh Earl of Aberdeen and Canada's governor general, 1893–98. In 1890 he bought the 500-acre Guisachan Ranch near Okanagan Mission south of Kelowna, and the year after acquired the 13,000-acre Coldstream Ranch near Vernon. In 1906 he set up a company and developed a sales and advertising campaign to attract British settlers who, as of 1892, 'poured into the Valley' bringing with them their upper-middle-class sentiments and unrestrained optimism regarding a fruit grower's life. Dunae, ibid., 103–4, 114, and passim.

6 The Reverend Thomas Bernard Greene 'travelled from Penticton each month to officiate, until 1897, when he moved to Kelowna . . .' where he 'carried on his parochial work with devotion and zeal.' F.M. Buckland, *Ogopogo's Vigil: A History of Kelowna and the Okanagan* (Kelowna: Okanagan Historical Society [1948], 98)

7 This drastic reduction stemmed from no simple cause such as orchards deteriorating during the owners' overseas war service. On the contrary, the problem was not too few apples but too many, with fierce competition from Washington and Oregon orchards. For an analysis of these fruit market complexities, see Margarget A. Ormsby, 'The History of Agriculture in British Columbia,' *Scientific Agriculture* 20 (1939), 66.

8 In an attempt to educate the working class, board schools were established in England under the 1870 Elementary Education Act which enabled elected boards to levy taxes in part support. These boards charged tuition fees as well, but excused poor children. Later surveys showed that in 1903, nearly a sixth of London's board school children 'received meals from charitable agencies,' that ill health of many board school children was 'the direct result of poverty,' and that to these schools were brought children sometimes suffering from 'the severer cases of physical impairment.' Not surprisingly, upper-middle class English immigrants aspiring to become gentlemen farmers were relieved to distance themselves from Old Country board schools and wary of British Columbia public elementary schools, despite a host of circumstances distinguishing the latter from the former. See David Rubenstein, 'Socialization and the London School Board 1870–1904: Aims, Methods and Public Opinion,' in Philip McCann (ed.), *Popular Education and Socialization in the Nineteenth Century* (London: Methuen 1977), 231–4 and passim.

9 Probably the two best known regional private schools run on English lines during Lord's Kelowna principalship were Chesterfield School, Kelowna (1912–24) and Vernon Preparatory School (1914–72). See Jean Barman, *Growing Up British in British Columbia: Boys in Private School* (Vancouver, BC: University of British Columbia Press 1984), 33–5.

10 Daniel Wilbur Sutherland took up teaching at Kelowna in 1893 and taught

for eight years before serving six years as alderman and seventeen as Kelowna's mayor. Less successful in federal and provincial politics, he received the Liberal nomination, but lost to Conservative J.A. McKelvie in 1921 and to Grote Stirling in 1924. As an Independent in the 1928 provincial election he lost to J.W. Jones. Despite these setbacks, his local contributions earned him the title 'Father of the City of Kelowna.'

11 That Elizabeth McNaughton and L.V. Rogers were appreciated for their efforts is further verified by Everett S. Fleming who, because his father returned for many years each fall to thresh his Saskatchewan grain crop, was left to harvest 'onions and other crops on the [Kelowna] ranch. This cut into my school program badly.' After starting high school in temporary quarters, his class 'moved with our two teachers, Principal L.V. Rogers and Miss Elizabeth McNaughton, to the spacious brick school on Glenn Ave. and Richter St. These two carried the entire curriculum for all three years of high school work. We owe them more than we can ever repay.' Everett S. Fleming, 'The Fleming Family,' *Twenty-first Report of the Okanagan Historical Society* (1957), 87-8.

12 Dr. Thomas J. Barnardo was a prominent English humanitarian whose involvement in child emigration schemes 'grew out of a deeply felt religious commitment.' Neil Sutherland shows that 'Barnardo developed his child-rescue work in the London slums, and by the 1880s his was the largest English organization in the field . . .' For somewhat differing perspectives of the Barnardo movement, see Neil Sutherland, *Children in English-Canadian Society: Framing the Twentieth Century Consensus* (Toronto: University of Toronto Press 1976), 29-30; Joy Parr, *Labouring Children: British Immigrant Apprentices to Canada*, 1869-1924 (Montreal: McGill-Queen's University Press; London: Croom Helm 1980), 67-9, 139.

13 Price Ellison was born in Durham, England, in 1851. As a youth he emigrated to Boston and later prospected for Cariboo gold. He came to the Okanagan in 1876, at length acquiring the Postill and Simpson ranches near Okanagan Mission, 'property near Swan Lake, meadows near Lumby, and the lease of the Winfield Ranch. In 1896 he was elected to the provincial legislature [E. Yale],' and was McBride's minister of lands in 1909 'and of finance and agriculture in 1910.' Gray, ibid., 134; Margaret A. Ormsby (ed.), *A Pioneer Gentlewoman in British Columbia: The Recollections of Susan Allison* (Vancouver, BC: University of British Columbia Press 1976), 121n, citing Myra K. De Beck, 'Price Ellison: A Memorial by His Daughter,' *Twelfth Report of the Okanagan Historical Society* [1948], 48-58.

14 The teacher in question was E.P. Duthie officially identified as a music and drawing instructor, appointed at a salary of seventy dollars a month, ARPS, 1914, ACxxvii.

15 Second primer would have approximated the second term of today's grade one, and junior third reader, the grade four year. However, since children

in England started school at 5 years of age and in British Columbia at 6, and given the fact that British elementary schools included board schools, voluntary schools, 'public' schools, preparatory schools, and others, classifying their pupils sometimes by 'forms' or at other times by 'standards,' Lord's predicament in devising a transfer placement policy satisfactory to all parties can readily be appreciated.

16 William Southon secured his Ontario teaching certificate in 1899. See 'List of Provincial Certificates Granted by the Education Department, 1899,' in *Report of the Minister of Education [Ontario] for the Year 1899* (Toronto: Warwick Brothers and Rutter 1900), 144.

17 During the Second World War, Savage played a leading part maintaining school services in heavily bombed areas, arguing for comprehensive high schools, and contending that in preparing teachers, 'all training colleges and university training departments become schools of education and ... be of equal standing.' P.H.J.H. Gosden, *Education in the Second World War: A Study in Policy and Administration* (London: Methuen 1976), 96–7, 302, 378, 399–400, 424, 440.

18 His and others' good opinion of Paul Murray is reflected in Lord's letter to the secretary of the University of British Columbia Senate Awards Committee. This appeal for UBC recognition of Murray's educational contributions enjoyed wide support in educational circles, but to no avail. Murray did not go unrecognized, however. He was awarded the King George Jubilee Medal in appreciation of his 'far-reaching influence in education ...' He died, age 94, on 10 January 1945. See A.R. Lord to Evelyn Farris, n.p., 23 January 1935; John Stager to the editor, Vancouver, BC, 24 March 1987; *Province*, 10 January 1945; *British Columbian*, 10 January 1945.

Clarence Fulton is remembered as the dynamic principal of Vernon High School in its early years. Though this institution was initially renowned for its accelerated matriculation class, range of extracurricular activities, and student morale, rumours of poor performance on government exams led to an investigation and Fulton's eventual dismissal. The town was nonetheless appreciative. A tribute portrayed him as one to whom 'wisdom was greater than knowledge,' who believed in laughter, and whose 'influence lives on in the lives of those who knew him ...' And a grateful board named Vernon's Clarence Fulton High School in his honour. *The Vernon News*, 1 June 1911, 1; ibid., 4 January 1912, 1; A.H. Sovereign, 'Portrait of a Schoolmaster,' *Twenty-fifth Report of the Okanagan Historical Society* (1961), 43, 45, and passim.

19 In fact, Murray, Jr. ran into difficulties not with the CBC which he left seven years later but for his activities as Director of the Responsible Enterprise Movement which organized labour interpreted as attempts to 'defeat the CCF and check the growth of the trade union movement.' See '"Big Shots" Fight CCF. $100,000 Trust Fund Backs High Pressure Propagandist,' *The New*

Commonwealth, 27 January 1944, 8; Barbara Clarke, Program Archives, CBC, to the editor, Toronto, 7 May 1987; B.M. Greene (ed.), *Who's Who in Canada 1949-50* (Toronto: International Press 1950), 542; *The Canadian Forum*, 23, March 1944, 271 and passim.

20 Before becoming provincial director of physical education, Ernest Lee was instructor in that subject at the Vancouver Provincial Normal School where Lord was principal.

21 The Mark Hopkins reference is attributed to James A. Garfield. For context and variations see John Bartlett, *Familiar Quotations* (Garden City, NY: Garden City Publishing 1882, 1937, 1945, etc.), 591, column 1; Frederick Rudolph, *The American College and University: A History* (New York: Alfred Knopf 1962), 243.

22 Indeed, the legal provisions regarding student refunds appear to have matched Wu Yuén's expectations, such refunds forthcoming 'on the production within eighteen months from the date of their arrival in Canada of certificates from teachers in any school or college in Canada showing that they are and have been bona fide students in attendance at such school or college.' For a historical account of the above regulation and of how doubt over its imprecision burgeoned into a full-blown, ongoing dispute among Victoria citizens and school authorities, see Mary Ashworth, *The Forces Which Shaped Them* (Vancouver, BC: New Star Books 1979), 64-73.

23 Dunn held the post of minister, Knox Presbyterian Church, Kelowna, from 1909 to 1913. At the time, provincial ministers of the Church of Scotland in Canada seemed generally opposed to union with Canadian Presbyterianism, but Dunn favoured such a move. Conversely, at a time when support for a Canada-wide amalgamation of Presbyterians, Methodists, and Congregationalists within a United Church of Canada appeared strong, Dunn resisted and Kelowna awaited his departure before Knox became a Union charge. See Rev. Alex Dunn, *Experience in Langley and Memories of Prominent Pioneers* (New Westminster: Jackson Printing 1913), 83; J.C. Goodfellow, 'Kelowna United Church History,' *Eighteenth Report of the Okanagan Historical Society* (1954), 124; *The Acts and Proceedings of the General Assembly of the Presbyterian Church in Canada 1912* (Toronto: Murray Printing 1912), 686; ibid., 1913, 593; ibid., 1918, 553; ibid., 1919, 582.

CHAPTER TEN: THE VIEW FROM HEADQUARTERS

1 Egerton Ryerson is best known as superintendent of schools for Canada West/Ontario, 1846-76, during which time he engineered a public school system in a tradition Child describes as 'free, universal, Protestant . . . , designed to promote nationalism and social stability, [and] controlled mainly at the local level.' Alan H. Child, 'The Ryerson Tradition in Western Canada, 1871-1906,' in Neil McDonald and Alf Chaiton (eds.), *Egerton Ryer-*

son and His Times: Essays on the History of Education (Toronto: Macmillan of Canada 1978), 279.

2 The full title was The Universal Spelling Book for Canadian Schools (Toronto: Educational Book Co. 1909), authorship unattributed. Its aims were 'to use only words that all children should be trained to spell,' and 'to make the most complete collection of such words to be found in any spelling book.' Ibid., iii. Its contents included commonly used words, homophones, etymology, pronunciation, and words employed in commerce and geography. Ibid., vii-viii. A section on frequently misspelled words contained such demons as 'abeyance,' 'asthma,' 'apparel', 'biennial,' 'apothecary,' 'axiom,' 'aggrieve,' 'aqueous,' 'arraign,' 'apprehension,' and 'abscess,' words calculated to trip many a latter-day elementary school child and perhaps their parents too! Ibid., p. 80-1.

3 The full citation is William J. Milne, Progressive Arithmetic (Toronto: Morang Educational 1906, 1908, 1915, 1916, etc.) published in three volumes. Book II, Part 2 covered review, denominate numbers, percentage, measures and equivalents, interest, and tables, as well as 'review problems in industries' touching on farming, fishing, transportation, mining, lumbering, banking, and other Canadian and world occupations. Ibid., 6. Book III elaborated on these, adding factors and divisors, problem-solving, the metric system, compound interest, promissory notes, banking, stocks and bonds, ratio and proportion, powers and roots, and mensuration. Ibid., 5-6. The pages omitted from Book III dealt with analysis by equations, exchange, and solids. I am obliged to Howard Hurt, Librarian, UBC Curriculum Laboratory, for bringing The Universal Spelling Book and Progressive Arithmetic to my attention and inviting my use of these rare books.

4 Lord's point is important for today's reader. As he showed, in 1909-10, 37,629 children attended British Columbia public elementary schools and 2,041 went to provincial high schools – about 5.4 per cent of the elementary figure. Timothy Dunn also draws attention to these proportions in his 'The Rise of Mass Public Schooling in British Columbia, 1900-1929,' in J. Donald Wilson and David C. Jones (eds.), Schooling and Society in Twentieth Century British Columbia (Calgary, Alberta: Detselig Enterprises 1980), Table 1, p. 26; Table 3, p.29. As Sutherland points out, however, in 1910, elementary school completion was widely considered as both a measure of educational achievement and an important credential. Many who took the high school entrance exam never even considered going on to high school, but stayed in elementary school – sometimes for extra years – in order to secure this 'public school leaving' qualification. Neil Sutherland to the editor, Vancouver, BC, 26 May 1989. By the same token, high school matriculation was accorded recognition not disproportionate to that afforded a university degree today.

5 The argument in support of the junior high school was that the transition

from elementary to high school could prove bewildering for adolescents and lead to a higher-than-desirable rate of high school 'dropouts.' The administrative solution, first officially proposed in J.H. Putman and G.M. Weir, *Survey of the School System* (1925), was a 3-year junior high school sandwiched between a 6-year elementary and a 3-year senior high school. Though a junior high school for academically weak pupils had been tried at King Edward High School, Vancouver, as early as 1922, the first junior high school reflecting the more general Putman/Weir recommendation was opened at Penticton, in 1926. Others followed in Vancouver at Magee, Templeton, Kitsilano, and Point Grey, as well as at Nelson, Kamloops, Nanaimo, and New Westminster.

6 This observation is consistent with Lord's opinion of the entrance examination during his maiden inspectorate. He recorded that results teachers in his rural inspectorate had secured for 1916-17 would 'compare favourably with those obtained in urban districts,' ARPS, 1917, report dated 9 October 1917, A43.

7 Two years remained to be completed, making four years in all for the McGill BA. See *Annual Report of the Governors, Principal and Fellows of McGill University Montreal, for the Year* 1906-1907 (Montreal: McGill University, 1907), 29.

8 In 1924-5 a total of 548 teacher candidates attended the two provincial normal schools, nearly a six-fold increase in 15 years. At the same time, provincial high school enrolment stood at 10.8 per cent of elementary school enrolment, twice that of 1910. See John Calam, 'Teaching the Teachers: Establishment and Early Years of the BC Provincial Normal Schools,' *BC Studies* 61 (Spring 1984), 51; Dunn, ibid.

9 Observers of the 1930s remember Weir as a dynamic provincial secretary and minister of education in the Pattullo cabinet, 1933-41, and in the latter part of the Hart coalition, 1945-47. Of his oratory, Bruce Hutchison writes about Weir's 'consuming fire of passionate protest . . .' Bruce Hutchison, *Times*, 12 March 1936, quoted in Margaret A. Ormsby, *British Columbia: A History* (Toronto: Macmillan of Canada 1958, 1971), 457.

Mann portrays King, the classics teacher and Kitsilano principal, as 'a strong supporter of junior high schools and particularly those facets of progressive education to which the label "scientific" could be attached.' For a thoughtful analysis of other sides of his and Weir's educational philosophy as it touched on progressivism, see Jean Mann, 'G.M. Weir and H.B. King: Progressive Education or Education for the Progressive State?' in Wilson and Jones, ibid., 91-118.

10 Harold L. Campbell enjoyed a long and varied career as teacher, principal, provincial inspector, normal school instructor, summer school vice-principal, municipal inspector, chief inspector, and deputy minister. Among some well-remembered contributions to provincial education

were introducing kindergartens, raising the status of art and music in the schools, helping initiate faculty-status teacher education at provincial universities, and overseeing implementation of the 1960 Chant Commission recommendation that intellectual development of the pupil should be the central aim of British Columbia public education. Campbell talks of his life on *Normal School Project*, Tape 78-T-19, University of Victoria, Special Collections. See also Department of Education, *One Hundred Years: Education in British Columbia* (Victoria, BC: Queen's Printer 1972), 36; Harold Campbell to the editor, Victoria, BC, 17 November 1988.

11 Lack of complete data renders this statement difficult to verify, but a single sample leaves some doubt. In academic year 1936-37, just prior to the implementation of curriculum alterations Lord describes, 252 UBC students sat the Chemistry I examination and 63 failed it – a failure rate of 25 per cent. But in academic year 1946-47, shortly before a senior chemistry course was restored to the provincial high school curriculum, 957 students wrote Chemistry 100 (first-year chemistry) and 221 failed – a failure rate of 23 per cent. Though variables at work remain unclear, these data reflect a comparative failure rate opposite to that which Lord retrospectively describes. See Office of the Registrar [UBC], Examination Strips, April 1937; UBC Class Roll and Record of Marks, General CHE list – Chemistry 100, 1946-47. I am indebted to M. Raphael, UBC Registrar's Office, for helping locate these materials, and to Anne Yandle, Laurenda Daniells, and Christopher L. Hives for permission and assistance in their use for this general purpose.

A member of the 1934 General Science Review Committee, Professor Emeritus Jack T. Young supports the view which Lord criticizes. The high school chemistry course, he wrote, was designed for 'a university chemist or science person.' The five-year general science program, he continued, was 'designed to provide students with an appreciation of science, and its influence on everyday life.' Nevertheless, Young contended, 'by the time people had taken ... five [general science] courses, they had had ... almost as much chemistry as if they had taken the two courses in chemistry in Grade 10 and 11 ...' J.T. Young to the editor, Vancouver, BC, 13 July 1987, 3-5, and passim.

12 Lord speaks here of that most difficult form of evaluation – identifying ex-students and somehow assessing the appropriateness to their present lives of the courses they once took. For a brief summary of several such follow-up studies, see George S. Tomkins, *A Common Countenance: Stability and Change in the Canadian Curriculum* (Scarborough, Ontario: Prentice-Hall of Canada 1986), 413-20 and passim.

13 Though by the early 1950s provincial high school science majors had available senior courses in all three of biology, physics, and chemistry, the concept of the high school Lord expresses here remained embodied in contemporary department publications. 'The secondary school of today,'

said the 1952 *Administrative Bulletin*, 'is no longer a selective institution for the intellectual, cultural or economic elite. It is a school for every . . . child and must attempt to meet the need for that pupil guidance and development which will result in happy and effective citizenship for all students.' See Province of British Columbia, *Administrative Bulletin, 1952-53 – Curriculum Organization for the Secondary Schools of British Columbia* (Victoria, BC: Queen's Printer 1952), 9.

14 Not only did the proportion of high school attenders increase during Lord's later years (44.2 per cent by 1947; 53.5 per cent by 1967, six years after he died), but also the social composition of high school populations altered radically. For the debate over the curricular consequences of these radical changes, see as examples S.N.F. Chant, *Report of the Royal Commission on Education* (Victoria, BC: Queen's Printer 1960), 283; Tomkins, ibid., 415; A.C. (Tasos) Kazepides, 'To Train or to Educate,' *The BC Teacher* (March/April 1987), 66; 2, 17, and passim.

15 Although teacher education was in place at Memorial University, Newfoundland, and the University of Saskatchewan as of 1946, it is likely that Lord refers here to M.E. LaZerte, dean of Canada's first University Faculty of Education established in 1945 at the University of Alberta. Dr. LaZerte was well-known among British Columbia educators, spoke at numerous educational events, and was renowned for his constructive wit.

16 At least 5 – each mentioned in Lord's manuscript – come to mind, notably, Alexander Robinson, S.J. Willis, George M. Weir, Harold L. Campbell, and H.B. King.

17 Thanks to Professor Peter L. Smith, Alexander Robinson has been rediscovered, his short term (1920-21) as principal of Victoria High School described as 'the stormiest in VHS history.' See Peter L. Smith, *Come Give a Cheer!: One Hundred Years of Victoria High School 1876-1976* (Victoria, BC: Victoria High School Centennial Committee 1976), 72-3. Robinson's *Letterbooks*, 138-191, 1899-1919, are also available, BCARS.

18 So nicknamed from a manner Ormsby describes as 'brilliant but egocentric, headstrong and brusque.' Ormsby, ibid., 320-1.

19 MacLean had held successive portfolios of provincial secretary and minister of education, railways, and finance before his year as Liberal Premier from 20 August 1927 to 20 August 1928.

20 Robinson's successor was S.J. Willis, principal, Victoria High School, 1908-16; associate professor of classics, UBC, 1916-18; principal, King Edward High School, Vancouver, 1918-19. Robinson described him as 'for the most part an excellent teacher' but not the 'progressive educationist' Education Minister J.D. MacLean considered him to be, 'Dr. Alex. Robinson writes to Minister,' *Victoria Times*, 11 November 1919, 5. True to his style, Robinson made no bones about naming the three candidates who, in his opinion, enjoyed 'superior qualifications.' They were 'Mr. Albert Sullivan, the Sen-

ior High School Inspector who, during the war, served with the Canadian infantry in France and Flanders; Mr. J.W. Gibson, the Director of Elementary Agricultural Education, one eminently qualified to direct educational growth along sane and progressive lines; and Mr. J.S. Gordon, Municipal Inspector of Schools, to whose untiring zeal and Christian character must be largely ascribed the high standard of the Vancouver Schools.' Ibid.

21 One might have expected that an ex-superintendent of education who for twenty years ran the provincial education system with an iron hand would run a distinguished high school the same way. Not so. Smith records that 'conditions quickly approached the chaotic. Students had a field day ... Discipline was soon non-existent ... At the end of the year, the general academic record on the government examinations was abysmal, and a public furore developed.' Smith, ibid., 73.

22 Teacher institutes were an early sort of in-service training which helped ensure 'uniformity of method' and stimulate discussion on such subjects as 'timetabling, curriculum, and methods of teaching.' As Johnson indicates, they were department-sponsored until the end of the First World War 'when the teachers petitioned the Department to establish their own organization, the British Columbia Teachers' Federation.' Johnson, ibid., 73.

23 Crummy was 'a scholar of exceptional literary tastes, and an eloquent preacher.' He engaged in educational work for six years under the Japanese imperial government and, during the same time (1888 onward), served the British and Foreign Bible Society and the Japanese mission of the Methodist church. See 'Aged Minister Dies at Home,' *Daily Colonist*, 15 August 1939, 3; 'Rev. Crummy Passes at 78,' *The Vancouver Daily Province*, 15 August 1939, 22; 'Noted Churchman,' *News Herald*, 17 August 1939, 4. Murray was first president of the University of Saskatchewan and archproponent of the concept of a state university conducted along the lines of American land-grant colleges, and serving 'the interests of the multitude and not of the select few ...' See *Canadian Annual Review*, 1914, 646, cited in J. Donald Wilson, Robert M. Stamp, and Louis-Philippe Audet (eds)., *Canadian Education: A History* (Scarborough, Ontario: Prentice-Hall of Canada 1970), 332. The 'Vancouver principal' retains historical anonymity!

24 The classical reference is to Ajax the Lesser, a conceited Greek whose violation of Cassandra during the sack of Troy 'caused him to be shipwrecked on the way home. Poseidon saved him, but Ajax, boasting of his own power, defied the lightning to strike him down and was instantly struck by it.' William Bridgwater and Seymour Kurtz (eds.), *The Columbia Encyclopedia*, 3rd ed. (New York and London: Columbia University Press 1963), 34.

25 Harold L. Campbell 'knew Dr. Robinson quite well and attended high school with his son and daughter and often visited their home' where, Campbell learned, Robinson was indeed 'a very kind person.' Campbell, ibid.

26 A fellow New Brunswicker, Robertson had met Willis at McGill where they both honoured in classics. Later, Robertson had become professor of classics at Vancouver College and 'while on a year's study leave at McGill' suggested to Principal William Peterson that, with adequate funding, Vancouver College could become 'a full-fledged college of McGill University.' McGill agreed. Sir William Macdonald promised $5,000 for three years and, in 1906, the British Columbia legislature passed enabling legislation. Smith, ibid., 40; Johnson, ibid., 79–81.

27 Smith remarks that 'as students and staff rushed to enlist, the quiet, orderly world of Victoria High School was severely shaken. Even more disruptive . . . was the opening [in 1915] of the University of British Columbia . . . To the chagrin of S.J. Willis . . . the school lost not only its McGill affiliation but also its right to offer any college-level work at all.' Smith, ibid., 42.

28 This truncated paragraph suggests that Lord intended to flesh out his portrait of Willis but never got around to doing so. An excellent remedy is Professor Smith's 'Samuel J. Willis: A Scholarly Administrator,' in Smith, ibid., 39–42, with photographs on 39, 40, 46, 51 and 54. I am indebted to Professor Smith as well as to Christopher Petter, University of Victoria Special Collections Library, for this and numerous other helpful references.

CHAPTER ELEVEN: LOSERS AND WINNERS

1 'Blind pigging' was the illegal sale of liquor, a devout practice along British Columbia's Grand Trunk Pacific right-of-way during construction.

2 The minister in question was the Reverend Melville Wright and the article to which Lord refers: 'Walked 350 miles from "The Very Gates of Hell",' *Toronto Globe and Mail*, 3 June 1913, 1, 4. For yet other versions, see Reverend F.E. Runnalls, *A History of Prince George* (Prince George, BC: F.E. Runnalls 1946), reprinted by the Fraser-Fort George Museum Society 1985, 127; *Fort George Herald*, 14 June 1913, 3. The length of bars is a popular datum in North American social history. For fuller accounts of this bar's dimensions and function, see also Guy Lawrence, 'Memories of the Cariboo and Central BC, 1908–1914,' in Art Downs (ed.), *Pioneer Days in British Columbia*, Vol. 4 (Surrey, BC: Heritage House Publishing 1979), 15; Lukin Johnston, *Beyond the Rockies: Three Thousand Miles by Trail and Canoe through Little-Known British Columbia* (London: J.M. Dent and Sons 1929), 113; Runnals, ibid., 127 and passim.

3 Some appraisals were less accommodating. Ex-student James Macalister wondered 'how they [ever] got hold of Sykes. He was hired during the great war when you couldn't get teachers. He liked to drink, and he got drunk down at the school . . . We kids told on him and he got fired.' Joan Adams and Becky Thomas, *Floating Schools and Frozen Inkwells: The One-*

Room Schools of British Columbia (Madeira Park, BC: Harbour Publishing, 1985), 141.

4 This was the community of Spences Bridge where, for the first term, 1915-16, Sykes taught 13 boys and 12 girls and was paid $60.00 a month, ARPS, 1916, Alxxxviii.

5 Following his stint at Spences Bridge, Sykes taught at Dragon Lake two stops south of Williams Lake on the PGE, ARPS, 1917, Aclxxviii. But the 'school on the Cariboo Road' was Macalister. Contrary to Robinson's threat, however, he did not lose his certificate after the Macalister fiasco, teaching at Bella Coola, 1918-21, Bamfield, 1922-24, and Lillooet, 1924-25. ARPS, 1919, Alxiv; ibid., 1920, C66; ibid., 1921, F72; ibid., 1923, F80; ibid., 1924, T84; ibid., 1925, M96.

6 Lord's account fits Wheeler's sketch of Jack Brown who arrived in Dunster in 1916, whose wife joined him the following year, and who homesteaded as of 1918. See Marilyn J. Wheeler, *The Robson Valley Story* (McBride: McBride-Robson Valley Story Group with Assistance of the Government of Canada New Horizons Program 1979), 360. For accounts richly contextual to Lord's Dunster settlers, see Jean Barman's recent *The West Beyond the West: A History of British Columbia* (Toronto: University of Toronto Press 1991), 176-201 and passim.

7 The teacher was A.A. Todd, who served at Dunster from 1915 to 1917. At the time he held a third-class certificate, taught 13 pupils, and earned $80.00 a month. ARPS, 1916, Aclxxvii, Alxxv; ibid., 1917, Alxxv, Aclxxviii. See also Wheeler, ibid., 262.

Index

THE PIONEERS OF BRITISH COLUMBIA